I0877371

Sarah Gilbert is a writer, producer and oral historian from Sydney. She began her career as a copy girl at News Ltd before moving to New York where she worked as a feature writer at the *New York Post*. She returned home to work as a reporter in current affairs television, but soon moved to Argentina where she wrote for Lonely Planet and *Time Out*.

Sarah's writing has been published in the *Sydney Review of Books*, the *Sydney Morning Herald*, the *Wall Street Journal* and *Marie Claire*. She works as a writer/producer across documentary film, television and podcasting, with a particular focus on Australian history, and she is the books columnist at *Galah* magazine. Sarah lives in Darlinghurst with her husband and their two children.

Sarah Gilbert

UNCONVENTIONAL WOMEN

The story of the last Blessed Sacrament Sisters in Australia

MELBOURNE UNIVERSITY PRESS

Melbourne University Publishing acknowledges the traditional owners of the unceded land on which we work, learn and live: the Wurundjeri Woiwurrung peoples of the Kulin Nation. We pay respect to elders past, present and future, and acknowledge the importance of Indigenous knowledge.

MELBOURNE UNIVERSITY PRESS
An imprint of Melbourne University Publishing Limited
Level 1, 715 Swanston Street, Carlton, Victoria 3053, Australia
mup-contact@unimelb.edu.au
www.mup.com.au

First published 2024

Cover design by Nada Backovic
Typeset by Sonya Murphy
Cover image courtesy the Melbourne Diocesan Historical Commission, Catholic Archdiocese of Melbourne.
Printed in Australia by McPherson's Printing Group

NATIONAL LIBRARY OF AUSTRALIA
A catalogue record for this book is available from the National Library of Australia

9780522880397 (paperback)
9780522880403 (ebook)

MIX
Paper | Supporting responsible forestry
FSC www.fsc.org FSC® C001695

CONTENTS

For Vianney, and for my grandmother.

'It's while it's being lived that life is immortal, while it's still alive.'
Marguerite Duras, The Lover

'God is a shout in the street.'
James Joyce, Ulysses

Aboriginal and Torres Strait Islander readers are advised that this book contains the names and stories of people who have died.

SERVANTS OF THE BLESSED SACRAMENT

AUSTRALIAN POSTULANTS AFTER 1950

Barbara Fingleton (Sister Marguerite/Sister Mary Margaret) grew up on a farm near Moree in New South Wales. She joined the convent in 1955, aged twenty.

Betty McMenamin (Sister Mary Francesca), a Melbourne woman who became Mother Superior in 1968. As leader, she guided the community through the great changes of the late 1960s and early 1970s.

Carol Hogan (Sister Mary Frances), a Melbourne woman who joined in 1953, aged twenty-two. She later became a feminist theologian.

Charito (Sister Maria Rosario Ungson), a Filipina sister who remained part of the Australian community after completing her training at Armadale.

Jill Thomas (Sister Mary Agnes), a Melbourne woman who entered the convent in 1951, aged seventeen.

Marian McClelland joined the Faithful Companions of Jesus in 1967 at age nineteen and soon after became a teaching nun at her former girls' high school, Genazzano. Marian left the Faithful Companions of Jesus and joined the Blessed Sacrament sisters in 1974.

Marie Philomena Grunke (Sister Marie Magella) grew up on a farm in Queensland before travelling and working in New Zealand. She joined the Blessed Sacrament sisters in 1966, when she was twenty-seven.

Mary Kelly joined the order in 1966, on the same day as Marie Grunke.

Maureen Flood (Sister Maureen) grew up in and around pubs in regional New South Wales before becoming a nun and later Novice Mistress. Like her friend Vianney, she joined the convent in 1957. Maureen later became an accomplished writer.

Maureen Monica O'Leary (Sister Monica), an Adelaide woman who was for many years the convent's main cook. She joined on the same day as Maureen Flood and Vianney Hatton, in 1957.

Melissa Jaffer, an actress both before and after her time as a Blessed Sacrament sister, joined the convent in 1965.

Sister Pete (formally Sister Peter Julian, and formerly Linda Wells), a Melbourne woman who in 1951 became one of the Australian community's first postulants.

Vianney Hatton, a Sydney girl who studied physiotherapy at Sydney University. She befriended Maureen Flood shortly before they both joined the Blessed Sacrament sisters in 1957, when they were each twenty-one.

FOUNDING MEMBERS OF THE AUSTRALIAN COMMUNITY OF THE BLESSED SACRAMENT SISTERS

Several sisters came from Canada to found the Armadale community, including:

Sister Berthe, a French-Canadian nun and founding Mother Superior of the Armadale convent.

Sister Mary Leonard, an Australian nun who undertook her training in Canada and who served as Mother Superior for many years.

Sister Mary Philomena, another of the Canadian sisters.

AUTHOR'S PROLOGUE

THE LIVES OF nuns have long held a powerful fascination for ordinary people, believers and non-believers alike. The idea of a group of women living behind high walls and closed doors, neither mothers nor wives, pursuing a life of the spirit, has aroused deep interest, suspicion, conjecture and fantasy for as long as the convent has existed.

Some of those fantasies and suspicions helped fuel bitter disputes over religion, from the Reformation in sixteenth-century Europe through to the sectarian tensions that plagued 1950s Australia. Others inspired a steady stream of pop culture entertainment, from steamy pulp fiction to classic films such as *The Nun's Story* starring Audrey Hepburn or *Sister Act* with Whoopi Goldberg.

Part of the fascination is surely the convent's mysterious separateness from the rest of the world. I was educated at Catholic schools, but the students never darkened the door of the convent itself. Most of what I imagined the inside of a convent to look like came from *The Sound of Music*. The nuns housed next door to our classrooms in Sydney's inner west had nearly all retired from teaching, and we rarely if ever saw them. In fact, the clearest sign of their continued presence was the occasional fire alarm that saw hundreds of girls marched out of class and onto the safety of the school lawns, all because the good sisters had burnt their toast.

In my 1980s childhood, we watched reruns of the 1967 TV sitcom *The Flying Nun*, where Sally Field's miraculous veil lifted her off the ground to attend to the everyday tribulations of the citizens of San Juan, Puerto Rico. As a teenager, I was glued to the screen and to one of Naomi Watts' first performances in the hit mini-series *Brides of Christ*, still the highest-rating drama ever made by the Australian Broadcasting Corporation (much of it was shot at the high school I attended). As I write, a new horror film starring Sydney Sweeney is in cinemas, set in a creepy Italian convent.

Monastic women retain a hold over our imaginations, even as they have largely disappeared from everyday life in countries like Australia.

This book takes us right inside one Australian convent. It offers an unusually candid and intimate account of the lives of the women who lived there: their vocations; their religious, personal and professional lives; and the ways they negotiated the profound changes of the late twentieth century individually and together.

The story begins in the 1930s and 40s, when the women who tell it were born and grew up. They all came from Catholic families, and all were educated by nuns. Their homes were in rural towns, on farms in Queensland or New South Wales, or in the city. They would eventually live together, under new names, at the convent of the Servants of the Blessed Sacrament in Melbourne—an enclosed order of contemplative nuns that was almost entirely shut off from the world. The story as it is told here is based on oral history recordings made with six women, all nuns and ex-nuns, as well as the writings left behind by two of their sisters in religion, now deceased. Much of the story is therefore told in the women's own words which gives us special insight into their vocations; their religious, professional and personal lives; and the ways they negotiated the profound changes of the late twentieth century individually, and together.

These women's lives, though, are part of a much longer story, one that began about two thousand years ago, when Jesus gathered his disciples around him. Among these were several women, and the Gospels attest to their central role in Jesus's story and ministry—a role that ran counter to the one assigned them by Jewish society at that time. When the first Christian communities formed after Jesus's death, women sought to retain this central place. They were the heads of households where the first Christians gathered and where the ritual of Eucharist was celebrated. The new religion offered women a role in the world that Roman law and custom did not.[1] Groups of women lived together and committed themselves to a life of poverty in emulation of Christ and in solidarity with the poor. Others retreated to the desert and pursued an ascetic spirituality, either as solitary hermits or in monasteries, and were equals in spiritual authority alongside the desert fathers who lived in the wildernesses of the Middle East in the first centuries after Christ's death.

These women were the foremothers of those who would come to be known as nuns. Whether they were wives who lived apart from their husbands, 'repentant prostitutes', young unmarried women or widows, and whether they lived in the desert or in the cities and towns, they all took a vow of chastity. Chastity offered an alternative to the life of wifedom and motherhood, giving women who chose it the independence and authority to pursue a spiritual life.[2] As Jo Ann Kay McNamara writes in her monumental history of nuns: 'No human institution is older than this sisterhood.'[3]

Over the centuries, congregations of women religious formed throughout Europe, each with its own character. The abbess led the congregation and enjoyed a position of power and influence both within the convent and, often, beyond it. But as the Church grew to become Europe's most powerful institution, women religious were brought under its centralised, masculine control. By the Middle

Ages, the vow of celibacy had become a cult of chastity, with clerical authority neurotically focused on the notion and protection of female sexual virtue. Rules for monastic life were established and imposed, and for women, many of them were more strictly enforced than they were for male religious. In particular nuns of all kinds were confined to the cloister: a strict enclosure behind impenetrable walls, separating them from the rest of society.[4] Yet the idea of women withdrawn into a world without men was also threatening to the clergy, and power struggles between abbess and bishop were not infrequent.[5]

Enclosure notwithstanding, convents often remained powerful and wealthy institutions and the women inside them participated in the larger world. Whether by writing, composing music or advising the faithful—from local believers to men of state—nuns wielded power both spiritual and material. Among them were some of the most influential figures of the Catholic church.

Saint Teresa of Ávila was a sixteenth-century Spanish noblewoman who became a Carmelite nun, theologian and reformer who wrote hugely influential texts about her mystical experiences and whose spiritual ecstasies were famously rendered in sculpture by Gian Lorenzo Bernini. Hildegard von Bingen was a twelfth-century German Benedictine abbess and polymath, who wrote what remains some of the world's most well-known and beloved sacred music. She was also a writer, philosopher, mystic, visionary and medical author. Juana Inés de la Cruz, a seventeenth-century Mexican Hieronymite nun, was a writer, composer, philosopher, poet and advocate for female education who was possibly the most accomplished author of the entire history of the Spanish Americas.

Some nuns directly disobeyed church officials to achieve their aims. Arcangela Tarabotti was an unwilling nun, forced by her father into a convent due to her disability and 'unmarriageability.' She became an early political theorist, exchanging letters with some of the leading intellectuals of seventeenth-century Venice. The books she published during her life included a proto-feminist manifesto called *Paternal Tyranny*, which Vatican censors duly banned. It wasn't until the 1930s that scholars rediscovered her work.

Nuns were sometimes among the most influential women of their times, but their important (and well-documented) contributions to political, cultural and spiritual life were often overlooked, unacknowledged or undiscovered by historians until recent decades. Convents were, from the Middle Ages, important centres of female creativity and intellectual labour.[6] Scholars now believe that convents across Europe and its dominions housed some of the artists, writers and scribes who were responsible for a large but unknowable portion of the Middle Ages' anonymous works of literature, including the detailed illuminated manuscripts that circulated during that time, and which convents produced as a source of income. (In 2019, researchers studying the human diet in the Middle Ages discovered a speck of blue lapis lazuli behind the teeth of a long-dead German nun, proving that she worked with what was then the most expensive pigment, one that only accomplished artists could access.) In our own time, we have the hypnotic blues piano compositions of the Ethiopian nun Emahoy Tsegué-Maryam Guèbrou, and Australia's very own Grammy-winning holy hit machine, Sister Janct Mead.

As for the traditionally feminine arts of cookery and textile work, the contribution made by women's convents are well known. Confectionary known as 'convent sweets' have been prepared by nuns since the sixteenth century, earning important income for the sisters while aiding their diplomatic and evangelical purposes.[7] Two French nuns, expelled from their convent after the French Revolution, were forced to bake and sell sweets to survive, thus popularising the macaron, while in Australia, the Carmelites at Wagga Wagga have long been renowned for their quality lamingtons. The fine needlework created by nuns decorated the robes of countless clergymen and there can be little doubt that nuns' hands wove many an unsigned masterpiece in tapestry. Convents have also commissioned countless works of art by composers, painters, instrument makers and architects—from the young Diego Velázquez's seventeenth-century portrait of a Poor Clare nun to Henri Matisse's Chapel of the Rosary, a modernist wonder in stained glass.

Women of all social classes became nuns. Some because they wanted an education and a life of the mind that was otherwise unattainable. These women had to bring a dowry in order to take their vows as choir nuns. For some destitute women, the only means of taking permanent shelter in the convent was to join as what was known as a lay nun—these women provided their labour in place of a dowry, working for their keep by cleaning and cooking.

Whatever their circumstances, most nuns were motivated by a powerful spiritual vocation. Some, though, were forced into convents. Fathers in Renaissance Italy, wishing to preserve the family fortune for a male heir, would often send their daughters to a convent, where the asking price for a dowry was significantly lower than it was on the marriage market.[8] On the other hand, many nuns were forced out of their convent homes during historical upheavals. The Reformation saw the dissolution of the monasteries in England and their suppression across northern, protestant Europe. Later, in France, following the French Revolution, Church property was nationalised and many convents forcibly closed.

We know a great deal more about the lives of nuns than we do about the lives of other ordinary women long dead and gone—the many millions who were neither queens nor duchesses worthy of having their histories recorded—because convents kept records. Along with prosaic data about who was professed on what date and how much corn was ordered for the winter months, convent archives are rich with women's stories. Nuns wrote hagiographies of their foundresses and accounts of their visions. They wrote dramatic plays. They wrote works of theology and natural medicine. And they wrote the stories of their own vocations and their lives as religious sisters. To quote Jo Ann McNamara again:

> [Convents] created fertile ground for the growth of a separate feminine sensibility and strengthened the bonds of sisterhood in religion. The trials and triumphs of the community resound through the literature of, for and about nuns in every age and environment … Foremothers who, for two millennia, have broken new paths for women in a hostile and forbidden world. They served their god and their church and in doing so they fulfilled themselves and laid a foundation for all women. Without the daring and sacrifice of these nuns, it is impossible to imagine the feminist movements of modern times finding any purchase in the public world. They created the image and the reality of the autonomous woman.[9]

This story, then, not only forms part of a long tradition of women's Christian devotion, but also of women's writing.

I was invited to produce this book by a group of sisters who I came to know through my family's connection with St Vincent de Paul's Church in Redfern. We became part of that parish when I was around ten years old, and during Sunday Mass, my curiosity was awakened by the women who sat together and quietly changed the words of the service, removing any masculine pronouns attached to God. They were different from the nuns who had taught me at primary school: they didn't work as teachers, and they didn't wear the habit. My family befriended some of the women, and they welcomed my questions about why they had become nuns, why they remained nuns, and what they thought God was. As I grew up, my own faith waned and my allegiance to the institutional Church was broken, but I retained a strong interest in religion and religious belief. I remained in touch with two of these women, and I always saw them as that part of the Church to which I could retain a sense of loyalty and kinship.

+++

The Servants of the Blessed Sacrament were established as an order in nineteenth-century France, amid a great revival in religious life. At that time, the Catholic Church stood in opposition to many of the intellectual and philosophical currents of the time: Enlightenment philosophy, evolutionary science, secularism, Marxism and nascent feminism. Women called to religious life hoped to realise the Church's vision of an alternative, 'perfect' society, starting with their own religious communities. Many new orders of nuns were founded, particularly in France and Ireland, which saw the work of nuns as lying well beyond the convent walls. These so-called 'active' orders (as opposed to 'contemplative' enclosed orders) offered women careers as teachers and nurses, or the opportunity to travel to far-off lands as missionaries. At a time when middle class women were increasingly confined to the domestic sphere, these professional opportunities were attractive.

So, while the Church sought to enlist women in its struggle against the dangers of modernity, these new orders of nuns became important agents of modernisation, educating girls from all social classes and laying the theoretical and practical foundations of what would eventually morph into the twentieth-century welfare state. In important ways, nuns formed the professions that would soon offer millions of laywomen the opportunity for self-actualisation and economic independence.[10]

By the time a small group of Blessed Sacrament sisters arrived in Melbourne in 1950, nuns had been part of Australian society for more than a century. The very first nuns to arrive in Australia were five Sisters of Charity, who sailed into Sydney from Cork in 1838. When they alighted in their full black habits, the Irish convicts who were laying the sandstone to build Circular Quay were said to have shed tears of joy.[11] The nuns soon walked from Sydney to Parramatta, where they established a school for the children of convict women working at the Female Factory.

Women like these became an important part of Australia's settler-colonial project and its mythology: hardy Irish nuns heading into the great unknown to educate the children of struggling farmers, keeping the old religion alive and planting its seeds in a new land.[12] While there can be little doubt about their hardiness, the land they were on was Aboriginal, and Catholic nuns played their part in the dispossession.[13] Yet their story is a varied and complex one. They educated many poor children who would otherwise have gone uneducated, and they set up institutions for the protection of single women, who faced unique challenges and dangers in the colony. Saint Mary MacKillop, who founded the Sisters of St Joseph of the Sacred Heart, the first Australian order, was dedicated to the welfare and education of the rural poor. She was briefly excommunicated after she blew the whistle on a possible case of clerical child sexual abuse.[14]

While nuns could be champions of social progress, they would also play their part in upholding and enforcing 'moral codes' that caused untold damage. In the late nineteenth century through to the 1960s, some Australian convents ran commercial laundries where 'fallen women' were shamed and often held against their will: their labour was exploited and their babies removed for adoption.[15] Missionary nuns played their part in the cultural genocide of child removal that gave rise to Australia's Stolen Generations. Yet the history of the First Australians' encounters with Catholicism and Catholic nuns is also complex. There was, for a short time, an Indigenous order of nuns in Australia (the one and only) at Beagle Bay Mission, in Western Australia, and its story points to the ways in which First Nations people adapted themselves to the imported religion and incorporated it into their lives, on their terms.[16]

In Australia and many other parts of the world, the lives of nuns were deeply impacted by two transformative processes that took place around the same time: the social changes that began in the late 1960s, particularly with respect to the roles women played in society, and the process of church reform known as Vatican II. Pope John XXIII called the Second Vatican Council, which was held from 1962 to 1965, to establish a process of renewal in the church that would affect the way nearly all Catholics experienced their religion. But no group was more impacted by the changes than women religious living in enclosed orders, who, for the first time in centuries, were able to cast off the 'rules, regulations, customs and community expectations' that circumscribed their lives.[17]

Since Vatican II many Australian nuns have been among the most enthusiastic and wise proponents of Church renewal, and of the adaptation of their own vocations to the needs of contemporary society. Some communities of nuns have consistently stuck their necks out for people who many Australians rejected and reviled. In 1984, the Sisters of Charity in Darlinghurst opened Australia's first HIV/AIDS ward, and in 1999 were about to open the country's first safe injecting room for drug users when the Vatican got wind of it and shut the project down. Others have been at the forefront of the peace movement, have worked in solidarity with Indigenous Australians and have fought tirelessly for refugee rights.

While most orders of nuns who came to Australia and those that were established here undertook work in the community, providing health care, welfare and educational services, the Servants of the Blessed Sacrament were different. They cleaved closer to the ancient tradition, remaining forever enclosed, praying for the salvation of human souls. Their founder, Peter Julian Eymard, was a French priest who had established a male congregation in 1856. Two years later, with the help of Mother Marguerite Guillot, he founded a women's order. Both were focused on Eucharistic spirituality and prayer before the Blessed Sacrament, which was understood as the material manifestation of Christ's presence among us on earth.

This is the story of one community of Servants of the Blessed Sacrament as it evolved to meet the demand for change that sounded in Australia and many other parts of the world in the second half of the last century. These women adapted their lives in response to the call for renewal set out by their Church at the Second Vatican Council, and to the changing world they discovered when they opened their convent doors in the years that followed. Up until those times, the ranks of Australian nuns were growing. They vastly outnumbered the priests, brothers, monks and bishops who made up the overwhelmingly male face of the Church (and they still do). But ever since that time, their communities have been shrinking, and now many female orders are dying.[18] This story is one chapter in a very long, rich history that, in Australia as in much of the so-called developed world, is slowly and quietly drawing to an end.

Many oral history recordings about the lives of Australian nuns have been made and archived—often by the nuns themselves. There was also a major project undertaken in 1985 by the Australian Conference of Leaders of Religious Institutes that sought to understand the post-Vatican II decades and the ways in which nuns and male religious changed their lives over that period.[19] This book makes a unique contribution to our knowledge of the lives of nuns by focusing on a small group of contemplative sisters—the minority among Australian women religious—and following their stories from the beginning of their lives until, for some of them, the very end.

The interviews for this book mostly took place in 2019. They built on interviews recorded by oral historian Jill Barnard in 2017, and I have included some of Ms Barnard's material in my text. I have woven together the interview material with records from the convent archives and the women's personal archives, as well from creative and academic writing left by Sister Maureen Flood, who was an accomplished writer and thinker, and a scholar of Judith Wright's work. Maureen wrote several personal essays, letters and reflections that are quoted throughout this book. Sister Carol Hogan, who completed a doctoral thesis on the community's evolution, became a feminist theologian of some influence in Australia and her writings provided very useful context and an additional point of view.

Both Maureen and Carol had died by the time this book project began. I relied for some historical detail on a small book by Mary Wilson, which was self-published by the community. These and other resources are cited in my bibliography. Many of the convent's documents that I refer to in the text are held in the convent's archives at the Archdiocese of Melbourne, along with the audio files of the oral history interviews on which this story is largely based.

The interview material is quoted in italics, a method modelled on Australian oral historian Alistair Thomson's in his book *Moving Stories*.[20] This is intended to make the work more readable by avoiding the repeated use of 'she said', and I hope it helps to highlight the substantial contribution each of the women made to the telling of their story. Personal letters are likewise quoted in italics, as are transcriptions of radio recordings. More formal documents are quoted using inverted commas or indentations.

An oral history is, in its original form, a sound recording. Transcribing it involves choices that are not always clear or simple, but I have endeavoured always to stay as true as possible to each woman's patterns of speech and the story as she told it. To make the material more readable, though, I have edited out words and phrases that don't affect the meaning—the 'ums', 'ahs' and 'you knows'. Where I have made substantive edits and deletions, I've marked these with ellipses (…).

As I drafted their story, the women corrected the drafts with me, usually in telephone conversations, and sought to clarify or edit their words on the page, so that the quoted material may not always precisely reflect the recordings. Since most of the women in this story have participated in the proofing and editing of the book as it has progressed, they are very much my co-authors.

And yet, this is my version of their story. It's a story the women wanted to tell, but it's also a story I wanted to know, and one that was told in response to my questions. As the pioneering oral historian Alessandro Portelli writes, 'the documents of oral history are always the result of a relationship, of a shared project in which both the interviewer and the interviewee are involved together'.[21] A different interviewer would have elicited a somewhat different account, and a different writer would have made different choices in the transcribing and organising of this collective autobiography. Memory, too, is unfixed, and changes over time, as well as from day to day. A different moment would have produced different memories.

Portelli reminds us that what makes oral history different from other forms of history is 'that it tells us less about events than about their meaning'.[22] It is made up of the memories that are transmitted, as well as those that are concealed. Indeed, 'the most precious information may lie in what the informants hide', and there were certainly questions for which I did not get an answer, as well as some I was too reticent to ask.[23] Oral history is unique in its ability to tell us about lives that would likely otherwise go unrecorded, and to tell us of those lives in the voices of those who lived them. It's that undisguised quality of subjectivity that provides oral history with its particular value. To quote Portelli once more, 'The importance of oral testimony may lie not in its adherence to fact, but rather in its departure from it, as imagination, symbolism and desire emerge.'[24]

I hope this story gives readers a rare insight into one group of women's unique experiences of God, the Church and their own unfolding spiritual vision as they grew from Catholic children into ardent young postulants; into women who experienced pain and loss, discovery and joy; and eventually into wise old nuns and ex-nuns.

BEGINNINGS

THEY COULDN'T EAT a bite of the roast Mrs Whelan had prepared. It was a Saturday, and it would be their last meal before entering the convent. Father Charlie Mayne had driven Vianney and Maureen down from Sydney on the Tuesday, and the girls had enjoyed being shown around town. Vianney supposed Charlie *felt that we should come earlier, to see a bit of Melbourne, since we were going to be locked up here for the rest of our lives.*

It was mid-May, and the year was 1957. The girls—and at twenty-one, they were hardly more than girls—had met once before, at a retreat for the Young Catholic Students, and both knew Father Charlie Mayne well. That week, he'd taken them to visit the Trappist monks at the Cistercian Abbey at Tarrawarra, in the Yarra Valley; to St Francis' Church (the oldest in Victoria and, until St Patrick's Cathedral was opened in 1897, Melbourne's most important); to the Catholic Library and the Young Catholic Workers headquarters. They visited the Blessed Sacrament Fathers' seminary at Lower Plenty, where they met Father Leonard (Len) McKenna, who promised to pay them a visit at the convent at Armadale, where the girls were soon to join a community of cloistered nuns. They also visited the Corpus Christi College, a Catholic seminary in Werribee, where Father Mayne was rector—an important job for a man who was an important Catholic figure in Melbourne and beyond.

Convents and monasteries were generally places of hospitality, and Vianney, Maureen and Father Mayne ate what Vianney described as a banquet lunch with the Trappist monks. At Corpus Christi College, they were welcomed warmly by the Sisters of St Joseph of Cluny: they heard a talk by one of the priests, met the seminarians and spoke with a young Hungarian boy who was one of several refugees the seminary was helping to settle.

Vianney sent a postcard of tree-lined Collins Street to her parents and brother Mick, recounting her adventures. The postcard reported that *Fr Mayne has been beaut* and that *Maureen is a super person, I like her better every hour*. They paid a visit to St Vincent's Hospital's maternity ward, and met the Mother Rectoress. There, they bumped into their new acquaintance, Father Len McKenna, who was arriving at the ward to visit Mrs Bob Santamaria (her husband, one of the country's most prominent Catholics, had played a key role in the then-recent split of the Australia Labor Party). When Father McKenna introduced Maureen and Vianney to that prodigious woman, resting after giving birth to her eighth child, she promised them she would bring her whole family to visit the girls at the convent.

+++

The convent in question was a fairly new establishment. It had been officially opened less than six years earlier, in the leafy suburb of Armadale, on 30 September 1951. A half-page report describing the auspicious occasion in detail appeared in the next edition of Melbourne's Catholic newspaper, *The Advocate*.[1] His Grace, Archbishop Mannix of Melbourne had stood before a 1200-strong crowd at an outdoor altar and bestowed blessings upon the building.

The twenty-five-room mansion, the former home of a shipping magnate, had been freshly reconditioned and adapted to suit the life of a group of nuns. The convent would be known as the Cenacle of Our Lady, Help of Christians—'Cenacle' so-named for the room in which Jesus and the Apostles were said to have gathered for the Last Supper. The women housed therein belonged to an order called the Servants of the Blessed Sacrament, founded in France about a century earlier. They were contemplative nuns, which meant they devoted themselves to a life of prayer, never leaving the confines of their convent, except to see a doctor. Only their chapel was open to the public, with Mass each morning (twice on Sundays) and Benediction—a devotional ceremony involving exposition and adoration of the Blessed Sacrament—in the evening.

It was a highly respectable crowd gathered there that afternoon. There were at least a dozen priests attending the archbishop. Archbishop Mannix received a warm welcome from Mr RE Hodgkinson, secretary of the organising committee, who declared that 'occasions like this afford us an opportunity to express our debt and warmth of affection to his Grace for all he has done for the people of Melbourne. For forty years, his Grace has championed the cause of the people and raised the status of the Catholic people throughout Victoria and Australia. The silent testimony to his great work are the convents, schools, homes, hospitals and religious orders of the Archdiocese.'

Indeed, Melbourne's Catholics had reason enough to feel a growing sense of cultural confidence. In the 1950s, more than 40 per cent of Australians were churchgoing Christians,[2] and among them were a growing number of Catholics. The sectarianism and anti-Catholic feeling that had predominated in Australia were on the wane. Australian Catholics were ascending from an Irish immigrant working class, with lower socioeconomic status and educational attainments, and were slowly becoming the equals of their Protestant countrymen.

Their ranks were swelling thanks to post-war migration from Italy and other parts of Catholic Europe.[3] Nevertheless, the Protestant majority still regarded Catholics as somewhat superstitious and eccentric, with customs such as not eating meat on Fridays setting them apart. Rules for Catholic living at the time were quite strict: the faithful had to fast before receiving Communion, and weekly Mass, always said in Latin, was obligatory. Confession was encouraged, and devout Catholics made theirs regularly. For Catholics like Vianney and Maureen, the church was at the centre of their cultural identity and their social world.

Those Catholics who stood out most in Australia were nuns. At once ubiquitous and mysterious, nuns were objects of curiosity for Catholics and non-Catholics alike. Their heads and bodies were concealed in all Australian seasons under veils and heavy 'habits' (long gowns). Oversize crucifixes and rosary beads hung from their belts. They famously took a vow of chastity, and their lives were mostly invisible, spent within the convent walls, where even the teaching and nursing orders lived in semi-enclosure. They were a common if fleeting sight in public, always traveling in pairs or groups as they moved between the convent and the parish church, the school or the hospital. Among Catholics, nuns were revered for their spirit of self-sacrifice and self-discipline, and for their devotion to God and the welfare of others. They were responsible for educating millions of Australian children and caring for the sick in their hospitals. It was quite usual in large Irish Catholic families for a daughter to go into religious life.[4]

The Servants of the Blessed Sacrament would not, however, be among those sisters seen in public—not even fleetingly. They would not teach in schools or nurse the sick or busy themselves with charitable work in the community. As Father R Ryder, Pastor of Armadale, remarked on the occasion of the convent's inauguration, 'one of the heresies of the age is the heresy of activity. Unless they are ceaselessly rushing around, many people think they are doing nothing.

The Sisters of the Blessed Sacrament have dedicated their lives to prayer. The unthinking regard the contemplative life as a life of ease. The truth is exactly the opposite. Their life of prayer is not haphazard, like ours, but a planned life of prayer and penance, day by day, year by year, until death.'[5]

As the rainclouds began to gather, the Very Reverend Father Leonard McKenna, leader of the priestly Congregation of the Blessed Sacrament, informed his audience that the new convent's renovations had incurred a debt of 25,000 pounds, which he hoped the faithful crowd would help defray. Appealing to their generosity, he assured them that the sisters were in 'a powerful position to attack the world and its problems, because they were praying for us at the fountainhead of grace, morning noon and night'. The sky darkened as the collection was taken, and Archbishop Mannix said he was delighted to see that the sisters had so many friends who were so generous in their support. Nobody was more pleased than he was to welcome them, he assured the crowd, 'and nobody more convinced that their coming would bring great blessings to the diocese'. Then the rain began to fall, and the archbishop cut short his remarks, hurriedly performing the Benediction as the faithful unfurled their umbrellas.

The crowd dispersed, and the nuns retired to their convent. The nucleus of the congregation was a small group of women who had sailed over from Quebec some twelve months earlier. Six of them were native French Canadians, and one was Australian. Sister Mary Leonard, a former organist for the Blessed Sacrament Priests at St Francis', had travelled to Canada to undertake her novitiate. These seven sisters had been joined just weeks earlier by three young Australian postulants.

Daily life in the convent revolved around prayer and household duties. The choir sisters recited the Divine Office in Latin and prayed before the Blessed Sacrament on a rotation system with an hour-long devotion every eight hours—two during the day and one at night. The coadjutrix, or lay sisters, prayed twice during the day and spent a greater portion of their time on domestic labour. Like countless women before them, the Servants of the Blessed Sacrament took vows of obedience, chastity and poverty, and that evening they faithfully prayed that their little community might soon begin to grow.

+++

Vianney and Maureen concluded their whirlwind tour of Catholic Melbourne with a visit to some friends of Father Mayne's—the Whelan family, in Coburg (its paterfamilias was the famous Whelan the Wrecker, who demolished many a historic Melbourne building and was later immortalised in an eponymous song by Nick Cave and the Bad Seeds). *I don't know*, Vianney recalled, *Charlie must have thought that we'd have a bit of female company or something or other.* On the Friday morning, Mrs Whelan decided that the girls had seen enough holy places, so she took them to the movies to see *Oklahoma!*, and afterwards they went to Hillier's for ice creams and milkshakes. The next morning, they got up early to go to Mass, though Vianney was less than enthusiastic. *I remember thinking, 'Oh look, I wish we could just sleep in this morning.' It was our last morning.* On the way home, Maureen and Vianney sang songs from *My Fair Lady.*

Then Mrs Whelan did this lovely baked dinner for us and none of us could eat it—neither Maureen nor me nor Charlie … We were all, I don't know—excited is not the word. Nervous, really nervous. It was a Saturday, and it would be the girls' last meal before entering the convent.

After lunch, on the way over to Armadale, Charlie took Maureen and Vianney to the Richmond football oval on Punt Road. *He said, 'If you live in Melbourne, you're going to need to know about AFL.' Little did he know, we'd hear nothing about the AFL.*

Vianney just remembers getting more and more anxious, *because we were supposed to be at the convent in time for Benediction.*

VOCATIONS

VIANNEY

VIANNEY HATTON WAS more or less raised in a convent from the tender age of seven. She and the other girls *were kind of brought up like little nuns. We went to Mass every day early in the morning. It was freezing cold.*

It was World War II that uprooted her from her family home in Bondi and exiled her to the Josephite nuns, miles from home. Soon after the Japanese Imperial Army had bombed Pearl Harbour in December 1941, the Australian government arranged a voluntary evacuation of children from Bondi and other areas they thought vulnerable to attack. Vianney and her little brother, Mick, were sent away—he to his grandparents at Kurri Kurri in the Hunter Valley, and she to a Catholic girls' boarding school at nearby Lochinvar, where her paternal aunt was a Josephite nun and teacher. A few months later, a Japanese submarine fired about a dozen shells over Bondi, one of them tearing a large hole in Simpson Street.

Leaving home at just seven years old was a big change. Vianney was a treasured little girl amid a large extended family. *I was the first grandchild on both sides of the family, and I have memories of lots of loving aunts and uncles, and of being spoilt with their love. I was so used to being loved and appreciated that, in later life, when sometimes I wasn't loved and appreciated, it was a bit of a new reality to have to come to terms with.*

School was a very austere place, not one bit softened by the presence of Vianney's aunt. *There wasn't anything warm and fuzzy or loving because she was there, and she would probably have been monitored to make sure she didn't give any special attention to me.*

The nuns were sometimes hard on the children. *They didn't have a lot of care for us as little girls. It was more a strict kind of life. When I think back to it, some of it was very hard. One thing that I remember, I suppose it was when I first went, I used to wet the bed—as any little girl sent away from home would. There was a toilet in the area where the big girls were, and this aunt made me go and sit on the toilet, and sit there for half an hour—it seemed like forever to me—and my memory of it is that it was very shameful. It was a very bad thing that I had done and very shameful.*

Vianney made do with letters from home—mostly from her Irish mother, who would occasionally come up for a visit. *All the girls would gather around and she'd tell them Irish stories. She was gregarious and very lovely.*

Back in Bondi during the holidays, Vianney spent her afternoons and weekends at the beach with neighbourhood children. Both her parents worked—her mother as a dressmaker and her father as a fireman. Later, the family moved from Bondi to a flat above the Kings Cross fire station. When she was at home, she relished the warm, lively family atmosphere. But when the war was over, Vianney stayed on at Lochinvar. *I got a bursary, and we got a telegram that said, 'Bishop's bursary—well done.' And now what I remember particularly about this is that I wanted to go up to the church to thank God for that.* She doesn't recall being asked whether she wanted to return home and attend school in Sydney. *Well, I presume that they asked me if I wanted to study there, but I don't have any memory of it. And in later years I've growled a bit about the fact that I did stay at Lochinvar, and that I didn't have the chance to come home and be part of the family. I regretted that very much.*

Though Vianney missed her family while she was at school, she enjoyed learning. She was clever, and her favourite subject was English. Vianney loved to read, relishing her study of Shakespeare—*A Midsummer Night's Dream*, *King Lear* and *The Merchant of Venice.* She also excelled at Latin and Ancient History. In her spare time, she devoured the regency romances of Georgette Heyer. *I read the whole lot of them, which were appropriate to a silly teenager. I just went to the library and got one after the other.* She also read *Little Women*, and her father cut each instalment of Ruth Park's *The Harp in the South* from Saturday's *Sydney Morning Herald* and posted it to Vianney at Lochinvar.

There was also religious education, of course, and religious readings. She read *The Lives of the Saints* and the spiritual memoir of Saint Thérèse of Lisieux, whose writings about her extreme spiritual exertions were very popular at the time. But Vianney wasn't especially inspired by those stories. *I didn't find myself attracted to what Saint Thérèse was doing, and I remember finding her suffering too terrible, and how hard the nuns were on her, and that all seemed to be very, very silly, extremely silly, not letting her take painkillers and things like that.*

It wasn't suffering that inspired Vianney, but beauty.

When I was about sixteen, I was doing English honours and we were introduced to the poet Gerard Manley Hopkins, and I became very caught up in this part, which is not so well known, of his poetry, but which really explained to me what my vocation was.

Vianney loved the maiden's song from *St Winefred's Well*—an unfinished play by Hopkins about a virgin martyr who is decapitated by her enraged admirer only to have both her head and life miraculously restored. The maiden's song was called 'The Leaden Echo and the Golden Echo' and it seemed to express how she understood her relationship with God.

Winning ways, airs innocent, maiden manners, sweet looks, loose locks, long locks, lovelocks, gaygear, going gallant, girlgrace—
Resign them, sign them, seal them, send them, motion them with breath,
And with sighs soaring, soaring sighs deliver
Them; beauty-in-the-ghost, deliver it, early now, long before death
Give beauty back, beauty, beauty, beauty, back to God, beauty's self and beauty's giver.
See; not a hair is, not an eyelash, not the least lash lost; every hair
Is, hair of the head, numbered.

It's quite important, Vianney explained. *The thing about it was that God is offered to us as beauty. And then, the only way that we could be given to God is as beauty. 'Beauty, beauty, beauty, back to God, beauty's self and beauty's giver.' I thought that I had beauty and that that's what I could give.*

By the end of high school, Vianney had decided she wanted to become a nun. It was quite a common path for girls at her school to take. *A lot of the girls entered the convent straight after they finished. The class ahead of us had seventeen or eighteen girls, and of those something like ten entered—a huge number.* The nuns who taught at the school were very keen to speak to those students who may have vocations, and to help direct them. But Vianney kept her feelings to herself. Though her parents were strong Catholics, they weren't pious, and she was fairly sure they wouldn't welcome the news.

MAUREEN

Maureen Flood was born in the same year as Vianney, 1935, but hers was a country family and a much larger one. Her father was a publican, and Maureen and her siblings grew up in a series of country hotels in New South Wales.

> My understanding of people and life came from life in the hotel, with all the characters who made up the cast.
>
> The men: boarders, drifters, drinkers, commercial travellers, businessmen, barmen, chefs, priests (mostly Irish), men from 'properties' in town for the day. The women: housekeepers, cooks, waitresses, barmaids, the women who drank in the Ladies' Lounge, boarders, wives of the men from the properties, with their children, nuns who ate in a room by themselves.
>
> This procession of people—flamboyant, eccentric, unconventional, down-and-out, proud, certain, lost—wound its way through my days and nights.[1]

Maureen's father was a proud Irishman. His brother, Frank—Francis Xavier Flood—had been one of ten Irish patriots hanged by the British at Dublin's Mountjoy Prison during Ireland's War of Independence. Maureen was surrounded by this and many other legends of her father's 'magical, mythical land'.

> All the heroes I knew about then were men. I didn't think that was strange. Now, I wonder about my grandmother, whom I never knew, the mother of these boy heroes. It was her blood nourished them in her womb. At hard times in my life I have strengthened myself with the knowledge that the blood of courage runs in my veins. Is this my father's blood or my grandmother's blood?[2]

Maureen adored her father, 'a vivid memory of care and fun, fairness and warmth. He really loved and even liked us kids'.

> Dad, tall, good looking, laughing, loving to sing and dance. It was he who taught us our prayers and he who came up every

> night to 'hear' our prayers ... He was the fulfiller of dreams. He achieved what he dreamed of for himself and he gave what he promised to us.[3]

Soon, tragedy struck the Flood family: Maureen's brother, Lesley, the youngest of the five Flood siblings, was run over and killed when he was just four years old.

> That was terrible. I'll never forget seeing my mother just lying still on her bed, with Dad kneeling beside her with his arm stretched over her. We were all sitting in our parents' room and I can hear myself say, 'Well, anyway, we know he's in Heaven.' That was actually consoling, but it was the piety of the girl that I was at that stage, when Heaven was a lovely place somewhere in the sky. We didn't have any other way to handle that death.[4]

While the pub provided Maureen's social education, the surrounding bush offered inspiration and awe. 'The bush, but not "out in the bush"; that was frightening for my Irish-English blood—frightening and fascinating. The promise was in the far hills and in the near hills, which surrounded us. I could never walk far in the bush alone.'[5]

Maureen's awestruck feeling for the bush sat alongside her faith in a very traditional Catholic God.

> Always the 'God of the Fathers'; my father's God. Love was here. Fascination too. And fear. I spoke to God in Church and in my prayers. I felt mystery in the hills and in the endless stars. Not in my body. Spiritual life had nothing to do with my body. God was not in singing and dancing, playing and running wild. Only in my prayers and in Church. With all that, I was drawn irresistibly into a world of mystery.[6]

Maureen gave an interview to ABC Radio National in 1996, and said, *I used to wonder about God and about eternity and one of my very earliest memories is on a little balcony at our hotel … looking up at the stars and wondering very, very seriously and deeply about God and about eternity. And the sense of eternity was conveyed to me through the immensity of the heavens, really.* But Maureen had not yet begun to consider devoting her life to that idea. *I thought I was going to be married and have lots of children.*[7]

When World War II broke out, Maureen's father couldn't join the army because he was slightly deaf, so the family was spared that worry and loss. He made them a promise that when the war ended, he would take them all home to see Ireland. That eventual trip was a very happy time for the Flood family, who were warmly welcomed into their big Irish clan. Maureen celebrated a snow-covered twelfth birthday there.

But back in Australia three years later, Maureen's father died suddenly. He was only forty-seven. 'He had a heart attack in the middle of the night. I don't think any of us really recovered from that blow. It was a huge adjustment to be without him and I had to give my mother a lot of support.'[8]

After leaving school, Maureen moved to Sydney to work.

> I went nursing for three years at St Vincent's Hospital in Sydney, but gradually I realised I didn't want to be a nurse for the rest of my life. I had thought of being a nun on and off. In those days I was pretty holy, believing in everything and going to church regularly. I used to go down to the church of the Blessed Sacrament priests in Haymarket. From them I found out about the Blessed Sacrament sisters in Melbourne, a very strictly enclosed order who had adoration of the Blessed Sacrament in the chapel day and night.[9]

Maureen made a decision, or perhaps it was the reaching of a realisation. *It struck me rather forcibly that in fact if I was going to live a worthwhile life, for me the best way would be to enter a convent.*[10] Maureen decided to join the new convent of The Servants of the Blessed Sacrament in Melbourne. And that was how she found herself staring at the roast dinner at Mrs Whelan's with Vianney and Father Charlie Mayne.

Maureen wrote that 'the idea of giving up everything and going a thousand miles from my family did not deter me. I thought that if you were going to give your life to God, you had to do the hardest thing.'[11] Her mother and siblings had no inkling of Maureen's hunger for holiness, and were shocked. Indeed, her mother was less than delighted, and Maureen knew her decision was hard on her family. She waited until she was twenty-one, and then she went. *Not without a great deal of pain, but there was nothing else I could do. My attraction was so strong.*[12]

BARBARA

When Maureen and Vianney entered the convent on 11 May 1957, one of the young novices there was Barbara Fingleton, known as Sister Mary Margaret—but mostly called Sister Marguerite. Like all the women at the convent, Barbara had changed her name upon entering the novitiate, marking the break with her former life and the start of her new one inside the convent walls. Women usually chose the name of a saint or other holy woman, and the central importance of Mary, the mother of Jesus, for Catholics meant that the convent was home to a very confusing number of Sister Marys.

Barbara was born in Moree in western New South Wales on 4 December 1934 and grew up on a large sheep station called Ogilvy. As the littlest of five girls, Barbara often felt overlooked, and even unloved. Her four older sisters were close together in age, but Barbara was three years younger than the second-youngest, Cathy, who, in her struggle to keep up with the eldest three, tended to ignore her baby sister. One of Barbara's earliest memories remains very clear. *We were going to Mass, and we were driving along and my father or mother said, 'Someone please wind down the window because it's getting warm,' or something. And I was nearest the window, so I stood up, and thought I was winding it down but I had actually opened the door. And I whooshed out like a feather and went under the car. And to my knowledge the wheels were going on either side of me and the car was going over my head. And I was in the middle of the road, but I felt as though I was landed on a bed of feathers.*

Lying in the middle of that empty country road, Barbara somehow imagined her family would go on driving to the church without her, leaving her there. *But my mother ran towards me ... She was running back, and I thought, 'Maybe I am loved after all.'*

Ogilvy was a remote property, and so while Barbara's parents were faithful Catholics, it wasn't possible for the family to go to Mass every week. There was an attempt to say the rosary together, but it didn't last. *We all gathered around the lounge room, with our backs to everyone, leaning on a chair or something. And I found it very strange and funny that we all sort of 'Hail Mary, full of grace ... Oh mumble mumble mumble.' And I was giggling ... I think some of the others were giggling, too. And so one day my father got up and said, 'That's the end of that. It doesn't work. I'm going to put these rosary beads on the mantelpiece.'*

Barbara was five when she and her sisters were sent to the nearest Catholic boarding school in Gunnedah, but it didn't last. Barbara wet the bed, which provoked the great ire of the nuns. Her sister Mercia wrote home to her parents that Barbara ought to go back home, and so she received a somewhat haphazard education via correspondence for the next few years. She envied her sisters, thinking *'They are getting to know how to be a human being. They're getting to know the truth about things, and I'm not.' I was even forgetting how to play. And even though I had two dogs that were my friends, I was the only one there. My parents were busy, Dad out on the farm and my mother doing things.*

Her solitude made Barbara a very observant child, and she came to understand that by watching something closely, really noticing it, it could reveal itself to her, along with deeper truths about the nature of existence. *Like, 'Why was that sheep out there walking around yesterday, and now a corpse I can see in the distance? Where did that life go?' I didn't know anything, but just by looking at it, I found out that truth comes to you. Because there was a sense that way up there, there was the Author of life. And that's what makes something that's living and something that's dead.*

It was during these long months or years at home that Barbara had two experiences that would change her life. The first happened during a visit from family on her father's side. They lived in Melbourne, and this was the first time Barbara had met them. Among them was a cousin, Paul. Listening to her mother and her aunt talking in the kitchen, Barbara learned that Paul, eight years her senior, and only sixteen years old himself, had decided to become a Franciscan priest. This greatly impressed Barbara, who perceived a deep spirituality in the young man. *And I stood behind Paul, and I thought, 'I'm going to listen, just listen, and take in everything about him' … And I thought, 'Oh he's very beautiful. He knows God loves him. You know—he's experienced it.'*

When Barbara went to bed that night, she contemplated what she had heard about Paul, and the feeling she had about his relationship with God. *How could the perfect Father turn his eyes away from the perfect Son to see and love someone else? And yet, I was convinced my cousin was seen and loved. Suddenly, a lightbulb came on. The perfect Father must see my cousin in the perfect Son, and the perfect Son in my cousin. I was transported and caught up in the love. I felt the Father bending over me with tremendous love and I was returning that love with the gift of myself.*

Not too long after Paul's visit, a priest was visiting the local area, and Barbara's parents invited him to say Mass at the farmhouse.

They invited all the Catholics from the district to attend, and to have breakfast afterwards. *And I thought, 'This is, you know, this is what Catholics have got to do—sit through this boring thing called Mass, just to get together and have breakfast.'* She was in the loungeroom while the priest said Mass, not taking too much notice of things, when she was suddenly overcome. *It's pretty hard to say, but I had this yearning, 'I want to know the truth. I want to be good. I want to be loving. I want to be lovable,' you know? But I added, 'But I'm powerless to do anything about it.' And then I saw the little host … This is what guided my life, really, this experience. I saw the host and I thought, 'That's strange. This is supposed to be a symbol of something very holy, really holy, Jesus or something. But it's more my symbol,' because I felt so insignificant, like a wafer.*

This strong message came to me with a very, very loving feeling: 'But I've identified with your nothingness'. Because I felt like a wafer, and that love that came to me, beautiful gentle love, it seemed to be totally identified with me, and I fell into nothingness. I just dived into that lovely presence I identified with, thinking nothingness was nothingness. I didn't care about the result of it. And, instead of nothingness, there was everything. There was the presence of the whole beautiful source of truth and love. And it was just … it was an experience that can't be really put into words … And when I eventually came back, that presence that identified with my nothingness was there, and said: 'Well, at least now you know your true self.'

Barbara would go on to refer to this mystical event as her 'experience'. She had thought that being sent away from school was the worst possible thing that could have happened to her, *but it ended up the greatest blessing by this experience that I had. It changed me from believing in separation to total oneness and love. I was bereft, in a sense, but I experienced perfection, love and joy and truth. I thought I had no truth and I experienced a wonderful feeling of truth: the real truth of oneness with God.*

By eight years old Barbara was beyond bed-wetting and was sent to board at St Philomena's in Moree. All her teachers were nuns, and she remembers them as being quite cold, and somewhat fearsome. Her parents gave her some very practical parting advice, including a tip about a natural anaesthetic that might help young Barbara withstand the trials of boarding school. *My parents, when I went to school, they said, 'Look, you will get the cane. There's no doubt about it. Everyone does. But you know you just rub some paper tree leaves on your hands before going to school.'*

The boys were all kept up the front of the classroom, where they could be more easily controlled, and the girls at the back. *You were just sitting up like a little soldier or something. And there was no real human touch or anything very loving about it.*

But Barbara enjoyed school, particularly religious education. What touched her most was the sense that Jesus reserved the most treasured place for those who Barbara calls *the lowest and the least.* She loved going to daily Mass, *and I loved the Latin because I didn't have to follow anything. I could just be in my experience.*

She completed her education at boarding schools in Sydney, where the nuns earmarked her for a future in religious orders. But Barbara wasn't interested in teaching. Instead, she noticed the lay nuns who polished the floors and dusted the furniture. *And I thought, 'That would be good because they're not expected to learn anything, teach anything. And they could be at home in their own truth rather than learning anything, rather than having to study.' And I thought, 'Well maybe that's a great thing.'*

But it was nursing where Barbara had her first job, rooming with the trainee nurses at the Children's Hospital in Camperdown. From there, she paid regular visits to the Blessed Sacrament Church at nearby Haymarket. *I knew the wonderful ways of going there and a shortest possible way from Camperdown to Haymarket. Whenever I wasn't nursing, I found myself going there to Mass.* And it was there that she discovered a pamphlet on the newly established convent of the Servants of the Blessed Sacrament in Melbourne, and there that Barbara found her answer. *The very name! I didn't want to know anything else. And I saw them, not looking at a saint, but looking at the host. And I had that great devotion, see, right from where I started to have my life turned around. And I walked out of that church like walking on air. 'Now I know where I'm supposed to go.'*

Not long after that, Barbara's father was in Sydney for a visit from Moree—her mother had died suddenly a few years earlier, when Barbara was at school. Barbara had already been accepted as a postulant by the nuns at Armadale. It was wintertime, and as her family all sat around a gas heater at the flat Barbara's sisters shared in Edgecliff, Barbara told them her news. *Everyone dropped their heads a bit when I said it, trying to take it in. But my sister, Mercia, piped up, and said, 'Oh, that's what I'm going to do! I'm going to become a nun.' And Mercia was a very social person—she'd had many boyfriends. Everyone swung their heads up and looked at her, because she was a most unlikely one.* Nobody seemed to take much notice of Barbara's news after that. *Everyone thought, well, I was a bit pious.* Her father didn't say anything. *He believed that we all had our seed within us, and his job was just to cultivate it, and look after us.* But years later, Barbara heard that he'd told other people, *'Oh if her mother was alive this wouldn't happen. It's like a death in the family.'*

Barbara and her father went down to Melbourne and, on the day she was to enter, her father escorted her to the cloister door on Hampden Road, Armadale. He was dressed up in a suit, *as if he was giving me away at a wedding.* Barbara was twenty years old.

JILL

Sister Mary Agnes was a young novice at the convent when Barbara arrived on 1 May 1955. Her real name was Jill Thomas and she had joined the Servants of the Blessed Sacrament in November 1951, at the tender age of seventeen, in just the second intake of Australian nuns.

Jill was born in the country, where the Murray and Darling rivers meet, but when her father found himself short of work during the Great Depression, he moved the family—including Jill and her older brother Terry—to Melbourne. *Yeah, it made you very thrifty. And you don't get over it.* But the family managed. *My dad always survived one way or another.* Jill supposes they were poor, but she never went without the necessities. *Most of the people we knew were just working people.*

A few years later, her father went off to war, lying about his age (he was in his early forties) in order to enlist. *I think it was because the Japanese were coming down to Australia, and they had probably hit Darwin by then, and he just suddenly said, 'I've signed up on going to war,' and so were a couple of his friends. And Dad was a man's man. So, you know, he was pretty happy out there.*

He was serving in New Guinea. *Mum was terrified. We all were. We thought he'd get killed. And one of my school friends' father had been killed. He was an airman. He died, and her mum was a widow. And Mum became very religious, and she and I used to go to Mass every day.*

Jill's mother took on work so that she could afford to send Jill to school at the Brigidine convent at Kildara. *You don't go far on a soldier's income.* She managed a store, and on the side she wrote articles for *The Monstrance*—a publication put out by the Blessed Sacrament Fathers at St Francis' Church on Lonsdale Street in central Melbourne. Jill often went there with her mother, to go to confession and to pray that her father would come home alive from the war. It was here that she developed the habit of prayer, trying to put in an hour of Adoration after Mass, *and when I went back to school after lunch, instead of going in and playing with the kids, I'd go to the church.* Prayer made her feel secure, and, even though she had many friendships she enjoyed, it allowed her to avoid socialising with her schoolmates. *I was two things: I was bold and outward, and I was also withdrawn.*

When Jill's father came home from the war, it was a big adjustment for the family. *There was a lot of friction there, because Terry had been head of the family since Dad went and he did not appreciate Dad coming home.* Her father had trouble getting work. *He was mending fences one week and trying to work in a shop the next week. It was hard to get a job if you didn't have qualifications.* After only a few short years back at home, her father took a job as a quarry manager in New Guinea, which was then under Australia's control, and she rarely saw him after that.

Though Jill had always imagined she would marry a farmer and have ten children, things changed for her when she went on a religious retreat with her schoolmates. She was about thirteen years old. *It was three days of fire and brimstone, with the dead coming back and printing their hands on the wall of the chapel. It terrified me, and I decided I wasn't going to go to hell. So the only way to save myself was to go into the convent. And the idea was there: I'm going to become a nun.* Her mother guessed right away. *When I came home from the retreat, Mum said, 'You're going to be a nun,' and I said, 'Oh yes, I'm going to be a nun.'*

Another thing that influenced Jill's decision was the sudden death of two of her schoolmates. One died of tuberculosis, and the other was swept away in the current at a local swimming spot. *I think to be religious you have to have a sort of experience of God. And I think in those times of stress and sorrow I realised there was more to it. And that definitely influenced me towards becoming a nun.*

Despite struggling a fair bit with her schoolwork, Jill hoped to become a Brigidine nun, like her teachers. But her confessor at St Francis' encouraged her to consider the Servants of the Blessed Sacrament, who had plans to set up a convent in Melbourne. This threw Jill into some turmoil as she deliberated about which order to choose. *I couldn't make up my mind. I thought, 'Hell, I can't stand this anymore. I'll go to the Blessed Sacrament sisters—it's the hardest thing I could do.'* Jill's faith was formed strongly by her awareness of life's hardships and losses, and her sense of God's presence gave her great comfort. *God made me to know him, love him and serve him here on Earth. And to be happy with him forever in Heaven. Wow, that'll do.*

Her mother was sorry to lose Jill, but glad for her vocation. Her father, who was not a Catholic, was not so happy. *He said, 'I will not come and visit you.'*

When she left school at fifteen, Jill was eager to join the convent right away, but she was too young and the convent at Armadale was not yet established. So she spent that summer holidaying with her boyfriend, Bill, and his family, before taking a job as a student teacher. *It was stressful, and I lost my voice. But I managed.*

She and Bill went out together for that whole year. *He knew I was going to be a nun. And I told him, 'Right, Bill, I'm joining the convent in November.'* It was 1951. Bill backed away, but he was the one driving the car to Armadale that November, with Jill and her mother on board. Another car drove behind them, packed with Jill's friends, all going to see her off. Her father, true to his promise, had gone back to New Guinea without saying goodbye.

MELISSA

Melissa Jaffer was born in South Australia on 1 December 1936, to young Catholic parents. Her father joined the RAAF when she was only three, and was away for the entire war and beyond, as he was one of the pilots charged with picking up the newly freed Australian prisoners of war left stranded in Sumatra and Java by the Japanese. *They literally opened the gates and let them go, and they didn't know where they were. So the aircraft used to fly in and get them, and spot them. And so Dad didn't really come home until the end of 1947, so I really didn't know him very well. And in those intervening years I lived with my mother, my grandmother and my sister—just the four of us—in Adelaide.*

Her parents shared a strong Catholic faith. Melissa describes them as deeply spiritual rather than particularly pious, and like all Catholics, they observed the main rules of the church. *Weekly Mass, of course, and confession every Saturday night before the pictures at the Star Theatre, Norwood—we always went to confession at St Ignatius*

Church before we went to the pictures. My father's faith particularly was very deep and strong, and my mother was something of a contemplative, I think. I think she really was, and she practised her contemplation all through her life, but mostly in her gardening. And she had a most glorious singing voice.

Melissa felt a strong pull towards God, or the spiritual dimension, from an early age. *I remember walking home from school, and being about seven or eight years old, and going into the church and kneeling down, and knowing that the source of my being, which we called God, was there.* But the Church was not her original calling. *I knew that I wanted to be an actor when I was eleven. I was at boarding school in Ballarat with the Loreto nuns. And they had a projector given to them as a gift.* It was there that Melissa first saw Laurence Olivier. *The senior girls were studying* Hamlet *and* Pride and Prejudice, *and they showed us those two films. And as soon as I saw him, I knew that's what I wanted to do. I knew.*

When she finished school, her family was living in Melbourne, so Melissa auditioned to join the National Theatre, and was accepted. *It was comprised of students who were on-the-job learners, really. We were in the shows, fortnightly repertory, but we were actually learning on the job.* Founded in 1938, Melbourne's National Theatre was one of a number of new companies, and the first to offer formal training and performance opportunities to Australian actors in their own country. But soon the Australian stage was too small for Melissa, and she sailed for London. It was there that the pull towards God became stronger. Melissa was about twenty-three, and *began to be drawn towards prayer, and drawn quite strongly. And so I would always go to Mass between the shows—do a matinee, go to Mass, go back and do a night show. I began to go to daily Mass when I was in London, and that's when the pulling became very strong. And the urge to seek a deeper … not understanding, but a deeper awareness of the source of being became very strong in me. It was a shock to me, because I'd never really considered that as a way of life. I was an actor. That was it.*

By the early 1960s she was back in Australia, performing in a play called *Under the Yum Yum Tree ... which was a very sexy sort of sixties romp for JC Williamson.* A 1962 review of the show in *The Bulletin* said Melissa was 'attractive, lively and very much at home on the stage,'[13] but she wanted something different. *And I suddenly felt this urge very strongly to retreat, to go into a convent. I suppose in broad terms that's what it was. I wanted to go into a convent. And it was very odd because at first I thought, 'This can't be right. Why would I . . . ? Why would I want to do that?'* It wasn't that she didn't want to continue acting. *My career was going gangbusters. I was doing very well, but I could not ignore this call, this urge—I think it was an urge—that even I didn't understand. But I followed it.*

When she told her parents, they were quite shocked and not at all pleased. *My father said, 'That's the worst piece of casting I've ever seen.' And my mother said, 'Well, you might change, but don't think we will.' They were absolutely stunned!*

Like many Melbourne Catholics, Melissa spent time at St Francis' Church, where she spoke to a priest about her vocation. He thought she ought to join an active order, since she'd been living such an outward, active life *and so he directed me towards the Missionary Sisters of the Society of Mary, I think they were called. They were mainly nurses in Samoa and all the islands surrounding Australia, or teachers. And I wasn't either of those, of course.* Melissa signed up as a postulant with the Missionary Sisters in Australia, but she quickly found that her vocation was not of a missionary kind. *So I went, and I was six months there. And the thing that I really loved was our time of meditation, which was only twenty minutes every morning. And I remember going to my Novice Mistress for my weekly chat, and she said, 'How's it going?' and I said, 'Well I love meditation.' 'Do you?' she said. 'Nobody else does.' I said, 'Yes, I do. I love it.' And she understood, I think, that my orientation was towards contemplation, the contemplative life, rather than active.* Melissa decided not to take her vows with the missionaries, but returned to the priest at St Francis' for guidance. He suggested the Servants of the Blessed Sacrament. Their convent was just around the corner from where the Jaffers lived—Melissa knew its chapel quite well. Her father was sick, and the family was going through a difficult period, and Melissa would often go to the Blessed Sacrament chapel to pray. *I started to go there every morning for Mass, and one thing led to another, and I applied there, and that's where I ended up.* It was 1965.

MARIE

In 1938, in the town of Goombungee on the Darling Downs in Queensland, Marie Philomena Grunke was born, the sixth in what would eventually become a family of thirteen children. Her parents were both of German stock, like many others in the district. Their forebears were shepherds who came to Australia for work, and soon took up small selections in the rich farmlands of the Darling Downs, where their knowledge of intensive farming saw them get the most out of their small acreages.

Marie was very happy on her family's farm. *It was a lovely way to wake up in the real world. We were fairly self-reliant, lived without electricity, so you just softly went from when you could see to where you couldn't, and in the twilight, you lit your lamps and you lit the fire.* It was what was known as a mixed farm, with milking cows, pigs and lots of chickens. Marie's father was both farmer and blacksmith, and even made shoes. *He always mended our shoes—I think in those days people just had to be able to do everything.* Nothing went to waste on the farm. Marie's mother was a wonderful cook, who tended a thriving vegetable garden and made all her own preserves, along with prizewinning cakes. *Every winter we killed a pig, and we all participated in processing the pork to get us right through the winter, so we'd have lots of German sausage. We had mettwurst and liverwurst—they were the two main sausages that we made from the pig.* The children all did their share of the work, making money selling whatever vegetables the family couldn't eat. *We were encouraged to grow things and then to harvest them and sell them in Toowoomba, and we'd go door to door with bags of peas that we had harvested. We were taught to be quite enterprising, really.*

The Grunke family would pile into the car and head to town for Mass every Sunday. *Every now and then we were the object of laughter from relatives and others who knew us because we were so many in this one little car! I knew they were laughing at us, and as a little girl of about ten or eleven it was so embarrassing.*

The children went to the nearest state primary school at Bergin, a little hamlet about a mile from the farm. *Every kid in our school was German. The only foreigners were an English teacher and his son.* For her final year of primary school, Marie boarded at the local Josephite school, thirteen miles from the farm. *I did fairly well in my scholarship year because Sister Gerard made me study really hard. I might have been a bit slack if she hadn't cracked the whip a lot around me.* Though she loved school, Marie was very homesick, and even hoped she'd catch polio so she'd be sent back to the farm. *I can remember looking out of the bedroom window, packing my suitcase to go back to boarding school and looking at the mallow grass. It's a particular sort of grass that grows really well in Queensland. It's got lovely big fluted leaves, with a little purple flower and tiny seed pods. I used to dissect them and they'd open like a mandarin. And I thought, 'I just want to remember what it looks like.' I was really just choked up because the car engine was switched on, waiting for me to get going.*

From her teenage years, Marie's teachers marked her out as a future nun, and so did some of her family. *My aunt Julia, who was my grandfather's sister, she was a Sister of Charity—a very regal woman, tall, dressed in black—and she had her eye on me. She said, 'That one's going to become a nun.' Unfortunately, she put that into my mother's head and my mother believed that that's what I should do. And I had moments where I thought that's what I should do, too.*

Yet when she was about to go off to Brisbane to study at the juniorate (a special kind of school for those who hoped to be nuns or priests), Marie was filled with dread. *My dear mother got all of my things ready, made some of the outfits I needed, including a beautiful dressing gown that she wanted me to have, and I'm all packed to go, and was to go next day from our little train station to Toowoomba to Brisbane. And she said to me, 'Do you really want to go?' and tears came to my eyes. I said, 'I don't.' Then she said, 'I don't think you should.' So that was the wisdom of my mother. I was so grateful. I remember the burden lifting from me, that I didn't have to go.*

Her mother, who was by now forty-seven, had just had her thirteenth child. The older children, including Marie's two older sisters, had all left home *and my mother had no one, really. My youngest brother, he wasn't even one, he was maybe five months old—and I thought, 'She can't manage,' and I think she knew deep down she couldn't manage.*

But by the time she was eighteen it was time for Marie to find her own way. None of the Grunke children stayed on the farm, as it was too small to sustain a second family. So Marie took a job in Toowoomba, at the railway station's refreshment room, *and I knew I'd be good at it. It was just simple work, making food for people and serving tables and things like that. It just came naturally to me.* Marie lived in the accommodations that the railway supplied. *You didn't have to look for a flat or anything so you could just bank your wage and save up.*

It was 1960, and Marie was about twenty-one, when she transferred to the railway station at Brisbane. Marie was still saving most of her wage, but she set aside enough to enjoy herself. She and the other young women who worked there and shared the accommodations would often go out together for a drink at the ladies' lounge at one of the local hotels, or to a dance. *We were like a community. I can remember in Brisbane when TV first came out and we got a set—well, the establishment got a set for us—and we all sat around the first night to work out what this thing was. And I remember after one night I watched until it faded out, because it stopped about midnight, and I thought, 'Well, if that's TV, I've had it.'* Marie left the television behind in favour of nights out with the other railway girls. *Oh, they were interesting young women. I loved them, and we'd go to dances and the hotels used to put on cabarets and visiting singers from different parts of the world would come through and we would jump on a tram in Brisbane down Queen Street and cross the ferry to Kangaroo Point or something like that.*

One day a young woman who worked with Marie confided in her: she was pregnant and was going to go to New Zealand to have the baby, and have it adopted. In the 1960s, there was a great deal of shame attached to unwed motherhood, and no provision at all for single mothers. Girls were afraid they'd be rejected by their families, or would be forced to marry. *I said, 'Are you going with anyone?' She said no. I said, 'You can't go on your own.' Everything in me felt for her. So I said, 'Well, I'll come with you.'*

Marie's best friend, Rusty, heard of the plan and decided to head across the Tasman with them. Meanwhile, the young pregnant woman, encouraged by Marie, had told her mother of her predicament. *I thought, there's a good chance that the mother will welcome her home—and she did. But you had to be a Protestant to get that sort of reception. Catholics wouldn't do that.* The plans having been made and tickets bought, Marie and Rusty went ahead without their friend. Marie spent the voyage playing table tennis and drawing pictures. She had a talent for art and had enrolled in a commercial art course by correspondence. Now, as the ship sailed out of Sydney, her skills came in handy. *I used to draw while I was up on the deck, and I'd be focusing, so that I wouldn't get sick.*

When they arrived in Wellington, she and Rusty quickly found jobs in the dining room of the St George Hotel. *And Dame Margot Fontaine and Nureyev, the ballet dancers, stayed there and I was very fortunate to have them on my table. So I thought, 'Well, this is pretty good. I'm getting to meet these extraordinary people!'*

The girls worked their way around New Zealand, from one hotel job to the next, living in staff accommodation and saving most of their wages, getting to know one town after another. Marie's memories of this time are detailed and very happy—it was a time of great freedom and adventure for her. *Rusty and I thought Queenstown was the most beautiful place we'd ever seen. It was still very tiny then. It was like fairyland, with the Remarkables that wrap around, and the ski slopes, and the little tiny chalets dotted around.* She and Rusty made friends with some ski instructors from the hotel, who gave them lessons during their time off. *So different from Toowoomba!*

Christchurch was to be their last stop before heading home, but there Marie met someone at a dance. By that stage, she had become weary of warding off men who *only wanted one thing. They didn't want to get to know you as a person. I was sick of wrestling for my life in a car with a bloke. I just didn't like it.* She went out dancing with no intention of looking for love, but there was Max. *And he was one of the funniest men I'd ever met.*

Marie and Max went out for a while, but *we were never really together as a couple. Catholics didn't do that if you weren't married. So, the thought was that we would get married—and he thought we would get married.* But soon Marie became pregnant. Max was very sanguine when she told him the news. *Max wanted us to live together. That's a totally normal and sensible thing to suggest. Here's me, being a very strict Catholic I said, 'No—I'd be living in sin.' The Catholic tradition dictates that if you're living in sin and you got killed in a car accident or something you'd go straight to hell.*

Marie kept going to Mass each day, placing her faith in God. *That gave me the comfort I needed, because my belief was totally that God would look after me. I knew that I made the mistake, but I knew God would forgive me … I can remember that I kept thinking, 'Oh I'll be alright. I'm not pregnant. And my monthly will return. I'll be alright.' And it didn't.*

Max wasn't willing to be married. *Well, he just felt he was too young, and he was. I mean, he was twenty-three and quite irresponsible. He was too young.* So, four months pregnant, Marie left Christchurch and Max, and headed to Auckland, with the ever-loyal Rusty at her side. The pair found work at another hotel and began saving up for the boat trip home.

As I always went to daily Mass wherever I was, I went to the cathedral in the heart of Auckland to find a priest I could speak with. After several weeks of speaking to him after daily Mass, Marie felt she could trust him not to censure her. *And so, with tears running down my face, saying 'I don't know what to do.' And he just said, 'Marie I'm going to look after you. Don't worry about it. We will get through. I'll get you through this.' Imagine what that was like to hear? And then after Communion each day, he would give me his blessing and bless the baby as well.*

Marie knew that unless Max showed up, she would have nowhere to turn. She did receive a letter from him, *you know, pouring out his heart and I thought, 'Oh maybe he's waking up, he's got to wake up.' But no.*

The priest at the cathedral arranged for Marie to stay with a local couple in the last weeks of her pregnancy. On 18 September 1963, she gave birth to her baby boy at the Women's Hospital in Auckland. *And still at that point I hadn't thought that I'm going to lose him. I still had hope that Max was going to turn up.*

For two weeks, Marie stayed in the hospital, recovering from the birth and taking care of her baby, feeding him from the bottle, because she'd been given medicine to make her own milk dry up. *I would hold him in front of me and I'd say, 'I'm going to remember you for ever.' I'd put his foot in my mouth and just kiss his toes.*

Within a few days a letter from Max arrived. *He was so happy to be a father. And that was it. No mention that he was going to come up and be with me. So, he was not going to come up from the South Island. He just was happy that I'd had our child. So that's when I realised it's finished. It's all finished, and I've got to lose my son … And I'm in the shower.*

I remember the day in the shower, and I started to cry. I thought, I can't afford to cry, because if I start crying now, I'll never stop and that'll be it.

Marie could see no way out of her predicament. Very few single women, and hardly any unmarried Catholic women, were able to keep their babies. There was no support for single mothers, and Marie couldn't tell her family. *I was completely backed into a corner. And one of the social workers said to me if I was 'selfish enough', were her words, 'to try to keep my child' because I'd need the child—the child didn't need me, according to her—if I was selfish enough to keep my child, social workers would keep a close eye on me and then I would lose my child, then he'd become a ward of the state … I still feel horror when I hear that.*

Marie left the hospital to take her son to the nuns at the Home of Compassion. After they took him, she headed straight to their chapel *and I said, 'You spared your own son. Why haven't you spared me mine?' I remember saying that, and I said, 'Just make sure that he's only ever loved, he's only ever loved.'*

Marie fell into a profound depression. *I couldn't pray. I found it distasteful … I didn't want to have anything to do with God anymore. I felt nothing. I looked out the window and looked at the trees, looked at the familiar sights, and there was no connection whatsoever. It was like I was losing connection with life.* But one evening she found herself at the cathedral, at Benediction. *I like Benedictions, with the incense and all the sensual things that are healthy for us, and I thought, 'I'll just go along to that,' and that was when it happened.*

I remember walking up to the church thinking, 'I feel so dead. There's no life left; it's all gone.' And there are moments in that ceremony when the priest puts a cloak around his shoulders, and he picks up the monstrance of the Sacrament and he makes the sign of the cross over the people. While he was doing that, I felt this movement inside me and I felt life coming back and I felt this deadness just begin to melt, and it kept melting. I felt tears running down my face. I thought, 'I'm getting my life back. What's happening?' I felt totally loved to the core of my being. Those are the only words I can find for that. To the core of my being, I was totally loved. It was the most amazing—call it a God experience—that I ever had, ever might have, perhaps, and it lasted for quite a long time. Normally they're just a fleeting moment, these things. And there was a procession around the church with the Sacrament and it lasted the whole time, and I thought, 'I've got my life back.' And I said to whoever it was, 'Whoever you are, I want to spend the rest of my life searching for you.' So that was that.

Marie wanted to keep faith with that experience, and to keep faith with her child. *I decided to go back to my old idea that I would become a nun. That way, I could maintain my connection with my son.*

MARIAN

In 1953, when Vianney and Maureen joined the convent, Marian McClelland was only nine years old. She was born in the same hospital as Vianney, the Waverley War Memorial Hospital, but the family (her parents, brother, Noel, and baby Marian) left their Coogee home soon after Marian's birth, moving to Melbourne. Marian's father had been a pilot with the Royal Australian Air Force, and before long he found a job flying with Ansett Airlines. A family home was built at what was then the edge of the city, and in 1949 the McClellands settled at East Ivanhoe. *The street only had a few houses in it—certainly there were no footpaths.*

The almost semi-rural flavour of East Ivanhoe was typical of the expanding post-war suburbs, where the Australian dream of the quarter-acre block was born. East Ivanhoe's streets sloped down towards the Yarra Flats, which were still a popular fishing and picnic spot, and where the local kids kept their horses in paddocks.

By the time Marian started school the family had welcomed another boy and girl. Their big sister walked herself down the street to the local primary school and back each day until she was seven, when she began to take the bus by herself to Genazzano, a rather upmarket Catholic girls' school in Kew, run by an order of nuns called the Faithful Companions of Jesus. *I loved school, I liked to learn and I was a good little girl. One of the other girls from school lived on the boulevard even closer to the river, so I'd visit her, and we'd go down and feed the ponies. And that led to my deep interest in horses. My grandfather paid for me to go riding when I was ten—that was terrific. I loved that.* By now there was a fifth McClelland sibling, a littlest sister, and having a pilot for a father meant they could all pile onto a plane and enjoy cheap flights to Sydney for holidays.

Marian was a good student but her education, styled especially for young Catholic ladies, was quite narrow. *You weren't allowed to do biology, for example. You never left the school grounds—you didn't go on excursions or any of that sort of thing. The whole thing was extremely regimented.* Most of her teachers were nuns, and Marian's favourite subjects were English literature, French, Latin, music and religion—she often won the prize for religious studies. *They called it 'Doctrine', for heaven's sake … I just loved the stories of Jesus. I thought he was a fantastic person. And we had Bible stories, which I found very interesting. They would have been severely edited, I'm sure of that, and carefully selected. There were too many juicy stories in the Old Testament.* Marian enjoyed going to chapel at school. *I was very attracted at an early age by … We always said, 'Jesus is in the tabernacle.' I wouldn't use that language now, but I was drawn to that. That sense that he was there, and you could converse with him. And over the years I came to make my own visits, especially when I was in the senior school from Year Nine, spending time there every morning.*

In her early teens, Marian was occupied with horses, and thought she might become a vet. But later, at *around fourteen, fifteen it just grew—that feeling that I wanted to be with Christ, I would say. So I would pray about all this. And that went on for a few years, thinking, 'What would I do? How would it be?'* She was surrounded by nuns at school, *and of course the nuns talked about being nuns, needless to say, because they wanted recruits and all that.*

It wasn't that Marian didn't want family life, or wasn't interested in boys, but *I would have felt very constrained in a one-person relationship. God was a bigger mystery, and somehow I wanted that. And I would wonder if it was a call.* Marian thought she'd become a teaching nun, since that was the sort she knew. *By the time I felt really secure about it all I would've been sixteen, and I'd have to say that my mother and father were a bit surprised. My mother said to me, 'Well, you know, I wanted to be a nun when I was your age, but then I met your father and that changed everything.' And I said, 'Well, that was you, not me.' My father said, 'Well, darling, you have seen your mother and me in marriage, but if that doesn't seem to be what you're called to, and if you have a calling, well we wouldn't stand in your way.'* They did, however, insist that Marian do one year of university.

By this stage, the late 1960s, Vatican II had taken place, but its revolutionary wave had not yet broken on Australian shores, and Marian was more or less unaware of what it held in store. By now, around 30 per cent of students at Australia's universities were women,[14] and Marian won a scholarship to do an arts degree at Melbourne University. She pursued her favourite subject, English literature, along with Indian studies, East Asian studies and political science. *I learned about Indian philosophy and the Bhagavad Gita and the Upanishads, and all those sorts of writings. And East Asian Studies introduced me to China, Chinese history, something of their art, modern Chinese history. And the Cultural Revolution was happening while I was studying, and later I got my copy of Mao's Little Red Book.* Marian made new friends and went on a few dates. *Yeah, I went to the pictures a few times and that. And the guys were nice, and if they got a bit smart, I'd say, 'Sorry, I'm going to the nunnery next year.' And so, on the second of February 1967, I 'left the world'. That was what you did in those times.* After one year of study, Marian entered the convent of the Faithful Companions of Jesus, next door to the school she'd left only twelve months earlier. The two other postulants who entered with her were likewise not long out of Genazzano. *So it was really just crossing from the boarding school to the novitiate.*

Marian would spend her first years as a nun with the FCJs before, some six years later, she joined the Blessed Sacrament sisters and began to share her life with the other women in this story.

VIANNEY

Towards the end of high school, Vianney was fielding the usual questions about what she planned to do after graduation. She wasn't ready to tell people her real plans, and had begun talking about a new profession called physiotherapy that she was interested in. But once Vianney finished school, the time came to choose a direction, and to let her family know her real choice.

And I remember walking along the beach—we were at Nelson Bay, which is a lovely seaside, bayside place up there in the Hunter Valley—walking the beach with my dad when the Leaving results came out. I had a really good pass and I knew I'd get a Commonwealth scholarship and all that kind of thing, and I was saying I thought I wanted to be a nun, and he's saying, 'But you could use this scholarship, you see?' And I said, 'But I don't know where I want to go with it.' He said, 'Well, what about this physiotherapy you've been talking about?' And I had been talking about it because nobody knew what it was in those days, least of all myself, but it was, you know, something to just hide behind, really. And my dad said 'Well, what about this physiotherapy? Why don't you try that?' So we hastened down to Sydney and I had to be interviewed and that's how I came to do it, and I was the least well-prepared for it.

Vianney began her studies at Sydney University in 1953. She recalls sitting in her first lecture, *thinking, I know nothing about this! I haven't done any of these subjects before and what am I doing this for? I should be doing Latin and English—doing something I like!* But she stuck with it, travelling from the fire station in Kings Cross to Camperdown each day, often on foot, to attend her classes. Her father would follow her around the apartment as she got ready to leave, proffering toast and other breakfast items. At home in the evenings, she'd practise her therapeutic techniques on young Michael.

Vianney, straight out of boarding school, found Sydney University almost overwhelming. No old school friends had gone off to university with her—those who went on to further study were at New England or Newcastle—and she wasn't living on campus, so it wasn't easy to make new friends. But by second year she had found her stride, and was finally growing up and out of her very sheltered, restricted childhood. Back in her early teens, Vianney's father would often take her to the art gallery while she was at home for the holidays, and he would gently mock her for squirming awkwardly before the nudes. Now she was studying anatomy by day, and cutting the rug at Sydney's famous Trocadero by night.

Most of Vianney's social life revolved around groups of Catholic students. She joined the Newman Society, which held retreats, prayer meetings, and social events like dances. The Church had just introduced the innovation of evening Mass, and Vianney and some of her fellow students began to attend a new chapel, built in an old warehouse on Broadway, run by the Blessed Sacrament Fathers. It was through them that she heard about the order of nuns who devoted themselves to the Blessed Sacrament, and who were eagerly seeking postulants at their new convent in Melbourne. Vianney felt straight away that she needed to go there. *For me, Jesus was in Heaven and in the Blessed Sacrament, so when I found this order, yes, it was pretty clear.* By the end of her second year, Vianney's father had been transferred to the fire department at Springwood, in the Blue Mountains. Vianney remembers walking around the garden there, *trying to tell my parents, but particularly my father—it's always he who is the dominant one in this—that I knew where I wanted to go. Anyhow, I finally got enough courage to tell him and he said, 'Well, alright, but you should finish your studies first.' Oh, dear, I didn't think that was good or easy.*

Vianney, without telling them exactly what she was up to, asked a friend if she could get a lift down to Melbourne with her family, as she had someone she needed to see. She went straight to the seminary at Werribee to meet Father Charlie Mayne. She knew Charlie from the Young Catholic Students retreats, and he took her to meet the Blessed Sacrament sisters. She had already been writing to Charlie about her vocation, and he often gave her guidance, suggesting books that might interest her. Together, they went to Armadale and knocked at the door of the convent. The heavy door opened as if by itself, and Vianney crossed the threshold to see a little grille in the wall, and the eyes of the Sister Portress peering at them from below her veil. In the parlour, she and Charlie spoke with the Mother Superior, again through a latticed grille, and thus Vianney got her first taste of the lives of the Servants of the Blessed Sacrament. *After that visit, I wasn't sure that this was the place.*

Her family was even less certain that the contemplative life would suit Vianney. *They thought that my personality was such that I wouldn't be very good. I mean, I was too gregarious, really, too used to a more enjoyable kind of life. So they thought that I'd be wasted on any kind of life like that.* Her father was worried that she'd be unhappy. *Very much so.*

But despite her own and others' misgivings, Vianney's longing to be with God only grew. She would visit the church on Broadway almost every day, to be as close to Jesus as she knew how. *I used to kneel in the back of that church and say, 'Oh, I want to be with you, God,' all the silly—not silly, they were appropriate to the time and who I was as a young woman—because it is very much like, well, a love affair. When you're that young, it is very much like choosing someone in a marriage, really.*

When at last she completed her studies, she thought she'd be able to leave for Melbourne. But again, her father, ever the voice of reason in Vianney's life, told her he thought she should return the Commonwealth's investment in her education. *Dad said, 'Well, you know, the government has educated you. You should at least work for the government.'* Vianney was dismayed, but she took a job as a resident physio at the Royal Prince Alfred Hospital, where she lived with a group of young female physios in a little cottage on the hospital grounds, just behind Missenden Road in Camperdown. Michael was by now at university, too, studying at the teachers' college, and he'd come over to the house or the hospital to have lunch with his sister, or to borrow a few pounds so he could take a girl out. Despite her impatience to enter the convent, this was a great year for Vianney, living with friends and earning her own income, much of which she put aside to pay the modest cost of her postulancy and novitiate—the two periods of trial and initiation—at the convent.

In the summer of 1956–57, Vianney knew that she'd soon be 'leaving the world'. She was nearing the end of her residency and began spending most of her weekends with a young man from Springwood. *When the relationship with a boy got to the kissing stage, you knew you had to stop then, but there was not too much stopping with the guy from Springwood.* His family loved Vianney, and they all seemed to hope the pair would marry. But in her heart, Vianney's plans hadn't changed. Her father, far from encouraging Vianney to pursue the relationship—he had never been keen to lose her to the convent, after all—was quite severe with her for giving the young man the wrong idea. Vianney, though divided, was sincere. *I fell quite badly in love with Harry, but I knew it was going to happen. It was a hard decision to let it happen.*

More than a little heartbroken, Vianney at last began preparing her trousseau to send down to Armadale. The nuns had stipulated a rather long list of everyday items she would need, and Vianney pondered the life ahead as she and her mother packed and folded the austere regulation clothing. *You had to have your black dress and your black shoes and your black stockings and oh, you had to have bloomers and all these kinds of things … I didn't have those romantic feelings when I started to put all the towels together. My mother said to me, 'What are you going to do with a dozen towels?'*

In May 1957 Vianney was once again at the threshold of the convent in Armadale, peering at the Sister Portress through the grille.

THROUGH THE CONVENT DOOR

POSTULANCY

ON 11 MAY 1957 Maureen and Vianney rang the convent bell and the door opened as if by some ghostly hand. The Sister Portress greeted them solemnly, and the girls were ushered through the heavy cloister door by another of the sisters, who urged them to get ready for Benediction. *So then they say, 'Where's your dress?' And my dress is in a big tea chest that I sent down with all my trousseau. So I had to run up—it had been put into the room that I was to have.* Vianney was dismayed to find her dress all crushed. *You know how you are at twenty-one, you wanted to look nice, but I didn't have the chance to iron it.* She got into her black shoes and stockings and raced to meet Maureen in the parlour, where Father Charlie was waiting to bid them both a final goodbye, and to have a look at them in their outfits. *Then they put a cape around us, because of course you mustn't show any shape of a woman, and then they put a veil on us to go into the chapel. And so in we go to the chapel with our veils down over our faces, because we mustn't be seen.*

The chapel was an intimate little church, with three or four pews for the nuns before the altar, and more for the general congregation at the back. The two sections were divided by an altar rail and a latticed screen, with a low door over which the priest served Communion to the faithful. The sanctuary at the front of the chapel was beautifully decorated. Pressed, starched linens dressed the altar, and fresh flowers filled all the spaces around the altar and tabernacle, where the hosts that made up the Blessed Sacrament—the Eucharist—were kept. It was like a *big throne for the Blessed Sacrament exposed.*

Straight after Benediction the sisters (at this stage there would have been no more than a dozen) filed out of the chapel, and *then we had to put on this little bonnet, this stupid bonnet—I don't know how to describe it.* The new postulants—Vianney, Maureen and a third young woman, Maureen Monica O'Leary (who, no doubt to her chagrin, was henceforth known as Monica in order to differentiate her from Maureen)—followed Sister Berthe, the Novice Mistress, into the refectory where the community gathered for dinner. In her letter home the next day, Vianney said they ate poached eggs on toast, followed by peaches and custard.

Sister Berthe was French Canadian, and had until recently been Mother Superior, but that role had now passed on to Sister Mary Leonard, an Australian who had spent her novitiate at the convent in Quebec. These two, along with five more nuns from Quebec, had travelled from Canada to Australia by boat to set up the Melbourne convent in 1950. Surrounded by substantial grounds and well-established gardens, the convent itself was an austere hulking grey building. But the chapel where the sisters prayed was beautiful. It was always decorated with fragrant flowers, and during the day, a soft light came in through the stained-glass windows, whose jewel-like colours seemed to glow. At night, the chapel was never deserted: at least two sisters prayed before the altar, their bowed heads lit by the warm flames of many candles. The opulence of the chapel stood in stark contrast to the nuns' living quarters: spare, cold and with impersonal furnishings, in keeping with the sisters' vows of poverty.

The postulancy was to last for six months, after which, if they were accepted, the young women would 'take the habit', and become novices. The novitiate was a second, more serious period of training, where the rules became stricter. If, after two years in the novitiate, a novice still felt sure that her place was in the convent, and the Mother Superior and Novice Mistress thought she was suitable and had a true vocation, then she could take her first, temporary vows and become a professed sister. Perpetual vows would come three years later, committing her to the convent for life, to remain within its walls until her death.

There was no conversation during dinner on that first night for Vianney, Maureen and Monica, nor on any other night. Instead, they listened to one of the nuns reading from a holy book. *I can tell you that the book they were reading that night was called* Life Everlasting *by Bishop Vaughan.* The sister read it in a heavy French-Canadian accent, and in a strange monotone called *recto tono*, which meant every word was spoken on the F-sharp note. *At first that is very strange.* Nobody explained the reason for this custom, nor its origin, but later Vianney learned that *one reason was so that nobody's voice would be outstanding. Everybody had to be the same.* After dinner, *they offered us a cup of tea and I asked them was there any sugar, and they got sugar for me—but that was the end of it. After that time there was no sugar.*

Half an hour of recreation followed dinner, and the three postulants met one another properly, along with the novices, who all exchanged polite, softly spoken conversation. Among them was Barbara, known now as Sister Marguerite, who was in her early twenties.

In the coming days, the new postulants would meet the other nuns—those from Canada, who had been fully professed, and a younger cohort of Australians who had taken their temporary vows. Among them was a beautiful, young, very quiet professed nun called Sister Mary Agnes, formerly known as Jill Thomas. Another was Sister Peter Julian (formerly Linda Wells of Hawthorn). She and Jill had both joined in 1951, the year the Armadale community had accepted its first local postulants.

Sister Peter Julian (named for the congregation's founder, Peter Julian Eymard) was part of the very first intake of Australian postulants in Melbourne, a few months ahead of Jill's, and was therefore the most experienced of the young Australian cohort. She became known as Sister Pete, though Barbara can't recall whether that moniker was already in use in these early days, when all the sisters' interactions were very formal. *She was so familiar and so lovely that as soon as we could, we called her Pete.* Barbara remembers Sister Peter Julian as a hard worker. *When she was in the laundry she would do the most difficult jobs, like stirring around the sanitary napkins—they were in a big bin that Pete took on cleaning. She would stir them and take over the washing of those things.* But she was also a free spirit, and was quite prepared to bend the rules at times.

Jill recalls *we had a code of silence—you could only speak for work or emergencies—but Peter Julian would put in a few words if she needed to. She was very strong-minded, very hard working ... She always had odd things in her pocket, like screwdrivers—she could fix things.* Sister Pete was quite a character. *One evening she was coming down to nocturnal Adoration, say one o'clock in the morning, and as she came down the big stairs—she was all dressed up in her habit—there was a rat running up the stairs,* recalls Jill. *The gong was sounding, and you had to be in the chapel as the bell sounded, so she jumped over the rat and proceeded to Adoration. She was just a hilarious person in that way.*

Perhaps it was Sister Pete's willingness to do whatever needed to be done, no matter how difficult or unpleasant the work, as well as her strong personality, that gave her a wider margin than some of the younger women enjoyed. As Barbara says, *I think she was respected, and they were pleased to have her. I think she must have helped them tremendously in the early days.*

Another of the younger nuns was Carol Hogan, known as Sister Mary Frances. Born in Essendon in 1931, Carol had entered the convent in 1953, after completing a Bachelor of Arts at the University of

Melbourne. Carol later came to write quite a bit about life as a Blessed Sacrament Sister, and she recollects the stir caused when Vianney and Maureen entered the convent and made some novel demands.

> Maureen and Vianney … started kicking up. They were smart: Vianney was a physio; Maureen had done some nursing. They were articulate, thinking women. I'd never been trained to think. They asked for a bath every day, which was agreed to when they were postulants. I hadn't done that. I just sweated away in my woollen habit and got rashes and stuff, but it was all for love.[1]

Jill can recall her jealousy when Carol Hogan entered. *When any of the girls from the university came, there were a lot of concessions made for them to help them adapt … When Peter Julian and I joined they were still very into the traditional European ways. You had a bath once a week. We had a jug and basin, and you washed each day in your room.* The weekly bath was less than satisfactory—the women had to bathe *in what was virtually a nightgown. Because if you happen to collapse in the bath you couldn't have someone come in and collect you naked. And I said, 'Right. I'd rather not have a bath.' So the good of Sister Mary Leonard* [the Mother Superior] *was that she fought for us and she made them change these old rules because they weren't acceptable in Australia. So we didn't have to wear the nightie.*

This degree of puritanism was quite unknown to Australian Catholics of Irish extraction, but Quebecois Catholicism, according to Vianney, carried strong traces of Jansenism—a seventeenth century theology focused on human depravity and original sin. *Our Novice Mistress told us that for them to go to a dance was a mortal sin. So that's where we were.* For Australian Catholics, *there was nothing wrong with dancing or having a glass of beer or having a good time.* The postulants found it all quite foreign.

Jill was fairly quiet, but she would occasionally assert herself via a silent rebellion of some sort. She resented the daily baths Maureen and Vianney enjoyed. As a novice she had had to ask permission of Mother Berthe every time she wanted to wash her hair. *Okay, so I go up to Mother Superior. 'May I wash my hair this Friday when I have my bath?' 'How long is it since you washed your hair, Sister Mary Agnes? Two weeks? Oh that's a bit soon.' 'Alright Mother Berthe.' So I waited a while. And I'm stubborn. I said, 'May I wash my hair?' 'How long is it, Sister Mary Agnes?' 'Three months.' 'Would you please wash your hair?!' Oh dear.*

Vianney's first letter home to her family recounts in detail her first twenty-four hours as a postulant, and mentions the evening bath: *we don't know how many we have but it's not as bad as we thought, apparently.* A somewhat disingenuous report: in fact, Vianney had simply told the Novice Mistress she wouldn't stay if they couldn't have a bath each day.

First impressions are difficult, almost impossible, to recover. But Vianney's mother kept a record of her daughter's first six months in the convent: a series of weekly letters from Vianney to her parents, bundled up, labelled and bound in rubber bands. They were addressed chiefly to her mother, with whom Vianney shared a long-standing epistolary exchange, thanks to her years in boarding school, when they would write one another several letters each week. In her fourth letter from the convent, though, Vianney gave her family the unwelcome news that letters were only distributed once a week. *We are given them only on Sunday—this was news to us all, but after the first surprise we have recovered and it's not too bad, really.*

Vianney received plenty of mail—from her physio friends, her aunts and even her old boyfriend, Harry. She occasionally got one from her brother, Mick. Sadly, Vianney didn't keep her mother's letters, but they must have been many pages long, and filled with vivid description (Vianney said she was a great raconteur). Vianney's letters home often ran up to sixteen pages, crammed with responses to her mother's many anecdotes about life at Springwood—Mick's football games, the bushfires ravaging the Blue Mountains and all the comings and goings of extended family and friends. *I was practically giving three cheers in my cell when I 'lived over' your description of the football … you're my very best correspondent, Mum.* Vianney would enquire after the trees and flower beds at home, describing in turn the convent's grounds, telling her mother which flowers were in bloom at any given time.

Of course, the letters were not private. *The Novice Mistress used to enjoy my mother's letters as much as I did. She read them all too, you know … I suppose that they had to read to make sure you weren't carrying on a love relationship with somebody or something like that—I don't know.* The receiving and reading of letters would remain one of the highlights of Vianney's week at the convent. As she wrote to her mother, *I don't know how I'll get on in Advent and Lent when we don't get letters!*

Given that they were scrutinised, Vianney's letters home cannot have contained a necessarily complete or accurate account. They express, in almost every case, the eager longings of a very fond daughter and sister to share her excitement at her new life, anxious to convince her family of that life's goodness and worthiness, and to reassure them of her own happiness. Vianney was very conscious of what her parents and brother had lost in her choice to enter the convent, and her letters are full of entreaties that they not worry about her. On 12 May, her first full day at the convent, she wrote: *Well it's Sunday afternoon, we're at Armadale and we're in good form. There is so much to tell you—perhaps if I begin by saying that everyone has been very kind and good to us and we are feeling fine, then you will be happy.*

The letters contain clues to the personality and preferences of the young Vianney. There are constant references to the food on offer, which by Vianney's account seemed both delicious and plentiful, though perhaps she exaggerated to cheer her mother up. In any case, she was clearly a young woman of healthy appetite. Her letters are filled with warm, well-intentioned family and local gossip, Vianney entering into all the details of her mother's reports as to who had been visiting and who was to soon be married, or to have her first baby. She was only allowed to write to her parents (and, once every six months, to her aunts Vera and Val, because they were nuns) but she received many letters from friends and family, and was always entreating her mother to reply to them on her behalf. She wanted a great deal of detail on the frocks her mother planned to wear to upcoming parties—Mrs Hatton was having all of Vianney's old party dresses altered to fit her, now that Vianney wouldn't need them. *I hope they don't look too young and frivolous on you—Dad and Mick will tell you.*

Vianney included Mick in her letters to her parents, giving her younger brother advice on how he ought to dress, encouraging him in his studies and chiding him for neglecting his books. She always wanted to know who he had taken to the latest ball, who he had met as he travelled around the state playing football, and who had won the match. She enquired after a large number of friends and relations, most of whom lived in New South Wales, miles away from the convent, and most of whom Vianney must have understood she would rarely if ever see again. She seemed very far from feeling removed from worldly concerns, and even mocked herself if she ever came across as too holy. *I am thinking of you, so often, you must know even when my letter doesn't arrive as expected that I love you all very much. You are in this as much as I am—right up to the hilt with me—in many ways it is less easy for you than it is for me, but we'll all offer it up for each other and pray with and for each other. Gosh, this sounds 'nunnish' and sanctimonious, but you know what I mean.*

Each Sunday afternoon the postulants received the letters that had arrived during the week, and were given time to write to their families. Vianney would retire to her 'cell', whose window opened to allow her onto a little balcony that was high enough to see Port Phillip Bay—the original mansion had been built by a ships' captain, who made sure his uppermost windows could see the boats coming in. Vianney would gaze out to the horizon as she composed long letters to her family, painting a picture for them of her new life:

We wear a black cape with hooks and eyes in front—comes just below the waist—and a cap on our head—it's of light black material, like a beret but with wide ruching in front. In the chapel we wear a long black cloak, not quite as long as our dress and a peculiar veil of white net with white material under the head part—I look a bit like a Quaker girl—this fastens up with a thin tape under the chin.

The three postulants did not have much contact with the professed nuns, mostly spending time with the Novice Mistress, Sister Berthe, and the novices. The day was organised around the sisters' great focus: Adoration of Jesus in the Blessed Sacrament. In her second letter home, Vianney recounted the general rhythm of the day, which was accompanied by the chanting, in Latin, of the Divine Office—a form of prayer based upon the Old Testament psalms—which has its origins in the earliest years of the Catholic Church and became a feature of monastic life in the Middle Ages:

6am—Get up, wash, dress, etc.

6:30am—To chapel for … some of the Office and preparation for

7am—Mass—followed by Office

8am—Breakfast—usually porridge (fairly nice and beaut and hot), apples, bread and butter and jam and coffee—much as you like.

8:30am—do your room. We don't sweep, only on Sat, but mop the floor with a piece of wool called a 'bat lain' I think—anyhow it's a jolly good idea—dust, then your duty. Mine is the Chapter Room and Corridor—mop, dust, tidy etc.

9:30—some reading and preparation for Adoration—which we've been taking usually in the mornings. Otherwise we have been helping with checking altar breads and general help—we spent two days—for a little bit each day—helping one of the sisters scrub and clean up a cell which has just been painted etc. Maureen moved into this when we finished—it was good fun doing it.

11:50—Examination, then

12—Dinner—pretty good—the meals are all pretty terrific, you help yourself with the food as it's passed round the table—much as you want.

12:30—Recreation. We've been playing a bit with the basketball and we're getting quite organised—someone suggested inter-convent comp, with Carmel our first opponents.

1:30—some prayers and reading then

1:50pm—Chapel for Vespers and Compline (Office)

2:10—Helping with altar breads etc—once we're organised this time I think will be for lessons, study, etc.

3:45—Afternoon tea. We have tea at all meals except breakfast (coffee), it is always beaut and hot—and weak which suits me fine—but not sugar—we don't have sugar on anything, porridge, crispies, etc. I don't mind these but can't go for the tea minus sugar. I dare say I'll get used to this too—even with my sweet tooth!! We have bread and honey or jam here—or sometimes biscuits.

5:15—Rosary, Benediction, Lauds (Office). This varies—we sometimes have Benediction at 7:15pm

6:30—Tea

7pm—recreation

The sisters went to bed at about 8 o'clock each evening.

Vianney still remembers enjoying the prayers of the Divine Office. *I'm one of the few who did. And because I'd done Latin, I was very able to … I don't want to say that I knew how to translate everything, but I had a fairly good idea about what we were singing about and what we were at, so I was very lucky in that point of view. And then I had an idea of the music because I'd done all my studies in violin. And so there was a whole lot there that I was able to grow with, you know, when I first entered.*

The Divine Office was said in the chapel, which was a very special place for those who prayed there—nuns and lay Catholics alike. Unlike a standard parish church, this one had the Blessed Sacrament exposed in the monstrance, upon the altar, at all times (or nearly all times—there were not always enough sisters in the convent to maintain unceasing adoration). At least two nuns would be found praying on their knees in Adoration of the Eucharist, day or night, and Benediction took place every day. Members of the public came to attend Mass and to pray, and the sisters maintained their cloistered state by only ever entering the chapel fully veiled, and separated from the general congregation. For the lay congregation, these nuns were particularly special, called by a higher vocation than those uncloistered nuns in 'active' orders (teaching, nursing and missionary sisters). The Servants of the Blessed Sacrament formed 'the court of the great King and His family of honour,'[2] as the order's constitutions declared. They sacrificed their whole lives—family, friends, freedom—to pray for the world, and save it by secluding themselves from it, and this was considered a particularly holy sacrifice.

Vianney's run-down mentions some of the nuns' other activities. One very important one, which took up a great deal of time and involved most of the sisters, was the production of altar breads. The convent had a kitchen which was a little factory for the making of the Eucharistic hosts for all of the Catholic churches in Victoria. The nuns worked in the steamy altar breads kitchen in their full habit, plus apron, mixing the paste, pouring it onto hot plates, punching out the round hosts and packing them into boxes. They had taken the work over from some other nuns, the Good Shepherd Sisters, who kindly offered it to the Servants of the Blessed Sacrament, so they could follow the recent papal directive for nuns to earn their own living. It was Sister Pete who ran the operation. As Jill recalls, *She was the one who made the altar breads a success. She dashed down as soon as she got up in the morning and made a huge paste of flour and water, then she'd do another pot after breakfast.*

Jill—Sister Mary Agnes—had been *dying to go into altar breads, because, you know, the Blessed Sacrament was going to be made out of these breads so it was sort of inspiring ... Well Sister Peter Julian went down and made the paste before Mass in a desperate rush—flour and water, flour and water, beating it up with a wooden spoon—and then rushed in for the Divine Office, and then went to Mass, Holy Communion, breakfast, and then dashed back down. It was all dash, dash. But the rest of us, we didn't have to make the paste. So we'd go down after breakfast and we'd start working then. The paste had to set before you could actually do the baking. So you baked and then they had to dampen down these sheets, and then we cut them on a cutter one at a time. Twenty thousand a day. And then they had to be boxed ... Sister Peter Julian had boxes that came from a lingerie shop and she cut them to size ... One had a half-naked woman on it and she sent it to the Jesuit school, and the boys got it. We got a message back from the Jesuits, 'Would you please send proper boxes, not naked women?'*

This labour provided the convent with an income, and Vianney took it on with enthusiasm. *Being the true daughter of my father, I was very strong on the fact that we did have to earn our living and it was our job to do so—not to be depending on the donations and gifts of the people who supported us ... The other thing about it was it was very Eucharistic work.* Via their labour, the Servants of the Blessed Sacrament provided the material for the Eucharistic ritual that would bring Catholics all over the state into communion with Jesus Christ, connecting the sisters' manual labour with their spiritual mission. In a sense, too, the work was contemplative in its rhythm, repetition and constancy. But it was hard, hot, repetitive labour, carried out six days a week. The altar breads kitchen became even busier in 1957, after Pope Pius XII relaxed the rules around fasting before receiving the Eucharist. Catholics once had to fast from midnight the night before, but now they only had to last three hours, and so many more people were receiving Communion, and that meant many more hosts to produce. During Lent—the forty days leading up to Easter, when many Catholics were more observant than they might be during the rest of the year—it was even more hectic. *I remember I baked all through recreation for the whole of Lent*, said Vianney.

Examination, which took place weekly, after lunch, was a public examination of conscience. This was the 'Chapter of Faults' where the sisters would confess their sins and ask forgiveness for falling short of the spirit of their holy vows of poverty, chastity, obedience, and for breaking the rules of convent life, including the important rule of silence. The postulants were receiving lectures on the order's constitutions, and the life of its founder, Peter Julian Eymard, but they were not given many practical guidelines as to the rules and expectations. Instead, they were just learning as they went along, and Vianney picked up some clues at the Chapter of Faults. *The first time I went to the Chapter of Faults, somebody came forward and accused themselves of lacking in modesty, and I thought, 'I don't want to hear this! What's all this about?' But one of the things of modesty was if you raised your eyes to look out a window maybe—that was very bad. Or you'd seen what was in the kitchen or something—that would be lacking in modesty. One of the big ones was being personal at recreation. You might have dropped a hint that, you know, your parents were coming down or something.*

Jill found the Chapter of Faults excruciating. *Well, what I dreaded—and I dreaded it so much that Mother Bertha made me do it—if you made some fault or other, you had to kiss the feet in the dining room as the sisters trooped in to their meal.*

Jill recalls that Sister Peter Julian must have recently made her first profession and was out of her novice's habit and into the new one. *And there was some old furniture outside the chapel in the back yard, and she pranced in front of the mirror in her habit. And Sister Mary Philomena, a French Canadian, dobbed her in. Because we weren't allowed to look in the mirror.* At the Chapter of Faults, a woman would drop to her knees and accuse herself of erring in some way. *Very rarely did you denounce anyone else. The Australians would only denounce themselves. You'd broken the rule of silence, or you'd broken the rule of detachment if you'd hung on to a pen when you shouldn't have.* On this occasion, though, *Sister Mary Philomena accused Sister Peter Julian of looking at the mirror.*

Barbara took the Chapter of Faults as another part of convent life to be endured, but not taken to heart, while she kept her own experience of God alive. *I really thought God saw us all as innocent. He didn't see us as guilty. But you had to kind of pretend that God really saw you as guilty. I did it quite happily because I thought, 'Well they're looking at my persona, my outward appearance. And that's not perfect, you know.' You could always make something up, something that seemed to be to do with your persona. But your true self was innocent. And that's what God was looking at.*

In the absence of personal conversation, recreation was spent in pleasantries, and, for the postulants, some gentle ball games. Vianney soon observed that sisters could no more exchange their thoughts and reflections on what they'd been reading, learning or observing about convent life than they could the latest news from their families, or stories from their childhoods. *We talked about the chooks—the chooks and the cat.* The logic underpinning this rule was to do with the women's complete devotion to God, to the exclusion of all other relationships—in this way, particular friendships between them were avoided and nobody's ego could be indulged.

This 'silence', and the prohibition on particular friendships, was part of the long tradition of cloistered nuns removing themselves from the world and its transgressions. The order's constitutions said:

> As a true servant is attached and bound exclusively to the service of the master, the Servants of the Blessed Sacrament shall subordinate all things to the service of Our Lord and refrain from any dealings with outsiders, even relatives excepting that which is required by necessity or Christian politeness.[3]

Christ the King was there, in the monstrance, and the nuns made up a silent court of adorers. Barbara didn't mind the silence so much, *because I was quiet, and didn't say much in those days. I often went to recreation and didn't open my mouth. I mean, I did try opening my mouth a few times, and then I decided, 'No, I'll just take something to sew or something.'* Yet remaining silent wasn't enough. Sister Berthe was still Mother Superior when Barbara was a postulant, and she had fixed a gimlet eye upon the postulants to make sure they were not being too expressive. *She always said I had a smirk on my face. She was telling me to wipe that smirk off my face. I don't know whether I was just musing about something, but I had a smirk.* Sister Berthe was so determined to discover the mystery of this smirk—indeed, to wipe it off the young woman's face—that she was driven to extremes in her effort to snap Barbara out of it. *And so one day I was walking down the stairs, and she grabbed my feet from underneath—you know, like put her arm through and grabbed them. And I didn't change my smirk, did I? And she said, 'Oh, sorry. That must be the way you have your face. You must have a permanent smirk on your face.' So she really softened about the smirk.*

Many of these rules were designed not just to reinforce modesty and self-effacement, putting aside individuality for belonging to the whole, but were opportunities to demonstrate obedience—one of the key rules of life as a nun. Barbara remembers *a lot of obedience ...*

We had to keep our eyes lowered. And your hands at your waist, and to walk on your toes. Barbara says it didn't occur to her to question these rules or customs or to wonder whether or not they were useful, or relevant to her faith and vocation. *I just had to accept it was God's will ... And I just wanted to be totally obedient. So that was it. We didn't look at one another. We just bowed our head if anyone walked past, but we didn't look at them.*

+++

Vianney, though, was a natural questioner, and as a postulant she freely asked when she was curious about something to do with convent life. There were plenty of customs that provoked her curiosity, and she laughs as she tells this story:

One of the things that used to happen at the Divine Office, if a person made a mistake—and I would have seen this as a silly thing in that first week—for reasons unknown to us, some people would get up and genuflect and then sit down again. So, I being me, said to someone in recreation, 'What does it mean when she gets up and does that thing?' and that person would have said to me, 'Oh I think you should ask Mother about that.' So, you ask Mother and Mother tells you that it's the penance for making a mistake at the Divine Office, you see. So I learned by asking questions, but they didn't always like that I asked questions. Monday was washing day, so they told me to hang the clothes out, which I was happy enough to do, but Mother Novice Mistress said to me 'Just take them out and ask the questions afterwards, would you?'

Vianney found many of these rules and customs difficult—her lively personality and her intellectual curiosity made her ill-suited to such strictures. She had never been attracted to the contemplative life per se, nor to the extreme personal sacrifice required of a cloistered nun. But the Adoration of Jesus Christ in the Blessed Sacrament made Vianney feel she truly belonged there at Armadale, and it made up for the difficult adjustments. In a way, they were the price she had to pay in order to reach that closeness to God that she so longed for. *On the morning after we entered the convent, Maureen and I were together in the pew and we came back from Communion and I just burst into tears ... It was joy. Joy that, at last, I was here doing what I thought I needed to do ... I thought Jesus was in Heaven and in the Eucharist. And for me to give myself to him was to be as close to him in the Blessed Sacrament as I could be.*

A roster system organised who would be praying in the chapel at what time, and soon the postulants would take their turn at nocturnal Adoration. Vianney wrote to her parents: *There is a buzzer in each room—when it rings you leap up and press yours, which illuminates a light in the chapel so they know you're up.* Vianney always woke at first buzz but said *Maureen had to be buzzed 4 times.*

While life in the convent was strict, they did take it easy on the postulants, and even easier on Vianney and Maureen.

The special allowance of the daily bath was only one of several things that seemed already to set Maureen and Vianney apart from some of their fellow sisters. By this time, the tradition separating what were once known as lay and choir sisters was ostensibly defunct, but in practice some remnant of it remained. For example, Monica, who entered with Vianney and Maureen, was not offered all the same privileges they enjoyed during their postulancy. Soon after they entered, one of the Canadian sisters went back home—she was used to central heating in Quebec and couldn't bear the unheated convent during Melbourne's winter. With her departure, a vacancy opened up in the kitchen, and Monica was put to work. Maureen and Vianney, on the other hand, were offered an extra half hour of study time each day, something that neither Monica nor any of the postulants or novices before them had been granted. Along with the way in which Monica had to relinquish her real name—Maureen Monica—this was one of the many signs that some postulants were favoured over others, maintaining an age-old hierarchy within the convent.

By the end of the first month, the girls were expected to have begun to understand the way of life, and to be following it more strictly. Vianney wrote home on Sunday 26 May, telling her family that *on Monday we are to begin in earnest—silence in all the right places etc.* She was worried all the good food and frequent distribution of chocolates would be over, too. *Maureen says she'll write a book called 'Sago and Silence'—it'll be a gem!*

The postulants now began waking at night to perform their turn at nocturnal Adoration, and they were required to observe a stricter silence at recreation. Sister Berthe, the Novice Mistress, and Mother Mary Leonard, the Superior, may have understood that Vianney would find this particularly hard. On 2 June, Vianney wrote to her parents:

Since we've been doing things properly I haven't spoken to Maureen except at recreation at which, however, we speak all together—Mother says that for a few weeks Maureen and I may see each other for one hour on Sunday—so that's beaut isn't it? Seems she is OK—gosh she's a terrific kid—I admire her open natural manner and her interest in and enthusiasm for whatever we're doing. She's beaut.

On reflection, Vianney believes *that probably meant more to me than it did to Maureen. I was more a person who needed that kind of company, you know. And though I accepted so many things from the way of life of a sister, I didn't accept silly things like that.*

Vianney's letters don't reveal much of what she and Maureen spoke about, but it's clear they enjoyed a growing friendship, sharing their letters from home, filling one another in on all the details of their earlier lives and their family members, and exchanging their early impressions of convent life—its joys and challenges. *Maureen was terribly shocked about the clothes we had to wear. Maureen found these clothes, so many clothes that we had to wear, really hard, really hard. You know, she's used to roaming around town in shorts and a t-shirt.*

To make matters more difficult, the postulants were not allowed to wash their heavy black dresses—they just cleared the dust from the seams and spot-cleaned any marks. Naturally, they would start to smell after a while, *but one thing that I managed to do, I don't know how I did it, for the whole of my religious life, I managed to always have deodorant. I don't know how I did it. I must have just said this is one thing that I'm just going to get my parents to get me, and too bad if I'm in trouble.* The nuns could never simply go out to shop for the things they needed, of course, and had to ask the Mother Superior for any little conveniences they wanted. Jill recalls that *it took me seven years to get outside the doors of the convent, and that was to go to the dentist. And the dentist said, 'Right, come back in six months.' He made sure we all came back every six months just to get us out of the convent.*

In June, Vianney's parents paid her a much longed-for visit. Vianney had been receiving plenty of visits during her postulancy—from Father Charlie Mayne, from Mrs Whelan, from a cousin in the navy who was passing through Melbourne, and from a young couple she'd met via the Whelans, who owned a nearby florist and were about to have their first baby. These visits would not be allowed as she approached the novitiate, she told her parents, *so you mustn't be sending other people along, or it'll be a case of 'given an inch they take a mile.'*

Visitors rang at the door, which opened by its curious disembodied mechanism, and, if their visit was acceptable, they would be admitted to the parlour. Vianney would meet them there, but would remain standing on the other side of a low wall with a lattice grille above it, separating her from her visitors, unless they were family, in which case the grille was raised so people could embrace (somewhat awkwardly, as the wall still kept them apart from the waist down). Vianney's birthday was coming up and her letters are full of anticipation of her parents' visit. But it was not all she'd hoped for.

When they came out to the convent, they were sitting in the parlour. There's no heat, there's no cup of tea. Oh, it breaks my heart. Even now. It really does. You know, for years my parents had been going into convents because my aunts were there and there was never a time that we went to a convent that there wasn't cups of tea. And even if it was just bread and butter sandwiches. And here they were, down at that place where their daughter is, and there was nothing at all. Nothing at all. Not even bread and jam.

She wrote to her parents the following Sunday. *It seems hardly possible that this time last week I was excited about your visit—for it seems much more than a few days since you left. It was really a big help to me to see you and to know you are happy for me to be here—I do hope Dad will be able to see things a bit clearer soon … I'm here for keeps. Heaven's the next stop … So I'm glad Mum that you said you don't want me home now.*

By July, just two months into their postulancy, Vianney and Maureen's intimacies had to come to an end. Vianney wrote home: *Maureen has just been over and this was by way of being our 'farewell.' We can't be seeing each other for 'our Sunday hour' anymore—this, of course, is not exactly a happy occasion, because we've really enjoyed seeing each other and it's helped us both so much but we realise it's been more than a privilege for us, and the Mothers have been beaut to let us see each other for this long.* Silence fell on their burgeoning friendship, broken only by the occasional visit from Father Charlie Mayne. Vianney wrote to her mother in October that their friend had been to see them, and *Maureen and I saw him together for about seven or eight minutes—M and I doing most of the talking!*

It was Father Charlie who gave them news of the Sputnik, the first artificial Earth satellite, launched by the USSR on 4 October 1957—the Cold War was on, and the space race between the United States and Russia had begun. But of course the Servants of the Blessed Sacrament did not receive newspapers or listen to the radio. Vianney looked out her window at night to see if she could spot Sputnik orbiting among the stars. With almost no opportunity now to share her innermost thoughts and feelings, Vianney would take off to the bottom of the garden, past the grotto with its statue of Saint Bernadette and the Blessed Virgin, and sing. *I'd sing my own hymns; I'd sing the things that I knew. Probably I learned them in school, you know. There was no one else to sing them to. I used to sing my heart out in front of the grotto.*

Despite Vianney's conviction that the convent was the right place for her, she remained a questioner. She had come to the convent to devote her life to Jesus, to return to him the love he gave her, and to *give beauty back to God.* But she often struggled to find a connection between that loving relationship she felt with Jesus and the rules of the convent. Sometimes its strictures led to situations that were quite absurd. In the leadup to her acceptance ceremony, where she and Maureen and Monica would enter the novitiate, the expectation was that the parents of the novices would provide the feast—a post-Communion breakfast of sandwiches and cakes that the novices' guests could share. The novices and nuns would only watch them eat—before the end of the 1960s, nuns were never allowed to eat with laypeople, even their own families. Vianney's letters are full of uncharacteristic ambiguity on this point, because she could never ask the Mother Superior exactly what was expected, nor talk it over with Maureen. She ended up suggesting that her mother write to Maureen's so they could work it out between them.

Father Charlie Mayne remained a great source of support to Vianney and Maureen—not only emotionally, as they got used to convent life, but also intellectually. He was a churchman of considerable influence, among Melbourne Catholics in particular. His role as rector of the seminary brought him into constant contact with young people and he was a great promotor of new ideas. As a senior cleric and a Jesuit, he held some sway at the convent in Armadale, and though the Mother Superior discouraged his visits, she couldn't really stop them.

Charlie encouraged Mother Mary Leonard to hold discussion groups of the kind he ran at the Catholic Youth retreats that Maureen and Vianney had attended, and during Vianney's postulancy he gave a talk on the Mass, and led a discussion afterwards. This innovation came as a bit of a shock to some of the older nuns. *I think Charlie told them we should be doing this and so when we were postulants, they started to have a gospel discussion with the professed sisters, and there were still a number of the Canadian sisters still there when we entered ... To those Canadian sisters we were these upstarts, you know, who were speaking up—well, unheard of to them that postulants would be talking in a group about the gospel or anything.*

Charlie also sent books to Maureen and Vianney. The convent itself had a small library, but the postulants and novices were by no means free to explore it at will. In any case, Charlie must have thought it wanting, as he gave the Mother Superior a list of books he thought she should acquire for the postulants, and brought Vianney and Maureen gifts of other books he'd selected, including one on the Mass, and one on the psalms *which is a great help when saying the Office, for this book gives the general idea of each psalm and we know what we are talking about more or less,* wrote Vianney to her mother. The Catholic tradition had never placed great importance on the faithful flock having any deep understanding of their religion or its texts. The Mass was said in Latin, which most of the congregation didn't understand, and Catholics were never encouraged to question or explore their religion. As Carol Hogan once said, 'No one knew much about Catholicism, really. Most Catholics didn't. It was the priest who knew everything.'[4] But Vianney wanted to know, and Charlie Mayne's parcels would help satisfy her curiosity, while providing her with that vital source of spiritual growth and intellectual development that reading had always been for her. Others, mostly her father, sent her novels, including *War and Peace.* Just as it had in her boarding school days, reading eased Vianney's solitude and homesickness.

Amid the adjustments to the challenges and hardships were frequent moments of levity. Vianney's letters describe certain diversions the nuns allowed themselves on particular feast days, like those of their founder, Peter Julian Eymard, as well as other important holy days in the Catholic calendar. On such occasions, Mother Mary Leonard, who was an accomplished pianist, would play, with Vianney accompanying her on the violin. Vianney's letters show that she and Maureen sang 'Just You Wait, Henry Higgins' from *My Fair Lady* at Sister Berthe's feast day. (Servants of the Blessed Sacrament did not celebrate one another's birthdays—this would be a mark of individual attention and an echo of family celebrations—but rather, they celebrated the feast days of the saints with whom they shared a name.) There was no dancing, but there were the occasional theatricals, such as re-enactments of Our Lady's apparitions, some gentle skits and humorous performances, as well as some mildly exciting parlour games.

A fuss was always made of visiting clerics, especially bishops. One such paid a call to the convent at the feast of Corpus Christi in June 1957, with Vianney writing home that *Mother told him where each of us was from, and we kissed his ring.* Vianney would come to deride this sort of priest-worship, but at the time, the ring-kissing would have been an honour.

Father Len McKenna, the Blessed Sacrament priest, was a regular visitor to the convent—the Mother Superior had known him for many years, as she had been an organist at St Francis' before she entered the convent. Vianney wrote a very detailed description of one such visit in a letter home. In what must have been a welcome break in the women's daily routine, the priest had brought along a slide show with which to entertain and edify the sisters. He showed them pictures of the new Blessed Sacrament seminary at Lower Plenty (Maureen and Vianney had already seen it, on Father Charlie Mayne's tour of Melbourne) along with some bonus slides of holy places in Rome and Lourdes. *And then the party—fizzy drink (I had red), sandwiches, cakes and two-on-one ice cream—nothing has ever been so good.*

While Vianney questioned and struggled as a postulant, Maureen always used to describe herself as having been 'the best possible nun of the worst possible kind'.

Well she was, you know—she was the perfect nun, she really was. In Vianney's mind, Maureen seemed to more easily accept the burdens and sacrifices of convent life, no matter how silly they seemed to Vianney, and even, perhaps, to welcome those hardships.

Well, Maureen—she's not here to tell you, but Maureen had a very strong element of wanting to be where things were very hard. She had a strong element of the crucifixion and the Passion of Our Lord ... She would often say that we come together and we follow Christ in the Eucharist because it's the hard thing to do and we choose the hard thing. I never chose a hard thing. No—not me.

Yet like Vianney, Maureen hadn't really understood what would be expected of her. As she told the ABC, *I think I wasn't really quite properly prepared for what I actually did walk into. Just as well, probably. There were very, very strict rules. We were not allowed to speak to each other apart from recreation time each day, which was presided over by the Novice Mistress first of all and then by the Superior. And all the conversation was meant to be directed by her and through her. We were not allowed to speak about ourselves personally, about our previous lives, about our families, about anything that would seem to be coming from ourselves as individual persons. That wasn't allowed.*[5]

Vianney had expected some of what came with life in the convent, but not the rule about sharing personal conversation. *Nobody said that we wouldn't talk. No, we didn't know any of those things.* Naturally enough, such strict rules gave rise to subterfuge. *Maureen and I had ways of letting each other know that our parents or family were going to be around.*

Maureen, like Vianney, felt the Servants of the Blessed Sacrament were lucky to have a way of earning their living, but it wasn't easy. 'The machinery was primitive, and it was hard manual work.'[6] That work was fitted in around the hours of prayer. *Prayer in chapel, in choir, singing all the Office of the Church in Latin. And then each one of us had a personal hour of prayer in the chapel every eighth hour, day and night, day and night, under a sort of a rotating basis. And we had our prayer in the presence of the reserved Eucharist, and we made quite a beautiful feature of that kind of prayer, with flowers and candles and everything focused on the altar. So life … and there was no going out. I mean we went out if we had to go to the dentist or the doctor and that might have happened about once a year. Other than that, no. No personal friendships of course. It was manual labour and prayer. That was my life for, oh twelve years. And it taught me a lot. It taught me a lot.*[7]

Maureen was soon appointed to look after the chapel, which meant working in the sacristy, a little room off the chapel's side, ensuring that everything was as it should be around the altar, where the Blessed Sacrament sat, enthroned and exposed. 'When you have perpetual Adoration in the chapel, there are candles and flowers to replace, lots of brass to polish and a lot of washing and ironing of vestments and altar linen.'[8] Maureen may have accepted the work as holy work and part of her offering to God in those early years, but she came to laugh ruefully about its ceaseless toil—at least, she laughed with Vianney, who recalls her bemoaning the *candles, candles, many, many candles. She thought her idea of hell was one more candle to light.*

Maureen's written reflections do suggest that she adjusted well to convent life, and was fulfilled by it. *It was a tough life, but I was deeply content. We were rostered to do an hour of Adoration in the chapel every eighth hour, day and night. Generally there were two of us … We had to kneel still. During the night, we stood up if we felt ourselves dozing off. We weren't obliged to just look at the Blessed Sacrament all the time. That hour of prayer was divided into four quarters: adoration, thanksgiving, reparation, and petition. I believed Jesus was there, listening to me, so that was easy enough.*[9]

Towards the end of Maureen and Vianney's postulancy, some new recruits arrived at the convent. Among them was Betty McMenamin, who was around fifteen years older than Vianney and Maureen. In a letter home, amid excited talk of the upcoming reception ceremony that would see her become a novice and take the white habit, Vianney wrote that Betty and the two other new postulants *seem much more sensible than I was and I guess they won't be as babyish as me—even though they'll feel things a bit strange at first.* Betty's maturity did set her apart from some of the other nuns—she'd had some professional experience working as a nurse in Australia and Asia. Vianney was delighted to welcome new women to the ranks, and wrote that *Betty is teaching us Burmese dancing, which we plan to do as an item for the celebration for Mother Mary Leonard's feast ... Betty plays fiddle, too, and we have a third violin here—Mother Berthe plays it—so we're going to have quite an orchestra.*

Vianney's final long letter as a young postulant was sent on Monday 11 November 1957, just before her acceptance to the novitiate. She wrote excitedly to her mother of having her new white habit fitted—there had been some earlier concern that the material wouldn't arrive, having been stolen from the warehouse in France. *Had a great fitting this p.m. Everything just perfect, Sister is a wizard! You won't know us—we'll even have different names!*

NOVITIATE

On 21 November 1957, Maureen, Vianney and Maureen Monica were received as novices. The ceremony took place in the chapel, with their families in attendance. Father Mayne reluctantly presided—he was not a very clerical type. According to Vianney's letters home, he would have preferred to be there in his capacity as friend and supporter, but since Maureen and Vianney had asked him to do it, he graciously accepted. Father Len McKenna gave the sermon, and Father Mayne blessed the young women's habits before the three of them filed out of the chapel to change, returning dressed head to toe in angelic creamy white.

They also received their new names. Each postulant had been allowed to submit three choices, and Vianney had exchanged ideas with her family. In one letter, she joked, *you know at one stage I was almost going to ask for Dolores as a name, but it doesn't sound like me, does it?!* She asked her family what they preferred: *Sr Mary Vianney, Sr Marie Vianney, Sr John Vianney—or maybe Sr Vianney Anne, what do you think? Tell me next letter—you too, Dad and Mick, 'family choice.'*

While her family insisted that her original first and second names, Vianney Anne, were the best choice, she received the name of Sister Mary Vianney (honouring both the Blessed Virgin and St John Vianney, a nineteenth century French priest). (Maureen was lucky enough to retain her original name, an Irish diminutive of Mary, while Maureen Monica was now known as Sister Monica, keeping her middle name while honouring the early Saint Monica of Hippo).

Vianney saw her parents for the second time since entering the convent at the morning tea, where she and the others remained behind the barrier separating them from their families in the parlour.

Now that they were novices, their preparation to become professed sisters began in earnest. The little forgivenesses and indulgences allowed to postulants had come to an end. They joined a number of other novices, including Barbara, or Sister Marguerite. Barbara's novitiate had been extended by Mother Berthe, who thought Barbara was not yet ready to take her vows. Vianney recalls that *Barbara was different—I don't know how to explain it—she was a bit more of an airy-fairy kind of person and, of course, she wasn't understood by the people in charge who have a kind of stereotype about what you ought to be. And so I think she probably had a pretty hard time in the novitiate.*

In fact, Barbara was different. Her other-worldly air may have been in part her natural temperament, and in part a hallmark of her path to God. Unlike Vianney, whose faith was linked strongly to an intellectual engagement with her belief and its meaning, Barbara was a mystic. But she never told Berthe or anyone else about it. *I was embarrassed to say anything about a mystical experience. Then they'd equate me with Saint Teresa of Avila or John of the Cross or something …*

These seemed to be up on a mountain, or put up on a pedestal. To say that I, Barbara, had a mystical experience would be sheer ... It would be the greatest embarrassment, because I knew I got it right down in the valley. I didn't climb any mountain.

Barbara had hoped the contemplative life would leave her free to meditate quietly upon her own transcendent experience of God's love, the one she still held close and that remained as real to her now as it was when she felt it in her parents' living room all those many years ago. *I entered just to be free to go within myself.* But the rules of obedience were not freeing in that way—if anything, they drew her away from that loving mystery. In her first letter asking to join she wrote, *I want my heart to be burning with love, on fire with love for God and Jesus.* It was not always easy to keep that fire alive in the cold, hard atmosphere of the convent.

Barbara remembers Mother Berthe as a loving sort of person, but she was a strict enforcer of the rules of obedience. *I only wanted to be the last and the least. I mean, I was overlooked in a way, you know. So I was vulnerable. I said, 'Just tell me what you want, and I'll do it.'* She recalls Sister Berthe teaching her how to walk like a nun. *I had to learn how to walk on my toes instead of my heels. I entered just to be free to go within myself, but she believed, you know ... Trying to teach me the ABCs of spirituality and that. I just wanted to be free ... But anyway, I'm sure it all was God's will.*

With her family many miles away, Barbara saw them only very rarely, but her cousin, Paul, who had made such an impression on her in her childhood, lived in Melbourne and he visited her from time to time. He had had a strong influence on her during her adolescence. *He asked me once, 'Are you happy?' And I said, 'Very happy.' Then he asked me, 'Why?' 'I don't know why. Maybe because I've only got one will with God.'* Another cousin, John Rafferty, was a frequent visitor. *I hardly knew him—he was ten years older than me, and I was in the country, and he was in the city. I didn't really know him but when he knew that all my other family was in New South Wales (in those days it was a long way away) he came along like a brother. He came out after his wedding and before the reception just to see me. I saw all the children and babies growing up. He and Paul were like brothers that I never had.*

By the time Maureen and Vianney had taken the habit and become novices, Charlie Mayne's visits were fewer and fewer. *They sort of, more or less, you know, gave him the word that he wasn't welcome all that much. So we got to the stage where he would perhaps come twice a year.*

Charlie continued sending books, and Vianney read every one of them. She relied heavily on these for both intellectual stimulation and spiritual development, work which she undertook almost entirely independently. Though the novices did receive lectures from Mother Berthe, their Novice Mistress, *they were mostly about the constitutions and about the way of life of a Blessed Sacrament Sister and all of that. And I don't remember that there was ever very much discussion at all.* Her only source of material on broader theological questions came from Charlie, and the books he sent helped her understand what little she could about the contemplative life—something that the novices weren't studying, despite intercessory prayer being at the heart of their mission.

In 1959, a new group of postulants joined from the Philippines. Just as the first Australian Servants of the Blessed Sacrament had travelled to Canada to take her novitiate before helping to found the convent at Armadale, these young women—many of them quite mature and university-educated—arrived in Melbourne to undertake their training, with a view to founding a Cenacle in Manila. The older Canadian nuns had mostly gone home to Quebec, and the new faces were very welcome, *but of course we weren't even allowed to talk to them. A whole other culture! A whole other people!* Vianney found it absurd.

TEMPORARY VOWS

On 21 November 1959, two and a half years after they had entered the convent at Armadale, Maureen, Vianney and Monica took their first, temporary vows as Servants of the Blessed Sacrament.

One of Vianney's early letters mentions a present sent from a family friend—the Ronald Knox version of the Bible. She was, of course, familiar with Bible stories from school, but Vianney had never read the book in its entirety. This was not unusual among Catholics, who rarely did any Bible study. *It was the Protestants who knew the Bible—we were supposed to know the sacraments.* Despite it being on the list of necessities, Vianney's superiors were somewhat disconcerted when she told them she was reading it. *I remember I'd go to Direction and the nun in charge would say to me, 'And what are you reading, Sister?' and I'd say, 'I'm reading the Bible, Mother.' And she'd say to me, 'Don't you need something else?' I think it was probably that they didn't know how to read it, either. And we didn't know how to read it.* Now Vianney did read it, cover to cover, *not with any movement towards spirituality but just as literature, and I found bits of it that I love, that were special to me.*

Many of the books Charlie Mayne sent contained quite new ideas. They were not widely shared or discussed, and certainly there was no discussion of them at the convent in Armadale. *These were all changing my idea of who Jesus is and who God is and where I meet God and where you find God.* Vianney was enriched by secular reading, too—not all of it authorised. She found Ernst H Gombrich's *The Story of Art* in the convent library, and her father sent her a copy of Boris Pasternak's *Doctor Zhivago,* which had just been translated into English. Reading novels, of course, was a proscribed activity for the nuns. *He was smart enough to wrap it in brown paper.*

Later, after final profession, Maureen and Vianney weren't allowed to see Charlie together in the parlour except on Christmas Day. The Mother Superior seemed wary of their friendship with

Charlie—almost disapproving of it. *I think we threatened her ... and she was a control person, you know. So that's sad. We've had some sad times in our story.*

Where Vianney might have questioned the need for many of the convent's deprivations, and struggled with an internal impulse to rail against them, Maureen drew strength from all the self-denial. *There was a lot of consolation in it, as normally happens at the beginning of a spiritual journey. There can be a great deal of consolation through prayer, through scripture. God I always thought of as the loving father, who was the endless mystery, who slowly was revealed mainly through daily and nightly pondering on the words of the Bible, the Old Testament and the New Testament ... Physically, emotionally, there was total denial, total self-denial. For me there was spiritual light through that kind of denial, sometimes an amazing amount of ... almost like bliss really.*[10]

Maureen also, of course, felt the burden of her sacrifice. As she told the ABC, *the pain came from homesickness, loneliness, missing my family, my friends, of whom I had many, not being able to communicate freely. I mean I've got a couple of friends who have been kind of faithful through the ages, come what may. They kept writing to me and keeping me in touch with what was going on without having received any answer from me because I wasn't allowed to answer. We were allowed to have visitors once a month for an hour, in a parlour. But, of course, my family lived miles and miles and miles away, so I normally didn't have any visitors. And on the rare occasion that I did have a visitor, like from a priest who was a friend who kept coming regardless of the fact that he wasn't always supposed to come—seeing people like him I was always divided from the visitor by a grille. There was a physical barrier between me and the people who, on rare occasions, I was allowed to see. So, the pain of it was having to learn to live entirely on one's own, when you're stripped really down to very basic things. This is what I do not regret, even though I would not want to go through it again.*[11]

All the women who joined the convent accepted its rules—and, to a degree, expected them—as part of the hard road to holiness. They had come here out of love for God and were offering themselves to him in a mystical union that would help safeguard humanity's salvation. They believed that their life of prayer could help redeem the world in God's eyes, rewarding the sacrifice he made when he, through his son, Jesus, took upon himself the burden of mortality and its suffering, dying to save us from original sin. They believed God loved them—most of them had experienced this love quite directly—and that he loved the world. They were young and ardent, and wanted to *give beauty back to God,* to be with him, as close to his real presence as possible.

Centuries of Catholic tradition held that these women were now becoming special people in the eyes of God—and would be perceived as such by others. The sisters understood the honour and responsibility this entailed, and knew it must be earned by discipline and self-mastery. The conviction that what might have appeared, on the surface, to be trivial trials of obedience were in fact important steps to the spiritual freedom that self-mastery promised was what helped some of the sisters to persist in the face of great difficulty.

There were particular tools available for the sisters, to aid them in this work of self-mastery. Jill recalls Sister Mary Philomena making one such item during recreation. *We occupied ourselves with our hands at recreation, and she had white thread and she was doing macrame and putting little knots in it.* Jill was curious.

When we said, 'What are you doing, Sister Mary Philomena?' she said, 'Oh, you'll find out.' Then you found out. Your superior handed you the discipline. 'You may give yourself the Discipline. Three strokes every Friday night. You're not to draw blood.'

The discipline was a sort of whip that was thought to have spiritual benefits, but Jill was shocked. *Now, I've never been struck in my life, except Dad, once—one whack. And you were told by your superior,*

'You have permission'. Well, okay. This wasn't a penance, or a punishment, *it was just, you know, a good thing to do. And I was terrified.*

Sisters were expected to retire to their cells and apply the Discipline as needed, striking themselves on the back.

I was very stubborn, and I didn't like being frightened. So anyway, I obviously told Mother Berthe how much it upset me. She said, 'Well, look, Sister Mary Agnes. I'm not going to tell you to do it three times. You just do it as much as you want. Right?'

Jill did it sixty-seven times *and Sister Mary Philomena was next door and she heard me. I just kept at it. I tried to beat it out of myself. Not hard. I mean, it can't have been that hard. But the fear! And then of course she took it off me. I wasn't allowed to use it again.*

The goal of becoming a fully professed nun helped Jill endure through these moments of clear ambivalence about convent life and of her deep emotional distress. *While you are aiming at final profession, you're sweeping everything under the carpet—you're just getting there.*

Vianney's feast day was the feast of Saint John Vianney (a saint to whom she had no special attachment—Vianney was named after her aunt). Jill's was the Feast of Saint Agnes of Rome, virgin and martyr, patron saint of girls and chastity, whose feast of 21 January falls not long after Jill's real December birthday. Despite the ban on birthdays, the sisters could sometimes guess who was celebrating. Carol loved crayfish, and each year on her birthday Carol's family would send a huge catch for all the nuns to enjoy at dinner.

Not being able to celebrate her birthday was something that stung Jill. With each new postulant who joined in her twenties, or later, Jill felt a painful stab of resentment at having entered the convent so young, just weeks before her eighteenth birthday. Her twenty-first birthday came and went without a visit from her mother, *and my mother sent strawberries for the convent for tea. That's the only thing I had for my twenty-first birthday.* At around this time, Jill would have been expecting to end her novitiate and take her first temporary vows, but

Sister Berthe wasn't sure she was ready. *I wasn't going to be approved for the next step … It was because I used to show my impressions. Now, 'show your impressions' means show how you're feeling. And you weren't supposed to. If you felt something, you weren't supposed to show it, and I did. I probably sulked. I have no idea.*

In the first years of the 1960s, while Vianney was in her temporary vows, a French priest called Father Julian Paul of the Virgin came to visit the convent. He had been sent by the Vatican to investigate small orders of contemplatives, to find out whether they were viable. He didn't speak a word of English, but it seems he was very satisfied with the Armadale community, noting that the thirty-or-so nuns in the community were happy, healthy and busy. The convent's numbers had been greatly increased by the steady stream of Filipinas who were coming for their formation (the postulancy and novitiate). These young women formed a significant part of the Armadale community from 1959 until 1964, when their own convent in Manila was ready to take them. Father Julian was delighted to observe Vianney's reading material. *I was reading a French book on the Eucharist and he nearly jumped out of his chair he was so happy about it.* Along with the Filipinas, new Australian vocations were also coming in. Altar breads production kept the nuns occupied and provided a steady income, putting them on a firm financial footing compared with other, smaller contemplative orders. Much later, Carol Hogan joked that Father Julian Paul was *the first and only person (and no doubt will be the last) to describe us as a community that was 'young, fervent, intelligent and breathing forth charity'.*

FINAL VOWS AND FULL PROFESSION

The worst thing that ever happened to me in the convent was that I was told I couldn't write any more letters except one page. It was really hard. When she took her temporary vows Vianney was told she could no longer write weekly, but only monthly, to her parents. She wrote eight, ten, or a dozen pages, just as she always had. But now, as a fully professed nun, she was restricted to just two sides of a single piece of regulation writing paper. The paper, folded into four, is marked with the letters SSS, representing the congregation's French name: *Les Servantes du Très Saint-Sacrement.* In the packets Vianney's mother kept, there are four such letters, each sent in 1963–64. Vianney, together with Maureen and Monica, had taken her final vows on 21 November 1962. They were now nuns forever, bound by a solemn vow to remain within the convent walls and keep to their Rule of Life always. This new status put them above the women who had not yet taken their final vows, but it did not confer on them any particular authority. There was no rule by committee at the convent—authority rested solely with the Mother Superior.

Just a few weeks before Vianney and Maureen took their solemn vows as fully professed nuns in 1962, the Second Vatican Council gathered in Rome. It had been called by Pope John XXIII in 1959, and since then the Vatican had been preparing for what would be the largest ever gathering of any council in the Church's history. The Pope believed that the Church needed to change. It had to leave behind its opposition to modernity and build a fresh relationship with a new and rapidly changing world. As he said at the council's opening:

> Our task is not merely to hoard this precious treasure, as though obsessed with the past, but to give ourselves eagerly and without fear to the task that the present age demands of us—and in so doing we will be faithful to what the Church has done in the last twenty centuries ... Christians and Catholics of apostolic spirit all the world over expect a leap forwards in doctrinal insight and the education of consciences in ever greater fidelity to authentic teaching. But this authentic doctrine has to be studied and expounded in the light of the research methods and the language of modern thought. For the substance of the

ancient deposit of faith is one thing, and the way in which it is presented is another.[12]

Change was coming, and over the three years during which the council met (it opened in 1962 and closed in 1965), documents about the Vatican's new teaching were distributed to clerics around the world. But the Mother Superior and many of her fellow sisters felt sure that the convent at Armadale would be insulated from these changes.

Despite Father Julian Paul's glowing assessment just a few short years earlier, the women were perhaps not as healthy as they looked. Life at the convent was, of course, difficult, and the sisters all expected it to be difficult. They welcomed self-sacrifice and discipline, but some members of the community were struggling.

Like Monica and Sister Pete, Barbara was by now earmarked as a lay sister. Her lack of confidence meant she struggled when it came time to take her turn at leading the chanting of the Divine Office, in Latin, in the chapel. *I did have a poor self-image about singing and intoning. I was very shy and very … feeling incompetent to get up and intone. So they decided that I was really not a choir sister after all. I should be taken away from there … Take off my gold ring and put on a silver ring.* This demotion came as a further blow to Barbara's self-image, once again making her *feel as though I was the last and the least. I had that feeling, that I was the last and the least. But because I was just happy within myself, that was not … Well, I think it did work on me a bit.*

Nonetheless, Barbara could stick up for herself when she felt she needed to. *There was a Filipina nun who was supposed to wake us up at night, and often enough I didn't even hear her. She whispered, and often enough she had trouble trying to wake me up … And Mother Leonard called me up, and, you know, gave me a scolding … 'You're not worthy to be a Servant of the Blessed Sacrament'. And she kept this up, and I said, 'Well, Mother, if you don't really think I'm worthy you'd better start following the processes for me to leave.' And that really threw her, because*

I was a meek and mild little thing. For some reason she just didn't want me to leave, no matter what, and she really took a backward step. She said, 'Oh, we're all unworthy.' And I said, 'Well Mother, you should get her to wake you up, and you might understand.' It was the first time I spoke up for myself. Because I thought, 'If I don't speak out now, this is going to happen for the rest of my religious life. I'm going to be really squashed.'

The Mother Superior never scolded Barbara in that manner again.

Jill, who had by now spent almost a decade in the convent, was becoming unwell. *I had a breakdown in the convent after my final vows—I was twenty-seven, I think … I was physically sick. I was shaking all over … I was strung out.* Jill began seeing a psychologist.

Doctor Seal was my psychologist. I saw him for nine years. At the beginning he diagnosed me as being immature and unstable. He put me on medication, then took me off medication—it was too much. Anyway, seeing him for the nine years, that was just a case of having someone to talk to once a month, and getting out of the doors of the convent was a help, you know, because we never went out.

Jill had been, as she says, *sulking*, and in part that was because she saw her fellow sisters being assigned special tasks and responsibilities while she was never given anything to do. *There was no fulfilment. You couldn't get ahead … I would have loved to have swept the carpet in the chapel but didn't get that job, either. I would have liked to have been sacristan—I never was given anything in the way of feeling good.* Mother Berthe could see that Jill was low in spirits. *I said, 'I just want to be in charge of something.' Well, they put me in charge of the altar breads. Sister Peter Julian had been in charge most of the time, and now I ran it. And that's when I had my breakdown. It was too much for me.*

Eventually, she settled for the modest job of putting out the bins at night. *I'd open the gate, walk out into the street and out onto the nature strip. There was a little dog there, a fox terrier. He looked up at me. And I was happy. There was a lot going on that never showed. A lot of mental anguish.*

Though she couldn't discuss her troubles openly with any of the other sisters, Vianney, at least, intuited that Jill was struggling. *She obviously had the brains to get a psychological book to help her, because she suggested I might like to read it ... And she gave me that book and it helped me a lot. So, she knew I was in trouble.*

Vianney had been at the convent for more than five years. Some of the fully professed sisters enjoyed a measure of responsibility, but Vianney, like Jill, was given no special authority over any element of convent life, despite her considerable talents and abilities.

Her four letters home during this period are addressed care of the Fire Station on Old South Head Road, Bondi. Vianney's family had left Springwood and were building a house at Blakehurst, in Sydney. Her letters were addressed just to Mum and Dad—Mick had married and moved away by this time. She was still asking her mother to thank the loyal friends who kept writing to her, though they knew she couldn't write back. Vianney's letters from 1963 and '64 show little of the exuberance of her younger self, but her sense of humour is still there, and her loving interest in all that her family was doing. She asks her mother whether the novelty of the new electric refrigerator has worn off yet, and says she is still struggling to master the art of baking altar breads. *I wish you could see me in my great white apron mixing up the paste for the bakers. We have a giant mix master but the flour and water have to be carefully measured. ... When I got to the baking, I was the 'problem pupil'—had paste all over the wall, stove, apron, shoes—to say nothing of my face and arms! ... Please God, with patience and perseverance I'll get there one day!* She also mentions she is putting on weight. *I am a much fatter person than the one you saw last. You should see the food I am devouring these days!* Vianney wasn't the only one. Jill, a petite woman of very slight build, said that she weighed 12 stone (76 kilograms) by the mid-sixties—*I was overcompensating, eating too much.* Food had become an important source of comfort to her, while vigorous exercise was difficult to come by and even harder to execute in the floor-length habit.

If Vianney wasn't showing her own frustration at the lack of responsibility she was given, her mother didn't hide her feelings. Vianney wrote, *You seem very keen to put me in one of the 'top positions' as you call it but that would be the thing I'd hate most—and most unlikely. Every mother thinks her daughter is the one for TOP but how immature and inexperienced little Sr M Vianney is in this house. Though I'm among the seniors by profession, I'm among the juniors by age and among the babies in maturity and holiness. So no fear. I'm very happy—after all, I came to give everything to Our Lord and though it is sometimes costly to human nature and the old ego our real happiness is in being nothing so that he can be everything.*

At around this time, perhaps in light of the growing number of postulants and novices at the convent, the decision was made to buy a weekend property, a place of repose for the sisters. It was called Moonyah and was on Victoria's Mornington Peninsula. The purchase of the beach house came as quite a surprise to the community, or, at least, to Vianney. *We didn't have any discussion—there was no discussion about any of this—we were just told it was bought. And about one Sunday a month it'd be your turn to be put into the car after the two Masses on Sunday to go down to Moonyah. We weren't allowed to talk. We must have taken our lunch of sandwiches or something with us—I don't remember a lot—and then by about four o'clock we were back in the car to come back. So I can remember myself writing home and saying what a lovely place it was and how lovely it was to come down but it was silly, you know. It was supposed to be a holiday.*

Jill loved going down there. *It was like an English style house—little attics—and we were to stay there for little holidays of a weekend and have a break. And we used to mow the lawn and cut back the hydrangeas and so forth.* Nature and a break in the routine really helped refresh Jill. *I was a different person.* Barbara, on the other hand, thoroughly disliked her weekends at Moonyah. *We had to sleep with someone else and I was very self-conscious about turning over. I had a squeaky bed. I was trying not to turn over. I thought, 'Oh, I woke her up again.' It was torture. I spent the whole day trying to walk around and get myself so tired I'd fall asleep.*

The 1960s were boom times for female vocations in Australia, with the number of nuns hitting a total of almost fifteen thousand in 1966. The convent at Armadale was also growing, despite the fact that the Filipinas now had their own convent and were no longer coming to Melbourne. While the numbers joining contemplative orders like the Servants of the Blessed Sacrament were smaller than those entering teaching, nursing and missionary orders, the community at Armadale had outgrown its original dwellings. In 1962, the twelfth anniversary of the convent's founding, a three-storey building was erected on the Armadale block, the top two floors serving as new sleeping quarters for the novitiate, while the ground floor was a larger altar breads kitchen with more up-to-date equipment.

In 1964, Melissa Jaffer, former actress, joined the convent, having discovered that her vocation was a contemplative one. Mother Mary Leonard was her first spiritual adviser. *I didn't have a great affinity with her. You know, spiritually, I couldn't really … I didn't quite feel that I could open my heart to her. A generational thing, I think.*

Two years earlier, in 1962, Mother Berthe had been elected Superior General and left Melbourne to preside over the global congregation of the Servants of the Blessed Sacrament at its general house in Paris. Mother Mary Leonard's term as Mother Superior should have come to its end by now—the system of senior sisters taking their turn at leadership usually guaranteed that authority didn't remain with a single sister for more than three years at a time. But instead of the role passing on to another senior sister, Mother Mary Leonard secured an additional three-year term. *And bingo. She got more time after that. She had longer than one would have expected, because she said she was the only one who could do it. None of us were capable,* said Jill.

With Berthe gone, Maureen was given a new responsibility. *I was made assistant to the Novice Mistress, then became Novice Mistress at a very young age. That gave me some freedom. Nobody could interfere with the Novice Mistress, not even the Superior. For my personal things I was still beholden to her. You had to kneel down before the Superior and ask for everything, even for new underwear.*[13] Maureen was not yet thirty, so she was young, but she had natural leadership qualities—she was very intelligent and had a certain unmistakeable gravitas. Melissa felt an immediate connection. *With Maureen, of course, it was wonderful … She understood my spiritual journey, and she understood where I was on that journey, and she was able to guide me if I needed guidance. It was heaven sent.*

The swinging sixties that Melissa left behind in London hadn't quite made it to Melbourne yet, but the times were undeniably changing. Australia, having committed its first troops to Vietnam in 1962, was by now involved in the full-scale war—compulsory military service was introduced in 1964, and conscripts would be flying to Vietnam the following year. John F Kennedy had been assassinated in 1963, and the Cold War was raging. While Australians watched news of the battle for civil rights in the United States, Indigenous people were making their voices heard at home. The 1967 referendum saw Australians vote overwhelmingly for greater civil rights for Aboriginal and Torres Strait Islander people. The following year the Yolngu people of Yirrkala in Arnhem Land sent painted bark petitions to the House of Representatives asserting ownership of their country, kicking off the movement for land rights. In 1965, Charlie Perkins led fellow university students in the Freedom Rides, seeking an end to discrimination against black Australians. Changes were also taking place in the Catholic Church. In a letter home on 21 June 1964, Vianney noted that next month Melbourne's parishes would begin to hear the Mass in English for the first time. *This is certainly new, but we were to expect something, and always be very open to whatever the Church decrees.*

It was a time when new ideas battled with convention. In 1963, the conservative Menzies government won an increased majority, and the election was the first to receive live television coverage. The following year, the Beatles and the Beach Boys toured Australia, while the editors of the satirical *Oz* magazine were gaoled for obscenity. The baby boom generation had grown up and was imposing its tastes and perspectives on an Australian culture that wasn't always ready.

As an actress, Melissa had been in the midst of all this social change, but now she put it aside in exchange for the life eternal. She welcomed the simplicity of the convent. *I must admit I was prepared to accept everything as it was. Coming from the world that I'd come from, thinking myself very lucky to be accepted into this world, I was prepared to do whatever came along. I rolled with the punches. I really did roll with the punches, and I didn't question things. There were a lot of … in retrospect of course they were stupid rules and regulations that we had … but to me, that was the way things were, babe. And you did it, you know?*

While the rituals and customs of the convent remained largely unchanged, some of the harder elements of the life were giving way. Just as Vianney and Maureen had had it easier than Jill and Carol, under Maureen's stewardship, postulants like Melissa faced less difficult conditions than postulants had done a decade earlier. Inside the convent, having swapped her knee-skimming early 1960s hemlines for the heavy black postulants' garb (by this stage it was at least made of cotton, not wool serge), Melissa was at peace. *Internally I felt I was home, spiritually home. I didn't quite understand it all of course, but I was there, and my main orientation was adoration of the presence of that source that I had been seeking all my life. Adoration of the presence indicated by the host in the monstrance—that was the form if you like, but under that it was the spiritual alertness to, and adoration of, the presence. The presence, yes. And that was our job, to witness to the presence.*

For Vianney, though, who was now approaching ten years in the convent, things were not getting any easier. In about 1966, she came upon a rare opportunity to send her fond wishes out more widely, writing personal notes to a variety of her family and friends. The convent had published a little pamphlet about the Blessed Sacrament and the Cenacle at Armadale, *and I said, 'Mother, could I send some to my place, to home, and my mother would send them to my friends?' She said, 'Sister, you do that.' So that's exactly what I did—on every little pamphlet that I was asking my mother to send to my friends, I wrote a little note.* Vianney wrapped them up and gave them to the Mother Superior. *About a week later she said, 'Oh, Sister I need to see you—I opened that parcel that you were sending away and I was horrified to find that you had written on all these pamphlets,' she said. 'That's a very serious offence and you will have to have a serious penance for these things.'*

Vianney was confused and heartbroken that her messages couldn't be sent. She could accept the penance—she had to kiss the feet of the first three sisters who came through the door of the refectory that night—but she found it humiliating to have to confess to disobedience at the Chapter of Faults. *People don't know what you've done, so the imagination can go to all kinds of places. I went to confession and I said to the priest 'I've done something wrong, Father, but I don't think it's a sin.' And he said, 'What? What have you done?' So I told the story and he said, 'I don't think it's a sin, either.' And the tears came to my eyes, you know. It was the hardest thing, and it came on top of my not being able to write except one page. And apart from me, what that did to my parents.*

By this stage Vianney was crying quite a lot. Jill—Sister Mary Agnes—had the room next door to Vianney's. *She cried all night. I think she cried for a number of nights and I knew she was crying. I was not allowed to go in.* The only person the sisters could talk to if they were having difficulty was the Mother Superior, and she was not always sympathetic. Nor did she really have the skills or training necessary to address some of the complex problems the community faced. For example, Vianney was struggling greatly with a nun, junior to her, who had developed a powerful crush on her. This woman had become possessive of Vianney, easily hurt and frequently jealous. *She was a moody person and she could be very hard on me. She could bang doors in my face. She was very difficult for me to deal with and I would go to what we called Direction, where you went to the Superior. And you know, you're supposed to say how your spiritual life is going on. And I would say to her, 'Mother, I'm not getting on with Sister Mary X ... We're not managing.'* The Mother Superior would respond dismissively. *'Oh well, you're too sensitive, Sister. That will all work itself out.' I finished up going to the parlour one time when Father Mayne came—Charlie—and I'd had enough of it and I think I came to tears, and he was lovely. He said, 'It's not you. You mustn't think that it's you. You're doing your very best and it's not you. It's that the other sister has got troubles.'*

Vianney and the others learned, much later, that before joining the convent this woman had had a child out of wedlock, and that the child had died. These were the sorts of intimate sorrows the sisters carried in solitude—secrets that were never spoken in the convent.

Vianney and Jill were not the only ones struggling. Barbara remembers seeing another nun, one who ended up leaving the convent, crying often. Barbara could not comfort her. *We were supposed to leave her and not interfere with God and herself. That was between God and herself, why she was crying. It wasn't anything to do with you.* Jill also recalls her psychologist asking her if she ever had a good cry. *'Oh no, no, you don't cry.' He said, 'It's good for you, you know.' So I went back to the convent and I cried for three days. I went down to the refectory with tears streaming down my eyes. No one batted an eye.*

Though Maureen was a very mentally strong woman, with a deep faith, Vianney believes she would have been feeling quite frayed at this time. Maureen had an enormous workload—she continued to take responsibility for the sacristy, while also fulfilling her duties as Novice Mistress. Maureen may have been handling things better than some of the others, but she no doubt sensed that some of her sisters were not doing well, and this would have worried her. She, too, perhaps, was finding the life less fulfilling than she had in her early years as a nun, and that her sense of deep contentment was beginning to fade. As she told the ABC in 1996, *Anybody who's walked this journey knows very well that those things don't last … Not everybody can survive that kind of discipline well, and I think you need to be fairly psychologically healthy, and physically healthy too, and otherwise people could break down under this kind of regime, and certainly did break down.*[14]

Maureen and Vianney's ideas and spirituality were growing from their own practice of contemplation and the readings Charlie was sending, which were making them aware of the developing theology of the Eucharist. They were moving beyond the understanding of the Eucharist as the static presence of Christ, the embodiment of his redeeming sacrifice, to be worshipped in the monstrance, and were beginning to understand it as a celebration. *We're learning that the Eucharist is a unification. And that it promotes unity and promotes community and promotes this wonderful Eucharist.*

But Vianney could see that the way of life in the convent wasn't reflecting that at all. Indeed, Mother Mary Leonard saw the new theology as a threat. And she saw Vianney and Maureen as a threat because they were learning about it, thanks to Father Mayne's deliveries. *I was really persona non grata. Charlie gave me a copy of the documents of Vatican II. So, as a good religious, I say, 'Father has brought me this book. May I read it, Mother?' and she, 'Well, leave it here, Sister, and I'll have a look at it.' So the next week I say, 'Mother, I wonder if I could have that book that Father brought?' 'Oh, I'm having a look at it, Sister'. So this went on for about four weeks. So finally I said, 'Would I be able to have that book?' 'Sister, I'll give it to you', she said, 'but will you put a brown paper cover on it and be very careful with it because it has essays in it by Protestants.' So that's our introduction to Vatican II.*

FRESH AIR: VATICAN II AND THE STRUGGLE AT THE CONVENT

ONE OF THE most important teachings for religious like the Servants of the Blessed Sacrament was issued in 1965, the year Vatican II concluded. Called 'Perfectae Caritatis' (Perfect Charity), it was a 'decree on the adaptation and renewal of religious life'. It required orders of nuns, brothers and priests to return to their roots, their founding inspiration and principles, and reshape these to suit the modern world. In 1966, Pope Paul VI sent out an apostolic letter (called *Motu Proprio: Ecclesiae Sanctae)* to all bishops, priests, nuns and brothers asking them to implement its guidelines, renew their spiritual lives and adapt.

The letter amounted to a command, not mere encouragement. Yet the convent community wasn't told about what it said, or what it would mean for them. Jill remembers *that we knew that Vatican II had been on, and the Pope had said, 'Let the fresh air in and let the spirit in'. And we received a communication from our mother house saying we had to update our constitutions. We had to come into the twentieth century or the order would die. And I had no suggestions at all in that way, but the initial reaction from the sisters was rather hostile.*

None of the new ideas were the subject of general, open discussion at the convent at Armadale. Yet by 1966, some of the nuns were attending lectures by Father Gregory Manly, a Melbourne

Passionist priest, who was explaining the new teachings and what they demanded of nuns. Vianney was not among the chosen. *Six of our people were allowed to go to that. I was not. Neither was Maureen. We were not considered worthy. But after about six months they did begin to tell us what was being said, and what was being said was joy to us.* Occasionally, a priest would visit the convent to give a lecture to all the sisters (at least, any who were not either hard at work in altar breads or serving their turn at Adoration). Vianney recalls that after one such visit, the Mother Superior dismissed what the priest had said, and told the community that *all of that didn't relate to us because we were Servants of the Blessed Sacrament and our way of life and way of understanding the Eucharist was such that it didn't refer to us—which of course was quite wrong.*

As Maureen tried to help the novices understand some of the new teachings, and to develop their spirituality as contemplatives, she was bringing to bear a perspective quite different from the more traditional one that Mother Mary Leonard upheld. Mother Mary Leonard, who was very sensitive to anything that might challenge her authority, bristled at the enthusiasm Vianney and Maureen expressed at the new possibilities the teachings represented—things that might fundamentally change the lives of all the Servants of the Blessed Sacrament.

It is not difficult to understand how these changes might have felt threatening, frightening or sorrowful for some of the sisters. They had dedicated years of their lives, the best part of their youth, to submitting their will to a steadfast rule of silence, in the deep belief that in doing so, they were purifying themselves for God. They believed that through prayer, hardship and discipline, they could become sacred instruments of God's will, offering intercessory prayers that would bring the world closer to Him. Any radical shift from this core set of beliefs would risk jettisoning all they had sacrificed, threatening to make it meaningless. The nuns themselves had had no say in the changes being proposed, which were decreed by an all-male Vatican Council half a world away from the convent at Armadale. For many, it must have felt like an unwelcome, perhaps unreasonable or even cruel, imposition.

For Vianney, though, there was no looking back. The new teaching represented a very profound truth that took Vianney beyond any consideration of whether or not she had been wasting her time in the convent all those years. It was much bigger than that. It was a revelation about the nature of the Eucharist and Christ's presence within it. *It wasn't dead. It wasn't static. It was the dynamic understanding of the Eucharist as the centre of our life and as a centre of our faith. It was this person in the Blessed Sacrament who was living and active and involved with all these people that we knew, and that we could be involved with, and that we should be involved with. And all of these things had to be part of the way we lived.*

The Eucharist was no longer a wafer stuck in a monstrance, the real presence of Christ held aloft on the altar as an object of worship. It was a nourishing food of sharing and celebration, bringing people together and encouraging them, giving them strength. It was *Jesus at work among us.*

In 1966, Marie Grunke finally made it to the convent. It was 2 February, and she was by now twenty-seven years old. After returning from New Zealand and losing her baby, Marie had decided to make a fresh start in Melbourne. Reunited with Rusty, the pair found jobs at a fruit cannery in Kyabram, in northern Victoria, where the hours were long, but the pay was good. Marie was happy to work at the expense of a social life, as she had ruled out looking for a husband. Although Max had pursued her all the way to Toowoomba, and Marie had introduced him to her family, she had lost all confidence in him, while her faith in God had only grown. *I had loved Max and I always knew there would be nobody else other than him ... And so that door was closed. So, I thought, I'll become a nun if I'm still able to become a nun.*

No one in Marie's family knew the story of her baby and how she was forced to relinquish him. *I'd always said to myself that I wouldn't tell anybody unless I found him. Otherwise, why open that wound? I can do nothing with it.* The only people who knew were a few friends she'd left behind in New Zealand, and Rusty, and the occasional priest. *I used to go to confession every now and then, just to talk about it, because it was safe. And I'd reminded myself that I couldn't stop what God wanted me to do. He took the child, and it's God, after all—who am I? So I have to trust that he knew what he was doing and he's going to care for my child. If I worry too much, it's like I don't trust him. I've got to believe he can care for my son better than I can.* She remembered the Bible stories she'd heard as a child—Abraham preparing to sacrifice Isaac to please God; and Hannah, who begged God for a son only to have to give him up to God when her prayer was answered. *God would ask these horrendously big sacrifices of certain people. And this was the one he was asking of me.*

Marie and Rusty decided to move into the city, and got a flat on Punt Road, Prahran. They both found jobs at the Melbourne telephone exchange, close enough to St Francis' Church that Marie could slip out and go to Mass each day. *I was still totally nourished by going to Mass.*

Thc flat she and Rusty shared was in a sort of boarding house, and the other rooms were mostly taken up by young medical students. *They were wonderfully alive people, and I loved that about them. They were real human beings and they were very broad in their outlook about life … completely free of the moralistic Catholic background that I grew up with. They were very moral, but they were more concerned about the bigger issues of life. They weren't hung up over petty religious stuff. And it wasn't my business if they wanted to have a different sexual partner from time to time.*

Marie joined the Legion of Mary, which was then a very popular organisation among Australian Catholics. She made weekly visits to the sick and needy, always with another member of the Legion. On one occasion, her companion mentioned that a friend of hers had just joined the Servants of the Blessed Sacrament, who made altar breads and prayed before the exposed Eucharist. Remembering her experience during Benediction—the ceremony where the Blessed Sacrament is exposed—in Auckland, Marie immediately asked to be dropped off at the nearest Catholic church. *So I went into the church and said, 'Thank you. Now I know the order I need to join. Thank you.' So that's all settled.*

The Blessed Sacrament priests at St Francis' introduced Marie to the Mother Superior at Armadale, Mother Mary Leonard. She said she would accept Marie as a postulant, and referred her to a doctor for a check-up, to make sure she was in good health. *The doctor picked it straightaway that I'd had a child—she must've seen the stretch marks on my tummy. And of course I cried, and she said, 'You'll be fine.' She gave me the highest recommendation.*

Marie gave up the room at the boarding house on Punt Road so she could go back to Queensland and farewell her parents before joining the convent. *I knew that when I said goodbye to my father, I'd never see him again. There was terrible grief.* In the months leading up to her postulancy, Marie and Rusty shared another flat with a young journalist who wrote for the local Catholic paper. It was this young woman, Avril, who introduced Marie to a major spiritual influence: Pierre Teilhard de Chardin, a French priest and a scientist whose idea of cosmic spiritual evolution attempted to tie together scientific knowledge and Christian belief. His theology promised a truce in the Church's centuries-old battle against modernity, but it was controversial, and the Vatican discouraged Catholics from reading his work. By the 1960s, though, his time had come, and Teilhard de Chardin's teachings began to resonate with people. In particular, it was his expansive understanding of the Eucharist that captured Marie's imagination. He saw it as an all-encompassing phenomenon that sanctified all of humanity and creation—it was not just a holy piece of bread that Catholics ate at Mass to sanctify their individual souls.

This was deeply compelling for Marie. It was what she had felt at Benediction that evening in Auckland, and it helped deepen her conviction that she belonged with the Blessed Sacrament sisters. Now living just around the corner from the convent in Armadale, Marie went to the chapel almost every day to pray, her eyes resting on the starched and ironed habits of the sisters as they knelt in prayer and chanted in Latin, catching glimpses of their faces through the grille that separated them from the other churchgoers. Marie understood their lives as involving great sacrifice, but also great happiness, *because this was the order that had this one emphasis: love … The Eucharist, the Blessed Sacrament, was the utmost proof of God's love, leaving himself for us for all time, historically, in the humble appearance of bread and wine … The only response to love was to love in return.*

But although Marie's mind was becoming more open, her spirit was turning inwards. It was as though she was already moving into a silent, contemplative mode. She began to find it difficult to connect with others on a social level, and casual conversation became a struggle. She felt separate, and strange. *If I was just on my own, I'd be fine. But dealing with human beings—I wasn't in a fraternal mood at all.* She was transforming, somehow, as though in preparation for the very difficult future she'd chosen. *It was this idealistic stuff … If you're going to join an order you may as well go to the one that's going to cost you the most … You know, why muck around with degrees? You may as well throw yourself into the burning fire and get burnt!*

Marie entered the convent in February 1966. Only a few months later, Melbourne would see the largest street demonstrations in its history as Prime Minister Harold Holt welcomed President Lyndon Baines Johnson to Australia and declared the country would be 'all the way with LBJ' in the United States's ambition to defeat communism in Vietnam. In her heart, Marie had already left the world. She was barely aware of the forces roiling outside the convent walls when its door opened to welcome her as a postulant.

When I got there, when finally I made it after all this toing and froing and putting it off for a year and finally getting there, Maureen Flood was fantastic. She told me to 'treat it as a motel for the first few days until you get used to it. Just try not to have any other serious concept in your head about it' … I remember thinking that was a very good thing for her to say, even though here's me, wanting to do it all the really hard way.

Her mother had very carefully prepared Marie's suitcase, filled with all the things she'd need at the convent. *And I remember getting into my lovely white cotton nightie. I'd never had a white cotton nightie in my life before and here I was in my very good white cotton nightie, lying in bed and I just remembered saying to God, 'Thank you. I've arrived home.' I am nearly crying when I say that. 'I've arrived home.' After wondering for years—half of my adult life—will I do this or will I not? Will I get married? And suddenly, finally, this final thing: I'm here at last I'm here for better or for worse. But I'd arrived home and it was such a deep feeling. This is where I belonged.*

One hour after Marie entered, Mary Kelly joined the convent as Marie's fellow postulant. *We were as different as chalk is from cheese but we both worked on it, and we made the best of our differences.*

But although Marie felt she was in the right place, that strange spiritual shift which had been building since she first decided to join the convent only intensified, and Marie was suffering. *It was as if I was painfully aware of the interconnectedness of everyone around me … I was swamped by an unfiltered sense of other people's presence, and I wanted to be relieved of this insight. I would pray to see less, for the feeling to go away.*

Though she trusted Maureen, Marie didn't tell her what she was feeling, saving it for the confessional, where a priest told her to just ignore it, assuring her that it would pass.

Marie heeded his advice, and as a keen new postulant, she was eager to get stuck into doing things the hard way, just as Maureen had been when she was a young nun.

So she was sorry to learn that the use of the Discipline was no longer part of the convent's spiritual practice.

They'd just phased the whip out by the time I came in and I was disappointed because I thought, how can you become a saint if you can't even use the whip? All the saints that I'd read gave their bodies a bit of a whack ... I bet Vianney didn't mention the whip ... Oh, and Maureen was so mortified at that whip—she hated even bringing it up.

Maureen's spirituality had grown beyond mortifications of the flesh by this time. *I found her to be very refined, a very thoughtful, caring person. You felt safe with her. I could tell that she had a relationship with the divine. Somehow it hits you between the eyes. And I used to see her about once a week in the very early days. If anything was a bit difficult, you could talk it over with her.*

Nonetheless, Marie didn't share everything with Maureen, and conversation with her fellow postulant and the novices never touched on personal matters. *People were so respectful talking to one another in the novitiate and they spoke fairly quietly and very respectfully. And I was used to rough and tumble in the real world and I thought, 'I've never seen anything like it.' Their voices were soft, and I liked that. It was so gentle.*

Maureen, despite the Mother Superior's disapproval, was sharing some of the reading material Father Charlie Mayne sent her. As Novice Mistress, Maureen had the authority to do so, and as a postulant, Marie soaked it all in. Her reading of Teilhard de Chardin had prepared her well for some of this new theology, and now she took to her books with great enthusiasm. She also did her share of the hard work of making altar breads, *and I was quite good at that because I grew up doing manual things and cooking and baking and all that stuff. So I was good, I got my head around that very quickly.*

All in all, Marie had no difficulty accepting the exertions and deprivations of convent life, the waking for prayer in the middle of the night, and the hot kitchen where she'd be sweating under her habit as she prepared the altar breads. Even the reading on the F-sharp at dinner didn't bother her. Marie knew what to expect, having read the lives of saints and mystics like Saint Thérèse of Lisieux and, Marie's favourite, Saint Margaret Mary Alacoque. *I loved her because she loved God so much. This is one example, that she was having her porridge this particular morning, and there were little grubs in the porridge. You know, maggots. She decided to eat them anyway for the love of God. And I thought she was amazing because my stomach—ugh! The mere thought of that! She's a total saint!*

When Marie happily entered the novitiate, she, too, chose a new name. *I took the name of Marie Magella, and I took Magella because he is the patron saint of mothers. That was the only way of acknowledging my son. It was a subtle way of honouring that I, too, am a mother.*

Marie felt sure she was where she belonged. But for others, things were starting to unravel.

The decision was made to sell the beach house, and the Mother Superior announced that a new property had been bought: Koorootang, a working fourteen-acre farm, again on the Mornington Peninsula. Vianney was horrified at the thought that, with the requirement to pay off the mortgage on the farm, she was now under a new financial obligation, and not one of her choosing, *because it meant that we were going to have to keep working as hard as we were working in altar breads to keep paying for these things … I just said to myself, 'We will never stop working like this … This is going to go on forever and we will never stop.'*

Her faith in God remained strong, she was drawing strength and inspiration from her study of contemporary theology, and her commitment to her vows was unwavering. But Vianney was deeply unhappy. *I can see that there's nothing for me to do or be. I was intelligent and I was curious, and I was generous and willing and so forth, but I'd been in the convent for close on ten years and I'd worked in the altar breads. And, look, there weren't many other jobs to do, but I'd seen other people given other jobs … and I think I was feeling that there was nothing for me. The best thing that they asked me to do was to teach Latin to the novices ... When I think back on it now, depression is often the other side of anger and I think it could have been anger that I was experiencing.*

General tension at the convent continued to build. Opposing factions had developed around what Vatican II demanded, and while the Mother Superior could not stop the coming changes entirely, she kept as tight a rein on things as she could. Jill stayed out of it, but she could see what was happening. *There were three or four of them opposed to the changes and they caused friction. A lot of friction. Thank God I was down on the farm and I wasn't aware of it all, but there was a lot of bitterness going on.*

Jill had now moved almost permanently to Koorootang, exchanging the strict routine of the convent and its sombre, and now palpably hostile, atmosphere for the rhythms of nature. Hard physical work in the open air relieved her anguish to some degree, but she was still struggling. She mended fences, milked the cow, mowed the lawn, sowed and harvested vegetables—all in her habit.

We were real farmers. We caught a fox just before Mass one Sunday—he was caught in a rabbit trap. And Sister Mary Jude and I thought, 'What are we going to do? Here he is in the rabbit trap and we haven't got a gun.' We got a spade and bashed him over the head until he died, and he was running in circles trying to bite us. We had lots of rabbits. Anyway, the veggies had to be picked, a whole paddock of beans. Lettuces, they piled up. We put them in the car, took them up to Armadale to a greengrocer, but he didn't want them. I think they all went to waste, the poor lettuces.

The other sisters all took their turn to join in the healthy outdoor labour and help maintain the farm. The idea was that it would become a second convent house, with plans for a chapel that would offer a place of worship to holidaymakers who flocked to the Mornington Peninsula each summer. At Christmastime in 1967, Vianney was at Koorootang with Sister Mary Francesca, (formerly known as Betty McMenamin) who was the convent treasurer. It was a particularly strange and memorable December, because the Prime Minister, Harold Holt, had just gone missing off nearby Cheviot Beach.

We were down there supposedly to water the plants and everything … And I remember the year because helicopters all came over and they were looking for Harold Holt. It was that Christmas. It was an awful Christmas. We had some records and I said, 'Oh look it's Christmas Day. Do you think I'd be allowed to play some of the records?' And she said, 'Oh, I don't know, I'd better ask Mother.' So, she rang back up to the convent and asked Mother, but Mother said no.

Vianney says it was *the worst Christmas I've ever had in my life.*

In March 1968, Mother Mary Leonard's time as Mother Superior finally came to an end. The freshly elevated Mother Mary Francesca was now Superior, but the exchange of power was less than smooth, and Betty struggled to implement her more progressive agenda. The community was thoroughly divided.

In August that year, a visitor arrived at the convent. He had been sent by Mother Berthe, who, as Superior General, was head of the entire Order. Father Marius Garail was a French diocesan priest who had helped the sisters in Paris to understand the new teachings from Vatican II, and Mother Berthe hoped he would now help the Australian sisters, too.

Father Garail arrived on the evening of 15 August 1968, and stayed for a month. Marie says, *I remember him as a fairly short, slightly chubby Frenchman, with this wonderful accent.* Marie had withdrawn quite willingly from the world, and even occasionally contemplated defecting to a stricter order—*I was thinking of joining the Cistercians who totally are in isolation in a little cabin somewhere on your own.* But she now found herself delighted with Father Garail and what he had to say, and was enthralled with the theology he was teaching the nuns. *He was just alive with the resurrection and the Risen Christ.* It came as a kind of revelation.

I had had the traditional image of the Eucharist of being the real presence—Peter Julian always talked about the real presence of Jesus in the sacrament. And it was like the Eucharist fully contained whoever Jesus was, in the sacrament. And that seemed extraordinary. Now it sounds a bit magical, but it seemed extraordinary that it had a personal presence, that little wafer. Then Father Garail came and he lifted the veil off the Eucharist. He lifted it up and revealed the whole of creation was somehow present in the wafer.

Father Garail helped Marie and the other sisters shift their focus from the Eucharist as sacrifice and memorial to something living and life-giving.

He emphasised the Eucharist as celebration. His strong emphasis was on the resurrection, and it was not such a strong emphasis on the crucifixion. We didn't do away with that, but we'd never had the resurrection emphasised like this before. We're talking about the God we believe in as the Risen God, the Risen Christ. And he somehow pervades the whole of the universe. The whole of the universe is Eucharistic.

Vianney remembers Father Garail as *a nice roly-poly kind of guy in his late forties ... He was warm. We related well to him.* During his month-long visit, he put the sisters through an energetic course of study on the new teachings, organising them into reading and discussion groups, and asking them for their individual thoughts and reflections. This was a totally new experience for Vianney—a connection she had never shared with others in the convent, an experience in the open, free sharing of her faith that she hadn't had since she'd been to those Catholic Youth retreats as a student.

For Vianney, Father Garail's visit was the change she had been longing and waiting for. *What we remember is only the excitement of it. Whenever we talk about Father Garail it's all, you know, positive and exciting. And he did a good thing. Those who weren't thinking this way were pushed on the way, and those who were, pushed further.*

Jill came back from Koorootang to attend some of the discussions about the future, including meetings about how the community would amend its Rule of Life to suit the new, post-Vatican II approach. Jill experienced Father Garail's visit as *three weeks' indoctrination. We were being indoctrinated. We were being told, 'You've got to change your way of thinking. You have to change your way of life and bring it into the twentieth century.'* Jill didn't feel she could speak or contribute in any way. *I was frightened of the changes ... I was immature and unstable, wasn't I? I wasn't really fit to be telling them what to do.*

While Melissa was happy at the convent and hadn't been seeking any change in her way of life, she was one of those who was very open to what Father Garail was saying. But the discussions were not easy, and tension would erupt. *Father Garail was talking to us one day, and he said, 'I'm assuming, girls, that you've read Karl Rahner.' And the Mother Superior said, 'Oh yes, yes.'* But Melissa declared she had never seen a book by the contemporary Jesuit scholar (famous among educated churchmen but unknown to her) in the convent library, much less read it.

And I stood up and said, 'No, I haven't. It's not there. The book's not there.' And I didn't realise that they didn't want me actually to be honest about that. And I thought, 'Oh well, I've said it, and it's true.' And I was called to Mother Superior's room and I was given a severe dressing down. And I said, 'But I'm telling the truth. We don't have Karl Rahner's book.' 'How do you know that it isn't there and I haven't removed it?' I said, 'I'm terribly sorry if I've embarrassed you.' And I thought, 'Now, that's interesting. All I was doing was being honest.' But I began to see from that moment the difficulties that other people were having, that people who'd been there for a long, long time suddenly were being asked to change, and couldn't see the reason for the change. And I thought, 'Uh oh! We're heading for a bit of trouble here.' That's what I thought.

Like each of the sisters, Melissa had a private meeting with Father Garail during his stay, to discuss her vocation and her future.

He said, 'What were you doing before you came here?' I said, 'I was an actress.' And he said, 'Well what are you doing here?' And I said, 'Well I think that God wants me to be here. I followed an urge to be here and I'm very happy.' And he said, 'What makes you think you can't have what you're looking for here and be an actress as well?' And I said, 'Well, first of all, I've never considered that possibility.' I had not ever considered that possibility. And he said, 'Well you can. What you want to be is a contemplative.' I said, 'Yes.' He said, 'Well, what makes you think you can't find it by being what God wants you to be, which is an actor? He's given you that ability. You should be doing that.' And I said … I got a terrific shock actually, but I took it on board, as I did everything. Everything that was done, everything that was said to me, to me it was God's will. I was just a really good nun, I suppose.

Marie had by now emerged from the dark cloud she had been under for so long. Her father had died on 2 August 1968, and Marie was the first of the sisters to be allowed to travel home for a funeral, reuniting her with her large family at the farm in Queensland. She hadn't seen her father since her farewell two years earlier, and with thirteen siblings living and working all over the country, it was the only time she remembers them gathering in the one place. While Marie still had to eat out of sight of her family, as nuns always did, the changes that were happening, and Betty's determination to embrace them, were what made it possible for Marie to make the trip home. *It was quite lovely to know we were all together for the first time ever in our history as a family. And he—well, he was sort of there.*

Back at Armadale, Marie took her first, temporary vows as a professed sister. Before the ceremony, Father Garail performed a very important, symbolic gesture. *Father Garail had the doors taken off between the sacred sanctuary of the altar and where the people gathered, the people's part of the chapel. And down came the doors, the grilles flung open.* For Marie, it seemed to symbolise the new theology of the Eucharist—that it was about connection, community and bringing people together. It was not about having the holiest of holies separated from the people, remote from them, and it certainly wasn't about separating the sisters from the community that came to their chapel to receive the Eucharist.

Shortly after Father Garail's departure, the sisters received a letter from Mother Berthe.

How much you are in my thoughts and prayers in these days following Father Garail's visit. I have received a few letters telling me how grateful you were for it. Being so far away it was surely necessary for you to hear ... what was the scope of the renewal demanded by the church ... The essential and most immediate point is to work to be a 'living community,' as you say so well.

Her letter encouraged the sisters to embrace change cautiously, judiciously, in the spirit of their vows, and to develop new interpersonal relationships with one another, and a more open exchange of ideas. She urged them to wait patiently for the results of a meeting of the General Chapter, where representatives from all the Blessed Sacrament congregations throughout the world (which at this stage included France, Canada, Brazil, the United States, Australia, Italy, Holland and the Philippines) would consider new rules to help the community adapt its traditions to the future. Soon after, Mother Berthe asked Sister Mary Leonard to make a trip to the mother house, which had recently moved from Paris to Rome, giving Betty greater freedom to help the community respond to the Pope's call for renewal. The convent at Armadale would soon embrace that call with vigour.

SMASHING THROUGH THE GRILLE

MELBOURNE UNIVERSITY, 1970

MARIAN STOOD OUT awkwardly among the students at the university. By now, like most orders of nuns, the Faithful Companions of Jesus wore an updated, less restrictive habit—they'd done away with the floor-length robes and the close-clipped hair covered by a bonnet, band and long veil. Now Marian wore a simple skirt and jacket and a greatly reduced veil that sat on top of her head and flowed down behind it, past the nape of her neck, *and you could show your hair, which was very nice.* But among the flared jeans and bright miniskirts, her drab nun's outfit still set her apart on campus. *I felt very peculiar in all this gear, especially the veil, at uni. No, I didn't like it at all. It was terribly isolating. People would steer clear. They'd think you were very strange, which was probably true.*

Sister Marian McClelland, twenty-two years old, had been in the convent for three years, and had made her first profession. She'd put off her studies to complete her novitiate, but now she was finishing her Bachelor of Arts in preparation for her career as a teaching nun. When she first entered the convent at Genazzano in 1967, the changes wrought by Vatican II were only just being felt. Now, they were reverberating powerfully through the Church, not least among Catholic university students.

By the late 1960s, the baby boomers had grown up. They were questioning the wisdom they'd received, and the picket-fenced Australia forged by more than two decades of conservative government. It was this generation of Catholics that took up the promise of Vatican II and connected its focus on celebration, inclusion and social justice to the broader cultural changes that were taking place all around them: a rejection of overbearing authority and the puritanism of both government censors and an older generation of clerics and religious leaders. Hippie culture was in full swing, and Our Lord and Saviour had been recast as Jesus the long-haired peacenik. The Broadway musical *Jesus Christ Superstar* was a huge hit on the Melbourne stage, and the Vietnam moratoriums—the first took place in May 1970—stood against the conscription of young Australian men to a distant war. Young people wanted change and were willing to march in the streets to demand it.

Marian wasn't really plugged into the political scene, and among her fellow Faithful Companions of Jesus, perspectives on the big questions of the time remained conservative, if they were voiced at all. Like many Australian Catholics at the time, Marian's community was influenced by the stridently anti-communist views of BA Santamaria, who was vocal in his support of Australia's role in the Vietnam war. *BA Santamaria was quite welcome at the FCJs, and I listened to a few of his talks. And to my everlasting sorrow I voted to not have the university join the moratorium, because at that stage I was thinking 'all the way with LBJ' sort of thing. I came to change my mind on that.*

Theologically, though, Marian's mind was opening to new ideas. She attended seminars in the new theology given to Catholic students by the Jesuits, *and don't forget, I had already had the experience of Indian philosophy. I knew about the Bhagavad Gita; I knew about the Upanishads. I knew they had this out-there, enormous concept of the divine.* This was what captured Marian's imagination: the idea of an expansive divinity, not restricted to arcane ritual or clerical authority, but present in everyday life, and available to everyone. She could see she was drawing closer to that bigger mystery that had first called her to religious life, but which she sometimes struggled to find in her daily life as a nun. That concept of the divine *was a bit crabbed into just the life of Christ in the convent ... I mean, that's my interpretation now. I don't know that I thought exactly that then ... But there was an awareness of enormity. And that drew me tremendously.*

The FCJs were a so-called active order, engaged in the apostolic work of teaching, rather than a contemplative one, like the Servants of the Blessed Sacrament. But the sisters at Genazzano were nonetheless subject to the strict limits set out by convent tradition. *Look, they were called active. They were semi-contemplative, because they never left the place, either. I never went out unless to the dentist or the doctor.* Marian, known in the convent as Sister Mary Xavier (she chose the name for Saint Francis Xavier's connection with India) had had to get used to *a very regimented schedule. Every minute covered. And you were not allowed—even when you went to bed—you were not allowed to think your own thoughts. You had to go to sleep. So that was how regimented it was ... If you were cleaning the corridors, you were in silence so that you could pray. What you were supposed to pray was nobody's idea.* Amid the silence, Marian learned to be in the moment. *I remember using an electric floor polisher, which I learned to do quite well, and sort of dancing around with it and waltzing around with it a bit and just making it a bit more interesting. But the silence was so that you didn't distract one another.* Every evening they had half an hour personal prayer time in the chapel, called 'the visit', but *they didn't really teach us much about praying—they didn't tell you what to do.* And afterwards there would be communal prayer.

Marian had certainly found the novitiate difficult, and the lack of stimulating conversation was hard to get used to. *You were not allowed to make any personal comments. The conversation went through the Novice Mistress and it was about the most ridiculous trivia you could ever have thought about … The sewing you were doing, or the weather … I must say the first year of novitiate I spent a lot of time crying—I think that's part of what happens—but I never wavered in thinking that this wasn't my life, that God was not calling me to that.*

Whatever the challenges, and despite her deep commitment to becoming a good nun, Marian was determined not to be unhappy. *What I said to myself was, 'If I can't laugh at least once every day, then I'm going to go. I'm leaving.' So I found ways of laughing.* In some ways, laughter came easily, as it does to children who are made to sit still and silent at Mass. *I suppose it's tension or something, but you do giggle quite a lot. And you regress, which is a terrible thing, but you do … They didn't really want you grown up.*

By the end of the novitiate, *I was getting a bit fed up with it. I wanted to do something else.* The loosening up of the strict rules for religious women was bringing small but important changes to the Faithful Companions of Jesus. One change was that just after taking her first vows, Marian was allowed to go home to see her family for the weekend, *which was very nice—very strange.* It was the school holidays in the late winter of 1969, and as soon as she got back to the convent she was told she'd have to teach the prep students, *with no training about anything! … So I got my baptism of fire with these kids. Poor little things, five-year-olds. I don't remember too much about that … I was terrified, though, because I didn't know what I was doing.* She prayed each night for assistance.

After a term of teaching, Marian spent her summer eagerly awaiting the autumn, when she'd be able to leave the convent each day for the bustling courtyards of the Melbourne Uni campus. From the Mother Superior's point of view, Marian's choice of politics and Indian studies as subjects was a little esoteric, but Marian was very eager to use her mind again and learn more about the world. She would major in English literature, which would serve her well as a high school teacher.

Along with the theology lectures given by the Jesuits, Marian had the good fortune to take special classes at St Mary's College, which was run by Loreto nuns. Her teacher was a woman who would become an important Catholic intellectual: *Veronica Brady was like the sun coming out over the clouds.* What Marian was hearing in those classes seemed directly at odds with what she'd learned from her Novice Mistress. She asked Veronica, *'How can you be a nun and say all this stuff?' And she said, 'Look, you know, you don't need to trouble the old nuns by some of the things that you're learning. They don't need to know about it, but you do.' And then she said, 'You will find fellow members of the underground wherever you go.' Oh, wow! It was very exciting.*

Marian graduated from her arts degree at the end of 1971, and the next year she took her diploma in education at La Trobe University, *a place of great experimentation.* The university, established in 1964, was part of a group of newer universities that were set to meet the growing demand for higher education in Australia. By this time, Marian had had enough of showing up in her habit, especially for her drama class, where the students needed to feel physically free. *I found ways to get out of it, I tell you!* On the days she had drama, Marian would leave the convent in her nun's gear, only to duck into the women's toilets and change into a sweater and miniskirt that her mother had bought for her, ready for class.

One evening, a paraliturgy (a liturgical celebration without the sacraments, which can be led by non-clerics) was being held at one of the Melbourne University colleges—it was a kind of ecumenical celebration to mark an ancient festival called the Feast of Fools, *which I'd never heard about in my life before.* The Mother Superior gave Marian permission to go. She wore her civilian clothing under her nun's outfit and her winter coat, and when she arrived at the party, she peeled the outer layers off and stashed her veil away somewhere. Then she caught sight of Marie Grunke from the Blessed Sacrament sisters. Marian had met Marie a few times at a course of lectures for temporary professed nuns, designed to help them understand what Vatican II meant for them, and to teach them some theology. Now here she was, dancing with a group of young students, dressed in the old habit of the Servants of the Blessed Sacrament, complete with white wimple and veil, and an ankle-length white habit. She must have dug it out of a cupboard at the Armadale convent. *And I thought, 'I wonder what she's making of all these young women.' The Feast of Fools!*

That event would be a truly memorable one for Marian. It gave her a palpable sense of what the future might hold for someone like her, and for all young Catholics. *This was such an awakening! All I can remember is there was a lot of wild dancing, which I took part in. And there were lots of theology students there, and we were just wild! And then, I couldn't find my veil when it was time to go. Somebody said, 'Who owns this?' And I said, 'Oh that's mine!' So, it was back into the habit … I was like Cinderella at the ball!*

THE CONVENT OF THE SERVANTS OF THE BLESSED SACRAMENT, ARMADALE, 1969

Marie Grunke wasn't the first of the Servants of the Blessed Sacrament to venture beyond the convent walls in search of an education, and perhaps some wild dancing.

After Father Marius Garail's visit, and with the conservative-leaning Sister Mary Leonard now in Rome, the new Mother Superior, Sister Mary Francesca was hard at work implementing the changes Vatican II demanded. To start with, Sister Mary Francesca was now known by her sisters as Betty. The old, saintly names had been part of the tradition that marked nuns as different from other human beings, something much holier. That was something the new changes sought to move away from and many, though not all, of the sisters reverted to their birth names.

One of Father Garail's clearest instructions upon leaving the sisters in September 1968 had been that Vianney and Maureen ought to be given the opportunity to study. *His words were 'Get those two educated', and Maureen and I were sent out to Assumption Institute the next year.*

The Assumption Institute (named for the feast of the Assumption, when Catholics celebrate the day that Mary, the mother of Jesus, was 'assumed body and soul into Heaven') was housed on the top floor of the old Mercy Private Hospital in Grey Street, East Melbourne. Its express purpose was to educate nuns about what Vatican II demanded of them, and give them the knowledge that would help them renew their vocations and update them in line with the Vatican's requirements. The Institute was really intended for novices and sisters in temporary vows—*but here we were, these two old contemplatives.*

Vianney valued her intellect and was very happy to be using it again. She and Maureen studied theology and moral philosophy, as well as forms of prayer and liturgy, or public worship. They even studied some literature. *English literature, yes—you know, I hadn't done any since I'd been at school, so I loved that.* Vianney recalls reading *Cry, the Beloved Country,* a novel set in apartheid South Africa, which reflected Vatican II's focus on questions of social justice—questions that Vianney had not been asked to consider since joining the convent in 1957.

Vianney and Maureen would attend for the whole year. *We went four days a week and then came home and made altar breads and did all the things that we needed to do, plus our homework and all that. So that was all quite demanding.* But amid the study and work there were the beginnings of a new place in Vianney's life for fun: both the thrill of intellectual engagement and the pleasures of social life. *It was fabulous, see—not just the courses that we did but that we mixed in with these other sisters.* When it was afternoon teatime, volunteers were needed to take the tea to whomever had given the classes that day, and Vianney and Maureen always raised their hands. *We'd be the first and we'd sit there, and we'd just plague the priest with questions. We were full of eagerness to learn, you know, and it was the first of any kind of real learning that had been offered to us ... Our postulancy and novitiate was very flimsy, I'd say, concentrating on our constitutions and on Saint Peter Julian ... It was all that kind of pious language and somehow or other most of us never related to it terribly well.*

Meanwhile, other sisters in the community were taking courses elsewhere around Melbourne, run by priests and senior nuns, to help them through the changes. It was a time of great hope and enthusiasm, and a huge amount of activity. The Church, despite having many very dynamic members within it, from progressives like Charlie Mayne to conservatives like BA Santamaria, had been hidebound for many decades, determined to resist modernity at any cost. The excitement and sense of possibility that Vatican II had unleashed was palpable, and nobody felt it more keenly than Vianney and Maureen.

While they were developing their minds, Maureen and Vianney's friendship was also deepening. Betty was still the only nun at Armadale who could drive a car, and four days per week, she chauffeured Vianney and Maureen the fifteen-minute drive from Armadale to East Melbourne. *Betty finally said, 'Look, I'm sick of this. Get the train yourself.' And we were very happy to get the train ourselves.* Vianney and Maureen were finally able to talk to one another, unsupervised. *It didn't matter now. They weren't going to tell us what to talk about.*

Back at the convent, discussions were underway about how to change the Rule of Life that defined the sisters' shared purpose and adapt it for the future. Slowly, the strict rules and customs that ordered the nuns' days were giving way, and the women were getting used to more natural interactions, as well as sharing in lively discussions about the future of the community and its spiritual direction. But Vianney remembers that it didn't come easily. *We had a whole year where we had sessions with a psychologist, virtually just learning to talk to each other—just to talk like human beings. We'd lost the skills.*

Marie recalls that at first, though they were permitted to speak more freely, they still avoided personal matters, both from habit and an ingrained sense of propriety. It took quite a while for them to loosen up. *It just faded bit by bit … We started to maybe have little meals together, and we could just sit and talk, and maybe even a meal with a glass of wine—that became not a taboo thing. So, just getting back to life as we knew it before we joined the nuns, I suppose. It was just more normal.*

But becoming *more normal* was, for some, a very mixed blessing. Marie recalls that *one of the lovely nuns said to me, 'Look, it was all right when we didn't know what the others were like but now that we can talk to one another, I've got to live with these people.' She decided to leave.*

Maureen mainly recalled both the excitement and the uncertainty of that time when she spoke to the ABC in 1996. *It was interesting. It was stimulating. It was fun. And then of course the hard things were that not everybody in the community agreed. We didn't know where we were going. We had a clear goal once, and that was gone.*[1]

The convent's archives have a document, 'Diary of Events April '68 to August '69'. A timeline, typed up on two sheets of paper, relates in bare detail a series of crises and striking novelties: several hospital admissions; an unspecified 'crisis' with Sr J; a request for dispensation by Sr R, who wished to abandon her vows and leave; the departure of several postulants and novices; the introduction of theology classes; new wardrobe purchased for the updated habit.

The document notes several novices and postulants leaving—in fact, nearly all of them left over the next year or so. Perhaps they could no longer match their contemplative vocations with the changes that were afoot. Some may have felt there was no point in becoming nuns, now that the Vatican had made it clear that holiness was equally available to everyone—nuns were no longer to be regarded, or to regard themselves, as closer to God or more valued by him than anyone else. For others, unacknowledged difficulties—including, probably, long-untreated mental illness—were finally brought to the surface. Individual women, and the community as a whole, had to grapple honestly with the question of whether convent life was really suitable for everyone living it at Armadale. Some who had been there for many years, as well as the postulants and novices who had entered the convent with the long-established image of a nun's life in their minds, found their expectations and ideals coming under intense scrutiny, and amid the silence and prayer were daily scenes of turmoil and transformation.

After years of struggling with one of her fellow sisters, Vianney went to see Betty in the hope of a different response from the one the previous superior had given her. *Betty had been a nurse, and I said, 'I don't have a lot of medical knowledge, but I have some, and as far as I'm concerned, that sister is sick. And if she's not sick, I am.' And Betty said, 'I know.' It was like the weight of ten years was lifted off me.*

For many members of the community, the idea that they might soon be able to cast off their heavy, restrictive robes and reconnect with the outside world was a thrilling prospect. The changes promised greater personal freedom, and the possibility of reuniting with family and old friends. Even more importantly, it meant spiritual growth: further study and an open engagement with others who sought a larger understanding of their shared vocation as religious women. But not everyone felt that way. For some, the idea of having to find their way in a society that they had left years, almost decades ago, and the vanishing of a way of life to which they had dedicated their souls and their youth, was daunting. Instead of freedom, it felt like a painful peeling away of layers of protection and security, of the parts of themselves they had felt were the most permanent and unassailable. It also meant an end to the specialness and status of being a religious sister, particularly an enclosed one. Some sisters welcomed the changes, but experienced a deep questioning of their vocation, and of whether they needed to remain nuns in order to continue their spiritual development. Carol remembered *being in one particular part of the convent between the newer building and the old house and thinking, my God, here I am. I've devoted the best years of my life to this. I could have married, and the thing to which I've devoted my life is falling apart.*[2]

The exodus was having a profound effect on convents all over Australia and beyond. In Armadale, it meant that the women could no longer practise perpetual Adoration in front of the exposed Blessed Sacrament. They needed eighteen sisters to complete the rotation, and soon there were not enough of them to complete the cycle each day. This had been the most important defining feature of the Servants of the Blessed Sacrament as a community. The change must have been hard for some of them to bear. Not everyone could easily invite a new idea of the Eucharist beyond its manifestation as the host in the monstrance, or understand Adoration of Jesus as something that didn't have to be undertaken as a separate, very special activity.

Marie found it hard to see so many of her companions leave. *It wasn't as though we came together and we were told, or they told us—you just saw somebody disappear. I remember sitting in the room adjoining the chapel, waiting to go for my hour of prayer, and I saw this young sister who hadn't long been in—she was a novice—and I saw her walking down the path in secular dress. I thought, 'What? She's going!' It was a great shock because I was very fond of Judy, and I thought, 'Oh, no!'*

Melissa had been observing the changes taking place, and she was among those who welcomed them. She was still committed to the life she'd chosen, but she was pondering what Father Garail had told her and wondering whether it was true—that she could nourish her spirit and do God's will by returning to her old life as an actress. *And then a member of my family was having a bit of trouble at home and they needed some help, some practical help.* Betty suggested that Melissa go home and help her family. *And I said, 'How can this be?' And she said, 'Well, we can perhaps arrange exclaustration for you.' Now, I was actually the first nun in Australia, I think, to be let out for a year, with vows, and they called it exclaustration. And she said, 'You can go home for a year, and in that time, you can consider what Father Garail said.'*

Melissa had taken temporary vows, so her one-year exclaustration would let her see those vows out, working in the theatre but remaining a Blessed Sacrament sister. She got a role in *a play called 'Hadrian VII', which was about Pope Hadrian. And because it was a religious play, and because I'd just come out of the convent, the publicity was unbearable …* The theatre company was delighted to have such an interesting young actress to promote. *You know, newspaper articles, proposals of marriage from all over the world—particularly Germany for some reason, I don't know why. They were fascinated by this person who'd been a nun and was now out and back on the stage. To me it was the natural thing, because that was my job.* Six months after that run, Melissa got a role in a comedy, *a West End romp, really. We did a warm-up season in Newcastle for two weeks before we opened in Sydney. And the renewal of my vows was coming up. And I remember sitting on the beach at Newcastle, really just praying about it, thinking about what to do. And I knew that there was no turning back, there was no going back.* Melissa had no regrets. *No, I didn't feel any sense of loss at all. Which is strange, isn't it?*

+++

In early 1969, Jill had to leave the farm on the Mornington Peninsula and come back to live at the convent at Armadale. Koorootang had a manager running it now, and soon it would be sold—it was too much work for the women to manage. *They were short of sisters because with the discussions on how to change the rule, all the postulants left, all the novices left. The temporary professed left.*

Returning to the convent plunged Jill into a fresh crisis. *When I got back, I knelt down by the side of my bed and I said, 'Oh God, why did I ever do it?' Coming back and being locked up—that was too much for me.* At the farm, things had been a little freer, and the rules a little less strict.

Betty quickly saw that Jill wasn't coping, and arranged for her to get some help. *Well, she said, 'What's wrong with you?' And I said, 'I'm frightened. I don't know. I don't know what's wrong with me.'* Jill couldn't hide her unhappiness, but nor could she see any way out of the convent and the holy vows she had made. *My fear was displeasing God.*

Betty arranged for Jill to see the Vicar for Religious, a senior Jesuit who was responsible for the wellbeing of priests, nuns and brothers. *And he asked me what was going on. I have no idea what I said to him. Now he summed it up. He said, 'Okay Sister Mary Agnes. Number one, you never had a vocation. Number two, they were at fault in accepting you. You can leave the convent in good conscience. What do you want to do?'* For Jill, it came as both a shock—one that dismissed her years of service to the order as a big mistake—and as a profound relief. *'I want to get out, and if I get out I'll never come back!'*

Betty was waiting for Jill outside the Vicar's office. *And I said, 'I'm leaving.' She looked as though she'd been punched in the stomach. Just like that. But then they really supported me. They got in touch with the family. They got a hairdresser in and straightened up my hair, because we used to just cut our own hair without a mirror.*

Jill asked for permission to say a personal goodbye to each of the sisters, and it was granted, which was highly unusual. *I was allowed to speak to them and say why I was leaving and what had brought it about—how I actually felt. And Sister Carol Hogan said, 'I can't believe it! I've lived with you all these years and I had no idea what was going on.'*

Jill still has the farewell notes each of the sisters gave her.

Within a week, Jill walked out the door. It was 1 August 1969. Just two weeks earlier, two US astronauts had walked on the moon. The Australia Jill had left eighteen years ago and the one she returned to were not the same place. In the 1930s, when Jill was growing up, her mother was among a tiny minority of mothers who worked. At that time, married women made up only 2 per cent of the workforce. By 1971 they would make up 18 per cent.[3] In 1969, women's right to equal pay was legally acknowledged, though it remained far from guaranteed. The advent of the pill made it possible for married women to plan their families and for single women to enjoy sex without the worry of an unwanted pregnancy or an illegal abortion. Women were slowly becoming part of public life in Australia—since Merle Thornton and Rosalie Bognor had chained themselves to the bar at Brisbane's Regatta Hotel in 1965, women were even drinking alongside men in pubs, a sight unseen in Jill's childhood.

Jill moved back into her family home, got work within three weeks, and her new life began. She struggled with a sense of failure—*I felt when I went out as though I've been divorced, and people would look down on me*—but much of her mental anguish had lifted: *I just was so relieved just to be myself.*

Back at the convent, the community was still shrinking. It seemed there was a new departure or two every month. It was not only novices and postulants who were walking away—longstanding members of the convent left. Even the former Superior, Mary Leonard, moved on, having come back from Rome to find the community completely (and for her, distressingly) altered. Vianney says *she must have felt that she couldn't live with us. She couldn't live with the way it was changing, I think.* Mary Leonard returned to her family and to work, leaving religious life behind.

For Marie, the departure of so many sisters prompted deep questions. *When you're seeing a lot leave, you're saying to yourself, 'Well, why am I staying?' So that was the question I had to live with for quite a while: 'Why am I staying?'—which is not a bad question.*

But Marie did stay and, like Vianney and Maureen, was filled with hope for the future in spite of the community's greatly diminished numbers. *We found it so exciting, and breathing life into this place that was so sterile and musty, and you could feel and smell it. This place needs new life, and there was the new life. You see why the spirit is breath—it was like a breath of life coming into our congregation.*

Barbara felt quite disconnected from discussions on how to change and adapt the congregation's Rule of Life, and in fact she has no memory of Father Garail's visit. It's possible that with her lay duties, like her work in the laundry, Barbara was left out of the study groups in 1968. In any case, *I never asked for any change. I was prepared to live my whole life in silence.* But when the changes came, she accepted them with equanimity. *The structures would not have diminished or added to who I truly was. My main cause was the truth of my true self and that will always remain, whether the structures changed or not. That was the most important thing.*

But as she began to understand the new Eucharistic thinking, Barbara saw more and more that it meant an end to separation—the separation of the nuns from the rest of the faithful, and of herself from the world. *So I was saying, 'Yes, I'll go along with what is all about unity. I'll let go. I'll accept the changes because it's all going towards unity,' which I put as first. The Eucharist is all about unity and oneness—we are all one!* The new way of thinking resonated with her own intimate knowledge of God. *I've experienced a oneness with God. And I was the last and the least who got the experience—from total separation, to feeling the oneness with God. That was my true self. My true self was one with God.*

One concrete benefit of the changing rules was that when Barbara's father had a near-fatal heart attack, she was allowed to go home to visit him in Moree. It had been fifteen years since she had been with her family, all together. *I was able to see my father and my sisters and their children, and I think they made a big fuss of me, because it was my first time home.* Barbara was given a bed in the sleepout, an extra room built onto the verandah, with windows that opened to the yard. *I was still in my habit, and my nephews somehow walked past, and one of them obviously peeped at me when I was in that bedroom, and he said, 'Nuns have hair!' That was a big revelation!* A year after that visit, Barbara's father died.

In late 1969, a Chapter of Aggiornamento (Italian for 'bringing up to date') was called in Rome, and delegates from each community of Servants of the Blessed Sacrament from around the globe were called to attend. The purpose of the meeting was to revise the congregation's constitutions and Rule of Life and adapt them to the edicts of Vatican II. Betty was elected delegate, and Maureen was to go to Rome with her to observe and help out. Maureen wrote that 'a lot of decisions were made about our congregation's lifestyle, giving us a little more freedom. Being there only to assist, I didn't have a vote. A young sister from the Philippines was there too. We were given charge of the dining room. We had to set the tables, do the washing and the ironing of the table linen, and clean the dining room. Hard work, but fun, especially with trips into Rome.'[4]

When Betty and Maureen returned home to Melbourne, one of the first things Betty decided was that it was time to get rid of the grilles in the parlour. This was a momentous event, of great symbolic resonance, and Marie recalls it vividly. *I got wind of it and I said, 'Betty, I just want to ask you one thing. I'd like to take an axe to those,' I said, 'I just feel I'd like to hack my way out of here!' And she said, 'Only if I can watch you.' So that tells you what a great woman she was.* Marie really did take an axe to the grilles—*I just did a symbolic chop or two*—before a handyman came around to finish the job.

The new Rule of Life agreed upon in Rome was now put into practice. There's a copy of it, dated 1971, in the convent archives. Its fresh emphasis is evident from the first pages. 'Allow yourself to be led by the Spirit,' reads an epigraph (Galatians 5, 16): 'The pages that follow have not only a theoretical or conceptual value, but also a value of life and experience, for they spring from the life of the sisters. They give the person the freedom necessary to grow into commitment, responsibility and true liberty.'

Maureen Flood, reflecting on this period, wrote:

> The work of renewal within was going on apace! I was happily 'returning to our origins and adapting to our times', as the Church had directed, not realising what the exploration of origins might turn up. Signs of radical change showed first in

> our central symbol, the celebration of Eucharist—a sacrament so reified that we had Jesus/God physically captured in a small piece of bread. Love was trapped and hard to recognise in this meal. Developments in Eucharistic theology and in the understanding of celebration effected a sea change in me.[5]

The emphasis had shifted, and the women's lives were now changing in earnest. Betty, as Superior and leader of the Armadale community, was heartily committed to preparing the sisters for their new life in religion, and for helping them find a balance between continuity and change, while arming them with the knowledge they would need to pursue the responsibility and liberty that the new Rule of Life offered them.

As part of this process, Betty thought it was time to give the sisters some important life skills. Marie laughs as she tells this story: *Betty was all keen that we do exercises, and she thought we should enrol in how to swim at a local pool. I can remember we got on this tram dressed in secular clothes … Betty would have got these from somewhere, and maybe I had one of Rusty's shirt dresses on or something like that. And so, when we got on the tram, I couldn't help feeling that the people guessed we could be nuns, coming out. And Barbara's up the front of the tram somewhere and she called out 'Sisters, is this where we get off?' And we're all ducking for cover. 'Sisters!'—it blew our cover completely!* The sisters also took driving lessons—everyone but Marie, who had attended a talk about the environment and was horrified at the news of the polluting effects of motor vehicles.

But the nuns needed professional skills, too. As Eucharistic sisters, they now saw their role as inviting the community to celebrate the Mass in a new way. As their updated Rule of Life stated, their mission was 'to live the Eucharistic Mystery fully in a Gospel community, while helping others to live it'. Where the priest once led the Eucharistic service alone, his back to the congregation, muttering in Latin with the assistance of some altar boys and perhaps a male acolyte or two, the idea was now that the sisters would take a more active role. The priest would, of course, be the one to consecrate the Sacrament and give the homily, but the sisters were no longer faceless choristers chanting in Latin with their backs to the congregation, providing a spiritually edifying soundtrack. They would now be planning parts of the liturgy, leading the prayers, doing the readings and inviting the lay congregation to participate actively. Maureen and Vianney could see that if they were going to take the lead in planning innovative liturgical ceremonies and teaching the new Eucharistic theology to the wider Melbourne community, they would need more training. Maureen went to London to do further study at Corpus Christi College. Vianney was keen to go abroad as well, and was accepted into a postgraduate degree in counselling in the Philippines, but Betty didn't think she could spare both Vianney and Maureen at once, so Vianney had to wait.

She didn't waste her time merely waiting, though. Vianney had come to understand how the lack of study at Armadale had made the contemplative life and the life of prayer more difficult and less fulfilling than it might otherwise have been. She began to explore rigorous study as a mode of contemplation and devotion.

Vianney would possibly have made a wonderful candidate for a mediaeval monastery, where she could have devoted her life to reading, learning and writing. But by the nineteenth century, scholarship was no longer an important aspect of monastic life for most nuns, and she had been offered little if any reading that would help her understand the meaning and purpose of the contemplative life, or the richly varied forms of prayer the Catholic tradition offered. She had relied entirely on what Charlie Mayne managed to smuggle into her hands.

Now that she was free to read whatever she liked, Vianney gained a fresh understanding of what she'd been missing in her life as a young contemplative. *You must have study time for the study of the poets and the writers through the history of the Church who are the contemplative role models. You've got to have access to that, and you've got to learn what contemplation is and the different forms of prayer. We were taught some forms of prayer, but it was mostly forms of prayer Saint Peter Julian prayed, which was according to what they called the four ends of sacrifice. So, we prayed according to adoration, thanksgiving, reparation and intercession. But we didn't use those ways in a creative way, and we weren't taught other methods and other ways of praying that we could have learned from or used.*

Now she made up for lost time, and was drawing great spiritual nourishment from her reading. Vianney, like countless other religious sisters around Australia and the world, began to plunge herself into the intellectual traditions of her faith, and hold them up to a new light. It wasn't a break with tradition (some certainly saw it that way, but Vianney didn't)—it was a 'renewal', as Vatican II said. Vianney forged close friendships with others who shared her interest in prayer and liturgy, and helped to offer courses at the Armadale convent, attended by religious men and women from other orders. Vianney also worked with Christians from other churches, as Vatican II meant a new spirit of ecumenism and openness, replacing the long-festering hostility Catholics felt—or were expected to feel—towards Protestants. Vianney and the others put their new discoveries into practice at the chapel at Armadale, where young, bearded priests showed up with acoustic guitars to say Masses, and the nuns were trying out new ways to celebrate the Eucharist and bring the new theology to the fore.

Meanwhile, Vianney was able to return to her practice of writing long letters, as often as she liked. She was receiving regular missives from Maureen in London, which only fed Vianney's appetite for adventure and study overseas. *We did correspond a lot. Oh, she was having a good time!* Maureen was now completely unsupervised, enjoying both a new freedom of the mind and the personal liberty to explore London and all it offered. *And instead of being there for the next lecture, she'd be hopping out to get theatre tickets, she'd be telling me.*

By 1970 it was Marie's turn to go to the Assumption Institute. *That's when I found out that it was possible for a young nun to actually fall in love, and I was scandalised that the priest would even suggest that that could happen. Of course, we'd forgotten that we were just human beings! And he said, 'If you fall in love, don't think that's the end of your vocation—just work through it.'* Marie and the other young sisters who were emerging from enclosure were being taught how to cope in the world, as well as how to understand their vocation in a new way. But for Marie, who hadn't had the opportunity to finish high school or attend university, it was the art history that really appealed. *I loved all that. I was starving for that sort of information—stimulation of the mind and imagination. It was wonderful.* At the convent, Marie found someone who shared her passion for the subject. Carol, who had been to university before becoming a nun, helped Marie raid the library for all the books she could find, and sat beside her as they leafed through the colour plates. *It was like journeying through an amazing museum in a way. She'd be pointing at the pictures of who they were, who did these works and why they were the way they were … I was getting soaked in history … I can't say to this day how wonderful that was for me.*

In the middle of 1970, almost a year to the day since she left the convent, Jill was married to Kevin Maher, a man she'd met at a local club for Catholics over thirty. The nuns had gotten to know him, as Jill had brought him to visit several times after they became engaged. *Yeah, and they loved Kevin. We'd go to visit and Mother Superior would say, 'Now come and sit beside me Kevin.'* Jill's parents insisted on paying for the wedding, but their budget only stretched as far as twenty-four guests. The nuns, who were still not allowed out of the convent to attend the wedding, helped make up for it by hosting a pre-wedding party at the convent, inviting all of the bride and bridegroom's friends. Not too long after, Jill and Kevin adopted a baby boy, Michael, and two years later a baby girl whom they called Michelle. Jill remained in touch with the sisters all through this period and beyond, maintaining a particularly close bond with Sister Pete, who, though she was a traditionalist who would never put aside her nun's veil and tunic, thrived amid the new freedoms for human contact the changes offered. *And Sister Peter Julian came to our house in Greensborough for Michelle's First Holy Communion. Peter Julian was very good with children—very rapt in children.*

+++

In 1972, Marian, who was completing her diploma of education at La Trobe, showed up at the convent in Armadale to attend a liturgy course. It was by pure chance that she was at that first class—she was only there because the FCJ nun who had originally signed up couldn't make it. Though Marian had met Marie a few times, she really knew nothing of the Servants of the Blessed Sacrament. *I got a ride over with Father Gregory Manly, who was a Passionist priest who had been studying liturgy in the Philippines.* Carol, Vianney and Betty were all studying with Father Manly, a much-loved teacher of theology, *and there was a group of other sisters from other congregations. So it was a meeting and mingling of about eight people, and it was to understand how the Eucharist, the new Eucharist, was done.*

Marian was greatly impressed with what she learned that night. She attended the course to its conclusion—a weekend retreat outside Melbourne. All the nuns left their habits behind for ordinary clothes, and Marian took long walks in the bush with Vianney. She could see that Vianney and others at Armadale were *moving in a different rhythm. Less mechanistic and more … contemplative is the only word I can think of, a more contemplative way of understanding and praying.*

Even though Marian had spent countless hours praying at the FCJ convent, this was something new. *With the sisters I was with, we had prayers which went at the rate of knots ... And in myself, I resisted. I thought, 'This doesn't mean anything.'* Marian could see that prayer could be much more than just a mumbling of traditional psalms, *and I began to see how through this public prayer you could lead people into a state of prayer, actually.* And then there was the Gospel, and a fresh approach to understanding and relating to it. *This is the word of God alive, and you listen and see what the invitation is. The invitation always came through the word, but it was up to us to see how we would respond to that.* To have a priest encourage a personal response to the Gospel was entirely new for Marian. Catholics had always been taught to listen to the sermon for the priest's interpretation, and to take that as the authoritative truth. At her convent, they still seemed stuck in that way of thinking.

Getting to know Vianney and Carol was a revelation to Marian. *They were so alive! ... And they seemed very human, like women ... They were starting to let themselves be more human and less regimented.* Marian was beginning to see that she could be a different kind of nun. She could be herself and be a nun at the same time.

Towards the end of that year, the people who had attended the liturgy course were invited to the convent at Armadale for a meal, and Marian met Maureen Flood for the first time. Maureen had returned from her studies in London with a head full of new ideas, and without its customary veil. Her fellow sisters soon followed her lead. Marian was immediately struck by Maureen. *She was completely at home. She was warm and inviting. She had a good sense of humour ... She was being a woman, and yes, there was a goodness about Maureen that shone out. That's all I can say. There was just something about her. It was a radiance.*

The next year, Marian, who had now graduated with a Diploma of Education from La Trobe, began teaching Latin, English, history and French to the Year 7s at Genazzano. By this time, Marian was one of the only nuns teaching at the school. There were very few new postulants at most Australian convents, and the Faithful Companions of Jesus were no different.

When Marian had joined in 1967, there were five young women in the novitiate. By the time she was ready to take her vows, she was the only one left from her intake group do so, and very few women joined after her. *The tap had just turned off.* Meanwhile, many more young Australians, especially women, were attending university.[6] Lots of them were studying to be teachers, and nuns were no longer so badly needed in Australian classrooms.

Marian recalls speaking to the mother of one of her students *and she said to me, 'You're young and you have your whole life ahead of you,' whereas I'd thought, 'Oh, I'm twenty-five. I've done everything now. All I have to do now is live it out.' That was a different way of seeing it.* Looking at her lay teaching colleagues, it began to dawn on Marian that just as there were perfectly good teachers who weren't nuns, there might also be perfectly good nuns who weren't teachers. The future she had imagined as fixed began to shift.

While Marian's community of FCJ sisters entertained only modest changes to their way of life and their understanding of their vocation, the community at Armadale continued its revolution. Maureen described a window opening onto the world in these years:

> Slowly interplay began between church and world and me and world. I went exploring. I felt quite safe. Everything I loved was still intact. God was in His heaven, after all. The first new world I entered was that of modern biblical criticism. Linked with that, the liturgical movement held sacred symbol up to the light for closer scrutiny. At the same time a stream of new theologies was expanding into a river. Liberation theology carried all before it and opened the way, and my mind, to feminist theology.
>
> Books of science, philosophy and psychology were available in a way they had never been before. Darwin, Marx, Freud came into my life as prophets. I heard, though still at a distance, the voices of Heidegger, Hegel, Kierkegaard and Nietzsche.

> Germaine Greer and Betty Friedan planted seeds that changed my life forever! The 'women's movement' gradually became for me the single most important vehicle of justice in our world … This was a time of liberation and joy.[7]

Greer's recently published book *The Female Eunuch* had made its way into the convent. While Maureen had been reading it in London, a copy arrived, wrapped in brown paper, for Vianney. Her father had sent it, and Vianney absorbed Greer's exhortation that her fellow women put aside their feminine delicacy and grab hold of their freedom with both hands.

Having missed out on her opportunity for further study in the Philippines, Vianney was resigned to remaining in Melbourne and forging her own path towards growth. She was working closely with her friend, Father Greg Manly, designing and delivering liturgy courses to the sisters at Armadale, and to other religious around Melbourne. The services at the chapel were changing and evolving. Carol was busy studying at what was then the United Faculty of Theology, forming part of a significant wave of nuns, both in Australia and elsewhere, who were taking advantage of the new opportunity to scrutinise their religion—the Church had effectively banned women from studying theology for centuries. Carol was bringing home the latest in feminist theology, which was influencing the liturgies the sisters designed. As Vianney describes it, the idea that *God was present in every person, and that in coming to us in the bread and wine Jesus was in every person* was something they'd always known, but it was now at the centre of how they understood their vocation.

And we were able to arrange our prayer life and particularly the celebration of the Eucharist in a way that brought that to the fore. We engaged more with the laypeople who came to our chapel, and we altered, say, the way that we were praying the Divine Office—in English, which was a big improvement. We didn't always try to chant it on the F-sharp. We used contemporary hymns, that kind of thing, and so those changes occurred, but the behavioural ones kind of followed that. And if Carol was here, she'd want to say that we became very influenced by the feminist emphases that we were hearing—in general, but also in our work.

While not all members of the community necessarily agreed with some of these changes, or saw the need for them, enough of them did, and those enthusiasts devoted their energies to bringing the more sceptical sisters along with them. While someone like Sister Peter Julian was not at the forefront of the changes to the liturgical prayers, she embraced things like the inclusion of the lay parishioners in the life of the convent. Photographs from this time show her delight in preparing feasts to celebrate First Holy Communions. Marie recalls that *Sister Pete loved baking and cooking. It was just part of who she was, and she loved little children, and she'd probably find out it was one little kid's birthday coming up and she'd do things like that—any excuse to make a cake.* While all the other sisters now went bare-headed, Sister Pete kept the veil on to the very last. As Jill says, *she was a toughie. And the thing was, when we had the old Rule, she didn't keep the Rule. When they changed the rules, she stuck with the old rules.*

When Maureen returned from London she became Mother Superior, and Vianney took over Maureen's former role as Novice Mistress. *It's all silly, really, because we had so few people.* Before long the two or three remaining novices had thought better of it, and left, *and Maureen said to me, 'Well, now you should go. You should go and study.' And by that stage I knew that I was much more interested in liturgical stuff, and she said 'Okay. If you want to do liturgy, find out where you can do it.'*

By this time, Marie was studying too. Betty had encouraged her to explore her natural talent and embrace it as a gift—something that did not lie outside of her vocation but could become an important part of it. In 1972, Marie had begun a full-time degree in graphic design at the Caulfield Institute of Technology, and she really began to flourish. *I was so happy that I was at art school with all these interesting lovely young people that I was enjoying immensely, but I was so happy that I was also with my community. They were such a wonderful backdrop to everything I was doing, and my friends would say, 'Can we have a look? We want to come and meet them. We want to see inside a convent. Can we come around?'* Visits could now be made much more freely, and many of Marie's friends did visit her at home.

On campus, Marie mingled with the students without any of the discomforts Marian had suffered—she wore stylish civilian clothes (many of them given to her by the always up-to-date Rusty—now the mother of three boys), and had her hair done in the fashion of the day. The program of study was rigorous: it was a full-time, four-year course that included curricula in the history of music, art and literature, as well as the technical side of graphic design. With so many of the women engaged in the hard work of earning tertiary degrees, and with the community's numbers substantially diminished, the convent invested in new equipment and hired laypeople to help manage and run the altar breads operation. The nuns still took turns to do their share of the work, but the burden was now significantly lighter.

Barbara, meanwhile, was enjoying her newfound freedom to visit family. Her cousin John had several children, and now she could spend much more time with them, in a much more natural way than the old parlour had allowed. She took her fellow sister, Mary Kelly, on many of these visits. *She was welcomed and appreciated. She was so easy, so comfortable to be with. Mary was the one I felt mostly connected with. I think we did have something in common. We sort of understood each other. She was always very true to herself and very easy to get along with and very nice. She had her spirituality and we were both country girls. I don't know. We seemed to have a friendship there and we liked going for little trips together. Anyone who got to know Mary and were her friends were lifelong friends.*

Barbara was also exploring her own spirituality, in her own fashion. She had never once spoken of her childhood religious experience with her sisters at Armadale. But sometime in the 1970s, she and Marie attended a charismatic, Pentecostal-style service at another church. Ecumenism was a big part of the response to Vatican II—the Council had specifically named 'the restoration of unity among all Christians' as one of its 'principal concerns.'[8] Catholics, who had once been separated from, and had seen themselves as very distinct from the other Christian churches, were trying to break down some of those barriers.

The Pentecostal church was an unfamiliar scene to Barbara and Marie. When the preacher invited members of the congregation to come to the front of the room, Barbara and Marie had expected everyone to volunteer, but theirs were the only hands raised. *We were asked to go up to the stage to be prayed over for the gift of tongues. But neither of us got the gift of tongues. And when we came back home, we were in the kitchen, and I think we fell into laughter about us putting up our hands and finding ourselves on the stage—we laughed our heads off.* Despite her mirth, something about that ceremony caught Barbara's attention, and she decided to connect with the Catholic charismatic movement. Having emerged in the late 1960s, this movement was growing—though initially dubious, the Vatican officially accepted the movement in the mid-1970s. In essence, its focus is on the personal relationship with God and Jesus, rather than on dogma, and takes an interest in phenomena like mystical experience, faith healing and prophecy. Barbara found a real connection there. *I was thrilled that people were able to talk about how they were touched by the Holy Spirit, because in the convent we couldn't say anything about Jesus or about spirituality* … But among the charismatics, mystical experiences were part of the everyday. *They were sharing that. They were jumping for joy. They would jump, you know. It was sheer delight to hear people—Tom, Dick and Harry—saying they had a mystical experience of the Holy Spirit. Oh, that was sheer joy.*

By May 1973, a turning point came for Marian with the FCJs. She ran into Carol and Maureen at an ordination Mass given for a mutual friend. Marian, wearing her FCJ suit and veil, was dressed quite differently from Carol, who was bare-headed and wore plain, cream-coloured clothing.

At afternoon tea someone said, 'Oh, are you two from the same order?' And Carol said, 'No, but I wish we were.' And I thought, how strange, why would Carol want to be part of my order? It didn't occur to me that she meant she wished I was in her group. Anyway, the afternoon went on and someone else asked the same question. And Carol said, 'No, but I'm trying to persuade her to join us,' and I thought, 'She's never said that. What does that mean?' And that night, it just overtook me. I always said it was like a train that I got on and couldn't get off, and it went through my mind over and over and over: 'What does she mean? What could this be?'

Because it was all she knew, Marian had always assumed that becoming a nun would mean a life of teaching. *But I could see that the Blessed Sacrament sisters were what I called a 'one thing'—not being, as it were, split into being a nun and a teacher.* She had not yet taken her final vows with the Faithful Companions of Jesus. *There was nothing to say I couldn't leave. I mean, these are big thoughts, and I was a Capricorn, and you don't make choices like that easily if you're a Capricorn.* Soon after that, it was Vocations Week at Genazzano, and Marian was supposed to talk to her students about her own vocation, to help any girls who might have felt a calling themselves. *I was terribly reticent at this stage, and I asked if Maureen would come over and just explain her life to the students as well as me explaining my life. But I wanted to hear what she had to say. It was really for me, not for the kids. And that really interested me a whole lot.* The spiritual life Maureen seemed to be living held a deep attraction for Marian. *Over that year it just became clear that I actually wanted that life—it seemed to me, I'd have to say, more like a purer form of religious life.*

Marian soon enrolled in another course, this time on symbol and ritual, knowing that Vianney and Maureen would be there. This gave her a chance to approach Maureen and see whether she might leave her order to join the Servants of the Blessed Sacrament. There was no other possibility for her to speak with Maureen, as Marian was still not free to leave her convent at will. *Heavens, no! No, I wasn't in charge of myself like that.* But she was free to contemplate the change within her. *I think that I saw it as a call inside a call—a deeper call. Because I didn't know anything about these nuns when I joined the other way. And I knew that it was to a prayer life that I was called. And all the other teaching sisters weren't having this trouble. They weren't being split. I was feeling I was getting split in half all the time.*

When Marian eventually worked up the courage to speak to her own Superior, *she almost dragged me over the coals about it, saying, 'Well this is ridiculous. You've made vows here. You know, none of the other people going to this liturgy course are saying all this sort of stuff that you're saying.' So, 'Forget it', basically, 'Forget it.'* But Marian couldn't forget it. She wrote to the Superior General of her order in Rome, and received some encouragement, and later she saw a priest in Melbourne who was the Vicar for Religious. He counselled her to listen to her inner conviction and be patient. But the Mother Superior remained firm in her opposition, *and she said, 'You're not to see those nuns anymore.' … I have never wanted to go against authority. This was very distressing and stressful, to have to stand up for myself and actually step out of line.* Yet Marian knew she had to. *If I couldn't do it, I felt I would be crabbed. Old and crabbed and unhappy. And inside me was like a ball of fiery energy that was just burning.* She wrote again to London, to her Superior General. *And about only a week later, she responded and said, 'If you want to go you can go.' So, I showed this to my Superior, and she said, 'Well, you go.'*

Her Superior asked her to make a novena—nine days of prayer—to be sure before announcing her decision. Marian did that, and she also agreed to see out the school term for her students' sake. At the end of 1973, she left the Faithful Companions of Jesus. *They gave me some money, which was very nice, and I got some regular clothes.*

She spent the next few months living with her parents at Maureen's insistence—she, too, wanted Marian to be certain that beginning a new novitiate, in a new congregation, was what she really wanted. *It felt like a pregnancy. Nine months!* But Marian didn't just sit around waiting. *I started a theology course, which was what Carol was doing, and I worked at the university in the tribophysics department as the tea lady.* In August 1974, she finally joined the Servants of the Blessed Sacrament as a postulant.

Vianney was now about to take her turn at an overseas adventure and further study. Vianney had looked into her options in various parts of the world. She applied to Rome, but the teaching there was mostly in Latin, which put her off a bit, and she also applied at Georgetown in Washington, DC. Vianney was working one day a week at the Liturgical Centre in Melbourne, where she heard about a new program at Berkeley in California, so she applied there as well. *I suppose just by the sheer fact that the post came back more quickly from Berkeley, I said 'Right. Well, this is the one—we'll take this.'*

Vianney boarded her first international flight in September 1974, landing in a California that was still being rocked by the enormous cultural change that began in the 1960s. Vianney had retained that strong interest in Australian politics she'd developed at her family's dinner table, and she often talked politics with Marie, who shared her interest in world affairs. *Well, it was great when I got there because it was just the end of all the protests that happened at Berkeley, but there was still a lot of the buzz there. And a lot of the Jesuit boys, because there were a lot of them there, were very caught up still in the protests and the discussion about Vietnam.*

Only months before Vianney arrived in the United States, the People's Army of Vietnam had marched triumphantly into Saigon, and Richard Nixon had just resigned in the wake of the Watergate scandal. The University of California's Berkeley campus and the nearby city of San Francisco were at the centre of California's counterculture.

The campus walls were decorated with posters of Patty Hearst (the young heiress and revolutionary who'd been recently kidnapped, then arrested) along with signs advertising talks by figures like Angela Davis. While the hippie movement was on the wane, the beginnings of the women's liberation movement were stirring. The United States's loss in Vietnam, and the devastating impact of conscription on millions of young men and their families, would reverberate for many years, and it was provoking intense debate about the place of the United States in the world.

Vianney was enrolled at the Jesuit School of Theology, just blocks from the main Berkeley campus, and she was to undertake three semesters of full-time study (it was essentially a master's program, but she didn't earn a degree—*the men all got a master's degree but the women didn't get anything at all)*. Her fellow students were a mix of nuns, priests and laypeople. Most of them were from different parts of the United States, but among them were six Australians, all there to study the latest in theology and liturgical practice.

Now, for the first time in her life, Vianney had a place of her own. *I lived in Presbyterian housing in Berkeley in a one-bedroom flat. It was great—it was wonderful!* (On the interview tape, Vianney almost breaks into song as she says this.) Before too long, she was hosting parties, inviting her new friends around and offering them libations from her well-stocked drinks closet. Dennis, a young priest from New Zealand, never arrived without a bottle of whiskey in his hand, and he and Vianney soon became friends. Gatherings would happen frequently at Vianney's or at someone else's place.

On every Saturday night the Australians all got together and had a Mass, and then we had a dinner together. And then gradually it got that other people wanted to come. And so gradually other people from the course joined us. The Mass became part of the festivities, really, and the Eucharist was more and more an everyday, human sort of thing that was part of the celebration of life for Vianney and her growing group of friends. Among the Australians was a Sacred Heart nun called Marnie Kennedy, from Sydney, who was living with other nuns from her order. *There were nine of them, and they were all scrunched into these three apartments and Marnie couldn't get out quick enough on a Saturday night to come and join us.*

Vianney also befriended Ray, a Canadian priest who was living in Oakland and drove up to Berkeley every day to attend his lectures. He'd complained about never being able to find a parking spot, so Vianney offered him her space in the building where she lived. While Ray was in class, Vianney would take the car to go and get her groceries or run an errand, and Ray would sometimes have a cup of tea with her before picking the car up and driving home at the end of the day.

Ray's car became a great boon to Vianney's newfound freedom. When any visiting Australian priest was in town, Vianney would take him into San Francisco to see the sights, have some dinner, or perhaps go to a concert, and Ray often came along, too. *I was driving over that Oakland Bay Bridge as often as could be.*

That Christmas of 1974, when Ray flew home to Canada for a visit, he left the car with Vianney. She and some friends took a road trip south, as far as San Diego, then headed west to Pueblo, Colorado, where they spent Christmas with some American Blessed Sacrament sisters who had a convent there. *I don't know what they thought of me, really. I hadn't met them before, and they were very conservative.* At Easter time, Ray left Vianney the car again, and she, along with Dennis the New Zealand priest, another Australian priest and an Australian nun, went on a camping trip to Baja California, Mexico.

While there was time for travel and enjoyment, Vianney by no means neglected her studies. Her liturgy professor was a priest, and he held weekday Masses where he expected his students to take over the entire ceremony and run it all, except for the Eucharistic prayers that only priests can say. *He expected us to do the homily and if there weren't any prayers there, special for the day, he expected us to make them up, appropriate to the season and all that kind of thing.* Although the sisters had become very active in preparing the Mass celebrations at their chapel in Armadale, this was a new level of responsibility and autonomy for Vianney—*it was the first time we'd done those things, and they were new skills ... It just felt like you were being part of what the Eucharist really is, an occasion when all people come together and all people can make the prayers.* The liturgy was no longer in the exclusive hands of the priest, and that offered an exciting opportunity for creativity.

It was quite a lot of work, too, and only very occasionally did Vianney's social life get in the way. *I remember one day I must have been out late or something and I rang the priest to ask could he do my Monday morning or whatever it was, because I was not able to get it prepared. And he said, 'No, I won't do it at all. It's your job and you have to do it.'*

Ray and Vianney became close friends, often going to the cinema or out to dinner, and Ray would occasionally surprise Vianney with a plan to take the day off for one or other of the American holidays. *They would have different holidays that wouldn't be on our agenda and he'd ring me and say, 'What are you doing?' and I'd say, 'Well I'm doing an assignment.' 'Oh no,' he said, 'you can't do that. I'm coming up to get you.'* Sometimes Vianney would prepare lunch, *and we'd go for a picnic up beyond San Francisco along the coast there, which was lovely.* On one memorable occasion she and Ray went to see Leonard Cohen in concert (he had just released his fourth record, *New Skin for the Old Ceremony*, with the famous 'Chelsea Hotel #2' its second track). Vianney's parents had sent her some money for Christmas, and she went straight to Zellerbach Hall in the centre of San Francisco to buy the tickets. *It was a lot of fun. And at the half-time interval a notification came over the loudspeaker that said there was to be no smoking. And then when the lights went down there was a big laugh, because everybody was smoking weed.*

Vianney excelled in her studies and was pleased by the end of her final semester to have achieved her goals. *It was really going to*

Berkeley that allowed me to feel a real person, and a person who belonged somewhere. And I belonged in my congregation, but I belonged as somebody who could contribute. Vianney took much of the US summer off. *I travelled across different parts of the United States, staying with people that I'd met and knew, and it was terrific.*

In October 1975, Vianney's American sojourn came to an end. She flew to Rome to meet Maureen at the General Chapter of the congregation of Blessed Sacrament sisters. Vianney and Maureen had plans to travel extensively as they made their way home (the community had healthy account books thanks to the many years selling altar breads), with a visit to the Holy Land first on the list, but Vianney was feeling unwell, and the trip to Israel had to be cancelled. *Well, it was a bit of a shock to be back from Berkeley and doing all these things and to find myself back in the convent. It was a bit of a shock. I came down to earth with a kind of a thud that made me seem to be sick. I didn't know what was wrong, and they didn't know, and we went to the doctor and the doctor thought I had an appendicitis ... Well, actually, I think I was sick because I had fallen in love with this priest. Really, that's what it was. It was leaving him.*

Vianney didn't unburden herself about Ray to Maureen. *She knew about him as a friend. I don't know that she knew how close I was to him. Maybe she did. Oh, people intuit those things, don't they, really?*

Though quite reticent on this topic, Vianney said, *It represents an important part of my growth and an important part of a challenge that I had to negotiate. That's true.*

Vianney soon became well enough to make a visit she had promised to another friend she'd made in California. Chris was a priest who lived in Karachi, Pakistan, and had insisted they come and stay. *And we did go there to see Chris—it was lovely. He was a lovely Dominican. Maureen was with me—we've got photos of us on a camel.* Vianney felt the dynamic between her and Maureen shift at this time. *Because I had sort of found myself there in Berkeley, I was less willing to let Maureen push me around … Oh it was just her way—her personality. We never stopped getting along well. But when we were going places, you know, I knew when to give in and when to say, 'No, I think we might try this or that.' So it was part of growing up, part of maturing.*

Not too long after returning to Australia, perhaps it was at Christmas time, Vianney paid a visit to her parents, who were living at Blakehurst, in southern Sydney. *They built a two-bedroom house when my dad retired. And when all we nuns started coming home—that includes my two aunt nuns and me—my father said, 'Oh this is crazy, I can't even get into the bathroom.' So they built another two bedrooms and a bathroom, which was called the Nuns' Wing.* Vianney confided in her mother, telling her about Ray and how hard it had been to leave him. *My mother had the front room, and she was sewing there. And I was maybe ironing … And I was telling the story, I was telling her about Ray, and it was pretty remarkable that I felt able to do that—I wouldn't have done that before. And my dad came over and she said—I just couldn't believe it—she said 'Now, don't interrupt us, Dad. Come and sit here. I'm listening to a beautiful story.' Isn't that lovely?*

For Vianney, this marked an important change in her relationship with her mother, a distance that was repaired by the work Vianney had done with a counsellor during the later, difficult years of enclosure, and by her own growing maturity.

Meanwhile, back in Armadale, things were still shifting and changing. Charito (her real name was Sister Maria Rosario Ungson, but everyone called her Charito), a nun from the Philippines who had made her novitiate at Armadale, came to live with the Australian community. Records show that there were several other women from outside the order living at the convent, including Betty McMenamin's aged mother. The sisters, each in her own way, were beginning to develop their own spirituality, and to seek forms of individual growth. Marie had finished her studies and was now teaching photography at the Assumption Institute while working part-time at the Catholic Education office, where she designed posters and laid out magazines.

In 1973, Sister Berthe and another Canadian nun came to join the Armadale community, and stayed for about three years. Berthe had been ousted as Superior General three years earlier—many in the international congregation didn't want to move in the new direction Berthe was taking. But Berthe was very inspired by what the Australians were doing, and wanted to learn from them. Barbara remembers that her former Mother Superior was open to change. *One night she knocked on my door. She came into my bedroom and knelt beside my bed and asked forgiveness for the way she treated me in the novitiate.* Barbara wholeheartedly gave it.

Barbara soon learned, to her surprise, that she and Berthe had some things in common. *Mother Berthe had become interested in charismatic Christianity as well. So she came out with the hope of introducing that, I think, to the community, with a priest. He was charismatic. And somehow the other nuns didn't quite catch on to that. But I was already involved.* By this stage, Barbara's sister, Mercia, had left her own order of nuns, the Little Company of Mary, and was living in Melbourne. She and Barbara would often see one another, *and she used to drive Berthe and myself to the charismatics. And we knew that the international convention* [of charismatics] *was talked about in Rome, so Mercia approached Berthe in the car. She said, 'Mother Berthe, is there any chance of Barbara going to the international convention?' It surprised me, because I never ever thought of asking. And Berthe said, 'Well, could be. She could very well be. She ought to ask at least.' And somehow or other I was told I could go.*

And so Barbara and Mercia took off for three months in the middle of 1975, starting in Rome and proceeding to other places in Europe. *We hadn't made any plans, but we made Jesus our travel agent. The best decision we ever made. It was wonderful. We had a wonderful time in Rome.* The charismatic convention was all Barbara had hoped it would be. *We sang and danced and we rejoiced. And I was particularly thrilled when people were talking about how they were touched by the Spirit and they were feeling so happy and joyous. I thought, 'That's marvellous! People can say it. People can say that they are touched by the Spirit.'* Barbara and Mercia stayed in a pensione with some of the other attendees, and managed to see many of the city's sights, jostling among the usual summer crowds—*we were packed in like sardines in Rome.* Afterwards, they stayed with a friend of Mercia's in Holland, where they rode bikes through the countryside, and then they went to France, where they visited the shrine at Lourdes and spent some time in Paris.

The next year, 1976, Maureen sent Barbara off to the Assumption Institute, and that was also the year that Carol gained her theology degree. Two years later, Carol was appointed one of the chaplains at Melbourne University. She was running a new Sunday evening liturgical service in the convent's chapel, using all that she had learned to create a very inclusive, progressive celebration. She was highly influenced by feminist theology and this new service attracted members of the local gay community, who probably felt less than entirely welcome at some Catholic churches. It was also the year that Vianney, to her surprise, was made Superior.

Vianney didn't really feel prepared to be thrown into the leadership role so soon after arriving back from the United States. Privately, she was still struggling with her feelings for Ray. *I didn't think much about whether … Oh, I did … about whether there would be a life for the two of us.* On her trip through North America, before joining Maureen in Rome, Vianney had visited Ray in his hometown of Winnipeg, and they remained in touch. *He used to write. We wrote a lot. He was a very good letter writer.* And the year after she came home, he flew out to visit her. But Vianney had her reservations. Ray could be jealous, possessive and even quite competitive—she had seen all that in California. *We both did the same course and we always had assignments and if I got a better mark than he did, he'd have something to say about that, because these priests think they know everything.* Most of all, though, Vianney didn't want to get between Ray and his vocation. *I had decided that he really needed to be a priest. And I'd been chosen as Superior. And really, I wasn't ready for it. But I knew that if I took that, I couldn't keep holding Ray in my heart.*

The letters petered out, eventually, and Vianney threw herself back into the life of the Armadale community.

In 1977, Marian took her first vows as a Blessed Sacrament Sister and was back in full time study. She had taken a year off from the United Faculty of Theology to complete her novitiate, under Maureen's guidance. *I had to start everything again. Start back being a postulant again, which was a bit of a bugbear, but I just said, 'It's worth it. It's alright.' And it was a different kind of training altogether.* Marian had a flair for ceremony, and she enthusiastically took part in all the preparations for liturgies. In her spare time, she worked making altar breads two or three mornings a week, using the much-improved machinery. *It wasn't difficult. I learned how to read quickly while the sheet of breads was cooking, so I read the whole* Lord of the Rings *series twice, I think, while I was doing that, because I'd got into children's literature while I was doing my Dip Ed., and I really enjoyed Tolkien.* The number of sisters at the convent had continued to dwindle, with two long-established nuns being granted exclaustration on compassionate grounds and returning to live with their families.

Now there were only about fourteen Blessed Sacrament sisters living at the convent, and while tensions had eased, they hadn't disappeared. There was still a division between those sisters who actively pursued change, and took up further study, and those who were less interested in that kind of thing, and who, perhaps, felt they were not offered the same opportunities. Monica, for example, remained largely in charge of preparing meals (the task was not as enormous as it had once been, but feeding over a dozen women, plus frequent visitors, every evening was no small undertaking), and Sister Pete (who never reverted to her birth name) remained very engaged in altar breads. While Sister Pete enjoyed the work, Monica might have been feeling that she had done more than her fair share. *I understand Monica a little bit because she was a lay sister,* recalls Barbara. *And I could see that her work was so hard in the kitchen.* For many years, Monica had worked with barely a day's rest. *She developed infections of the ears but she wasn't allowed a day off—she was needed in the kitchen—so she didn't get the treatment she needed. I was watching it, in a way, and I thought, 'Will I offer to do the kitchen? That would be too much for me.' But she needed relief. I think she felt resentment about it. I have a feeling she felt resentment. She didn't feel loved, and she felt used. She needed a break.*

Mary Kelly, who had entered the convent on the same day as Marie, was another sister who was sceptical of the merits of some of those changes the community had undergone.

Marian remembers that *at meetings, they wouldn't say much. I always remember, Mary would bring knitting. I think it was because it gave her something to do during the meeting. She was good at knitting. And that was the funny thing, because, even from the start, I thought, 'All those women that are not interested so much in the intellectual—they have got really practical and very good talents.' It's hard to sort of … you couldn't actually compliment them too much on that, because it seemed like you were talking down to them. But I could see and appreciate their good things … I think they possibly felt a bit undervalued. And they might have been happier in the old way of things, but they came along—to their credit, they did.*

Marian's relationship with Maureen, her spiritual director, was very important. *Well, she made demands on the spiritual life … She was known as sort of 'have your guts for garters'. There were high standards. But she'd always listen very intently and could take you into the psychological places where you needed to go. And for me, I had to try and get over the break in my whole self that happened when I left the other order. I mean, I couldn't help that. It was there.* Marian likens it to a broken lifeline on the palm of her hand. She was really struggling to reconcile her years in the FCJs, and her departure from that life, with her new direction. *I had done something totally against my nature, and it was getting back at me, and she was helping me to sort of bring it back together to heal it.* Despite being sure that leaving to join the Blessed Sacrament sisters was the right decision, *I felt guilty. I felt I'd sort of perhaps betrayed something … I suppose like a broken marriage, if you want to put it that way, that you thought that was your life and then it wasn't. And I imagine women feel like that if they leave a relationship that's not perhaps working, as well.*

While everyone was pursuing their individual projects and interests, a common purpose still prevailed in some important ways. The sisters were each receiving an allowance that they could spend as they liked—they no longer had to ask permission—and could come and go from the convent as they pleased. But everyone came together for the morning prayer, the morning Mass, the midday prayer and the evening prayer. Thought and creative effort was put into preparing the prayers, so that the Divine Office was now more meaningful. A lot of energy was brought to the Sunday Mass for the local community, with three or four sisters forming a liturgy group to plan the ceremony around the usual Church calendar. These Masses drew young Catholic families who wanted to experience their religion anew. And plenty of Jesuit priests who wanted to learn the latest in liturgy came along, knowing that the Blessed Sacrament sisters were extremely skilled in that area.

Some of the changes were as simple as setting the prayer space with pictures that Marie had made, and using symbols that corresponded to the Gospel reading for that time of year, but other changes were related directly to shifts in the sisters' theology. Marian recalls that *Vianney came back very sensitised to the language, so we started realising that God is neither male nor female, and so we shouldn't be saying 'Him' all the time.*

Christmas and Easter were huge celebrations, requiring lots of work, and Marian remembers them vividly. *Beautiful, beautiful singing. And we would introduce more contemporary elements. I remember singing from* Godspell *at one of the Good Friday liturgies. And the community responded very well. It somehow was feeding our spirits very much. Yeah, they were very special, those celebrations and ceremonies … The emphasis went back onto the Eucharist itself as the place where we gathered as people who have a history together. We have this Christian history and it goes back, and takes in the Jewish culture in the Old Testament. So we were there to tell our story and to remind ourselves of who we were and to go forward in love for each other. You just felt close to people, doing things where you were all singing together and praying together.*

ANOTHER FACE OF CHRIST: THE MOVE TO NEWTOWN

THESE YEARS IN the late 1970s were in many ways the final years of togetherness as a community for the Servants of the Blessed Sacrament in Australia. Their convent and chapel were at the centre and the forefront of the new liturgical practice, serving as an example to many priests and nuns while nourishing a thriving community of Catholics who attended Mass every week, filled with hope for all that Vatican II had promised.

Having achieved so much, the sisters would now seek new challenges, while others would present themselves, with or without warning.

Maureen Flood had emerged from the difficult early years in the convent to take full possession of her natural leadership abilities. Renewed by the spirit of enquiry and growth that Vatican II ushered in, she now found herself on a path that she could not get off. It was leading her beyond even the radical changes she and the other sisters had established in their community at Armadale. A woman of considerable intellectual powers and personal strength, Maureen wanted more—a deeper and more intimate knowledge of both God and the world.

As we began to change and as we began to learn more about the spirituality of the Eucharist, it was clear that the Eucharist is really meant to be the food of the poor—the food of the broken people—and we had made it into a fairly elitist sort of a thing. I was asked after a couple of years after we changed to coordinate a project that was looking at the links between contemplation and social awareness, and I realised that I hadn't had any direct experience of social injustice.[1]

As part of her exploration of that link, Maureen helped establish a newsletter called *The Smouldering Wick* that she edited for several years, beginning in 1976. It published contributions from a variety of people: Christians who were living a contemplative spirituality in one way or another, as well as those who were working directly for social justice. The idea was to explore the connections between the two—in Maureen's words 'to pray more deeply and to act more strongly by being with people in their struggle for justice.'[2] The Blessed Sacrament sisters' archives contain some copies of this newsletter, printed on foolscap paper in the pre-computer age, along with a draft essay, several pages long, that Maureen wrote ahead of one of the group's meetings. She reflected on where her own life of contemplation had led her, and on the challenge she hoped to meet:

> I don't think there is much left of the myth that says that contemplatives live in a kind of blissful cloud of peace and light. The mental anguish that occurs when all the usual props are taken away and one is left entirely to one's own resources is closely akin to … 'helplessness.' It is strange that in that helplessness there is the possibility of the discovery that our own resources are far greater than we've ever dared think! But that kind of suffering becomes liberating only when we are able to accept helplessness and need as something not to be afraid of or avoided or denied. 'Liberation' occurs in the acceptance of weakness. Personal freedom comes not so much in doing anything but in surrendering in trust to life, to God: to a mysterious rhythm of life that is greater than we are and which is,

finally, trust-worthy. This 'surrender' and 'passivity' go hand in hand with courage and the ability to risk.

The question that arises is what part have surrender and passivity to play in working for justice? And how can we integrate surrender and passivity with resistance and action?[3]

Meanwhile, sometime between 1976 and 1978, Vianney visited her family in Sydney and was busy meeting up with all the many friends who wanted to see her. It may have been only her second trip home since being allowed to leave the convent. One friend, Jo Dirks, was a Blessed Sacrament Father at Haymarket, and *Jo said to me, 'You need to come up and meet Ted.'* Jo was talking about Ted Kennedy, a diocesan priest who had been the chaplain at Sydney University during the 1960s, and since 1971 had been a parish priest at St Vincent's Church in Redfern. Ted had drawn very close to the local Aboriginal people, and they were having a profound effect on his theology. A very erudite priest, Ted was steeped in the Gospel and in Church history and poetry, and his sermons attracted an interesting and curious crowd. As it happened, Vianney knew a couple of other priests who would be there with Ted, so she was looking forward to the visit, and she was keen to meet Ted. She was surprised to find that he was equally interested in speaking with her. *I had the impression of Ted eager to talk about the possibility of our coming there. He was very keen for any kind of nuns, I think. I don't know why he was so keen to have some nuns around (you could say because they would do the work, that would be one very good reason). I don't know why he was so keen to have us around, but he certainly talked that way.*

The idea of the Blessed Sacrament sisters forming a second, separate prayer community, closer to the poor and marginalised, had been discussed among the sisters. Armadale was now an even more affluent neighbourhood than it had been in the 1950s. During their time overseas, Maureen and Vianney both studied some liberation theology, which had worked its way into the mainstream of church thinking. Pope Paul VI, in 1971, spoke clearly of the preferential respect owed to the poor, and he told Catholics that 'the more fortunate should renounce some of their rights so as to place their goods more generously at the service of others.'[4] The sisters had few goods to speak of, but they had themselves, their time and energy, their prayer and their good will. Some of them wanted to give of these things where they might be most needed.

Vianney thought Maureen should go up and see Ted, too, so the pair made a visit, and Maureen heard what Ted had to say. Maureen reported on this visit in *The Smouldering Wick* in 1978.

> I travelled from Melbourne on an overnight train, took another train from Central to Redfern (one stop!) and struggled out of the station with my bag. As I stood at the corner, waiting for the lights to change, a large truck pulled up and a black man leaned from the cabin shouting to a man beside me, 'Hey mate! Pick up the bag for the lady!' The black man and I laughed. The man beside me looked uneasy as I assured him I could manage; my friend yelled again, as the lights changed and he moved, 'I'd do it for you, love, if I could!'
>
> It's like that in Redfern. There's a strange mixture of the friendly and the open, where you can talk to anyone, against a darker background that suspects the stranger and the newcomer who may be there just to 'observe.' I went not to 'observe' but to participate in the life of the community …
>
> From my first day in Redfern I began to be aware of two apparently contradictory feelings or impressions that were with me whenever I stopped to reflect. The first was a great feeling of happiness: of how good it was to be there and of how beautiful the people were. The second was the deepest possible sense of shock—that people could be in such a plight. There

> are a good number of justly angry people around St Vincent's but I was more aware of distress than of anger, both in myself and in those with whom I can into some close contact …
>
> One day I went with two black men and a black woman, to visit in a general hospital. As we walked through the corridors I began to realise that something was happening that I'd never experienced before: everyone was looking at us. There was not a single person who didn't glance in our direction. I became fully conscious of what was happening only when we four were in a lift which stopped at the floor before the one we wanted. Two people stood ready to come in. As the doors opened there passed across their faces expressions of surprise, hesitation and, most of all, fear. They just didn't want to get into that lift.
>
> I was totally unprepared for this kind of reaction. I hadn't anticipated it but I couldn't mistake it. And I had to recognise that the ability to react like that was in me too. I wondered what it must do to people when this kind of reaction meets them all the time.[5]

When Maureen and Vianney returned to Armadale with their news, Marie was one of their most enthusiastic listeners. *Contemplation close to the streets was Ted's concept. A contemplative order close to the streets, not locked away, but close to the streets—close to the most broken people.* It made sense to Marie, both as a natural step in her exploration of her faith, and as an opportunity to be of real use in the world. *We were contemplative, but we were nowhere near broken people, except if people rang you up and told you to pray for somebody.* Soon Marie and Maureen took another trip up to Sydney to investigate what they might do there. Marie had no doubt that it was the right move for her, and for the Blessed Sacrament community. *On the way back on the plane to Melbourne, I said 'We've got to go. This is extraordinary.' I think*

Maureen's eyes filled with tears because she was so happy to hear me say that. She didn't want to influence me, which I admire her tremendously for. So she wanted it to come from me: 'We've got to go.'

While some of the sisters back at Armadale were enthusiastic, others were sceptical. It was the same old division—now the women who had studied abroad and taken time to think about where their vocation could lead were the ones most supportive of the Sydney move, while the others—*more practical and pragmatic and commonsensical,* in Vianney's words—were not so sure it was a good idea.

Marie Grunke reflected on this difficult period in a document dated 2 February 1981 and entitled, rather uncompromisingly, 'Have we really recognised as a congregation, our experience of dying?' She describes her own gradual awakening in a convent that was being asked to resituate itself in the real world, offering its sisters greater access to the media and a new awareness of the suffering in that world.

> I was being confronted with the pain and misery of millions of people living in poverty and dying of starvation. I searched my soul for ways of bridging the gap between my three wholesome meals each day, a bed at night, medical attention whenever I needed it, and the fate of over half the world's population.[6]

Marie contemplated her vow of poverty, and what it meant in light of this new knowledge. 'And so began a yearning in me towards greater voluntary dispossession. I could not feed the hungry of the world, but I could at least take a step towards them in their poverty.'[7]

While Marie struggled to face her fears about the implications of such commitment, at least half the community opposed it altogether. Not only were they unpersuaded by the philosophical arguments for voluntary poverty, but many of these women, some of them several years older than Marie, were looking forward to retirement. After years of self-denial and hard work—making altar breads, cooking, cleaning—they had brooked the changes to their religious life, but they were not prepared to make themselves uncomfortable, nor did they see it as essential to their contemplative vocations.

It all came to a head at a very tense series of community meetings, presided over by a professional counsellor and mediator. Vianney's second three-year term as Superior was due to be confirmed as part of those meetings, but she was very reluctant to continue in that role. *All I can say about my time as Superior was that our prayer life was very vibrant; that's all I can say. But as for being of service to people, I don't think I was a very good Superior because it became really evident to me that there were two groups in the community ...*

I raised the question again of another community, and I think I was of the opinion that the only way to make this thing work was to divide these two groups, if I can put it that way. Not divide them, but give them a chance to be the kinds of groups they wanted. But I came in for a lot of criticism and so one day, on the last day of this probably three-day thing, I just took myself off and thought 'Oh, I can't sit there and take all this. I'm going.' It shook up the thing, but I was almost of the opinion that it needed to be shaken up.

Soon after, the Superior General paid a visit from Rome to help sort things out, and she made Vianney an offer. *She said to me, 'Would you like to go to the United States?' and I said 'Yeah, okay. I'll do that'. My agreement to do that shocked them, too.*

Vianney travelled back to the United States in 1979 and moved in with the Blessed Sacrament sisters in Pueblo, Colorado. It struck her immediately that they, too, needed some shaking up (perhaps this was becoming Vianney's unintended speciality). And so, despite driving the move to Redfern, Vianney was overseas when a small group of nuns left Armadale to set up a new convent on Forbes Street, Newtown.

SYDNEY, 1979–2006

The new place where Maureen, Marie and Betty would make their home was just a ten-minute walk from St Vincent's Church on Redfern Street.

Aboriginal people had been coming to Redfern for decades, first to find work at the Eveleigh Railway Workshops, and later to find community and seek family members lost to them during the many decades of forced child removal: the Stolen Generations. By the 1970s, the railway works had long closed, and the community was suffering unemployment. The 1967 referendum that had seemed to promise a new beginning for Indigenous people, with an end to discrimination and greater inclusion in the political life of the nation, had not delivered—people were experiencing the same levels of poverty and marginalisation they'd long suffered.

When it came to the private rental market in most Australian cities, Indigenous people faced stubborn discrimination. Such was certainly the case in Redfern, and when a dozen or so black squatters were thrown out of abandoned houses along Louis Street, they took refuge with Father Ted at the presbytery. 'It was in the days when there were no Aboriginal hostels, no Aboriginal housing of any kind, and the numbers quickly built up to about a hundred on cold wet nights,' Ted wrote.[8] When the Sydney City Council pressured Ted to evict them, he supported Bob and Sol Bellear, two young black activists, as they joined with the squatters to form the Aboriginal Housing Corporation. A grant from the Whitlam government saw them buy the first row of houses that would soon be known as 'the Block'. The Block on Eveleigh Street became a vital centre of Aboriginal community and political activism, and a spiritual home for Indigenous people from all over Australia. Ted was a frequent and most welcome visitor there. Ted was also instrumental in the decision by the Sisters of Charity to hand over their property on Redfern Street, next door to the church, to the new Aboriginal Medical Centre—the first of its kind in Australia.

Ted understood very clearly that Aboriginal people were suffering the ongoing blows dealt by colonisation. The grief and pain of the frontier wars, the dispossession of land and the destruction of family, culture and language were still creating powerful aftershocks, and there was also the daily burden of racism and its detrimental impact on people's health and wellbeing. 'The pride and pain of their race is transmitted directly to them. The pride and pain of their race is being held almost in sacred trust, but always unfiltered and undiluted. It is humanly unbearable to hold that sort of fire in one's heart,' he observed.[9] Ted saw the consequences of that pain first-hand—he performed at or attended countless funerals of young suicide victims, sometimes at the rate of one per week.

Over his first decade at Redfern, Ted had gathered around him a group of priests, nuns, brothers and laypeople who wanted to hear what he had to say, and to help in the work he was doing with Aboriginal people. Ted's chief collaborator, though, was Shirley Smith. Known to nearly everyone as Mum Shirl, she was at the heart of Redfern's black community as an elder and activist, and she often spoke to the congregation at St Vincent's about her work, bearing witness to the situation Aboriginal people faced, and casting it in the light of the Gospel. Ted described Shirley as 'the greatest theologian I have ever known'.[10]

It was into this dynamic, with all its complexities, that the three Blessed Sacrament sisters, Maureen, Marie and Betty, threw themselves—ready or not. Their new convent on Forbes Street was made up of two side-by-side terraces. A wall had been knocked out between them so that there was a very large front room, which served as the chapel. The house had been the home of a community of the Little Sisters of Jesus, who had recently moved out (their charism meant they had to be among the poorest of the poor, and Newtown was already gentrifying). The idea of this new Blessed Sacrament community was to provide a place of retreat and prayer for those working alongside Aboriginal people in Redfern and standing in solidarity with them to fight racial injustice. The sisters were to offer spiritual support to a hard-working activist community, but they quickly found that things in Redfern didn't always run to plan.

Maureen, Marie and Betty moved into the house just before the end of 1979. 'It was a nice old house, so that was where we started, with Tuesday night Mass and a meal afterwards. Dozens of Aboriginal people came in and out of the house and if they needed a bed there was a bed, even if we were sleeping on the floor. After that, we could never walk away. You see another face of Christ.'[11]

Marie remembers her first Mass at Redfern that Christmas. *After midnight Mass with Ted, this Aboriginal man came up to me and he said, 'Sister, I'm cold. Could you get me a blanket? And I'm hungry. Could you give me a sandwich?' And I thought, 'Oh my God, that's straight from the Gospel: "I was hungry and you fed me. I was cold and you clothed me."' I thought, 'I'm on holy ground.' This is what we were meant to be here for.*

The local people soon got to know the nuns, with many calling at the house at Forbes Street regularly—some of them, daily. Maureen, Marie and Betty were open to this new experience, but they had no particular training in how to support people struggling with addiction, mental illness or trauma, much less any training in what we might now call cultural awareness. They had to make it up as they went along.

Growing up in rural Queensland, Marie had had no contact with Aboriginal people—none of those who lived in or around Toowoomba ever attended the local Catholic church on Sundays, and she had grown up surrounded by casual racism. In fact, her mother *warned us children if we were naughty she'd put us outside, and the blackfellas would come and eat us.* The community that had gathered around the

Armadale convent since the nuns broke down the grille was, likewise, very middle class and very white.

Now Marie was with Aboriginal people every day. *As we got to know these people, they would come to our home and we'd feed them and just be with them. You'd laugh and cry together. So, suddenly here were these people who had been invisible for all those years … I mean, I think I was probably a teenager before I ever met an Aboriginal person.*

Ted's commitment to this community was total, and his standards were exacting. For both Maureen and Marie, this was a completely new life—a new way of living day to day, and a new demand on their personal, spiritual and psychological resources. The physical comfort of the convent at Armadale had been left behind. Along with Betty, they maintained their communal prayer life, rising and meeting in the chapel early each morning, but life became a lot less predictable, and a lot less possible to control, than it had been at Armadale. The little contemplative community discovered that there was scarce time for contemplation as they'd long understood it.

While Marie knew this was where she wanted to be, she felt quite vulnerable and unsure at times. *One of the challenges for me was coping with some of the people who used to call in regularly. And one of these people was Harold. Because Harold had a mental disability, I didn't ever quite know where I stood with Harold, and I was probably just a little bit nervous of Harold. I remember Ted saying to us when we came there, 'You have to just be sensible.' In other words, 'Don't be afraid of it. Just be sensible in how you deal with it.' And I think the only other rule he had was don't call the police. And I honoured all of that.*

Harold Young was usually in attendance at Sunday Masses at Redfern, and was very well known to the congregation. He would often pace up and down the back of the church, barefoot, his back as straight as a line—the legacy of a childhood spent in institutions. Like so many of the Aboriginal people drawn to that church, he regarded Ted as a friend, and Ted regarded Harold in the same way.

The scene at Redfern on Sunday mornings was nothing like the scene at any other Catholic church in Australia, possibly the world. It had none of the pomp, very little of the ceremony, and was less like a Catholic Mass than like a chaotic gathering of a large and diverse extended family. Ted emerged, dishevelled, from the sacristy, his hair and robes askew, shortly after 10am. And he was open to whatever happened. Baptisms would take place in the course of the Mass, often quite at the last minute. Newly baptised babies were handed about the regular Sunday crowd for people to bless. Dogs would sometimes wander into the church. After Communion, members of the congregation were free to stand up and deliver news of the latest anti-nuclear action taking place, or ask for help with whatever community or activist project they might be undertaking. Luminaries of the Aboriginal rights movement were invited to speak to the community, including Michael Mansell and Bob Bellear. Shirley Smith would frequently address the congregation and did not hide the raw emotion of what she shared, often weeping openly as she discussed the plight of her people and called on the community's help and solidarity. Sometimes someone who had been drinking would break into song. Patty, a young Aboriginal woman, had a beautiful voice, and Ted would not merely tolerate this interruption, he would welcome it. He used to beam at Patty when she sang. For Ted, it was people like Patty who brought to life the essence of Christianity, and sanctified the Mass.*

+++

Marie, while gingerly navigating her possible place in the world of the poorest black people of Redfern, was soon forging other connections.

---

* Attempts were made to trace Patty's family and consult them for this story, but they were not successful. Her surname has been withheld out of respect for Patty and her family.

One was with Lilla Watson, a Murri woman, and an artist and activist from Queensland. Lilla had impressed Marie greatly with her advice to white people, like the nuns, who wanted to work with Indigenous communities: *'If you've come to help us, you're wasting your time. If you've come because your liberation is bound up with ours—let's work together.' That's profound, isn't it? She was a wonderful woman, and she befriended us all at Redfern.*

Marie was still working on her photography—*I'd set up a little darkroom in a room upstairs*—and from time to time she produced work for the Catholic Education Office. When Lilla saw Marie's work, she suggested that Marie might set up a photography school to share her knowledge with Aboriginal people. Lilla had contacts in Kempsey, on the New South Wales north coast. The community there liked the idea, so Marie applied for a grant and, over the next year or two, she travelled back and forth to establish the school and deliver workshops to get the place going. *It took me a while to set up the school. I had to buy all the equipment in a photography shop in Pitt Street in Sydney and transport it all on the train up to Kempsey. I think I bought a few enlargers and developing tanks.* Marie made lasting friendships with families who welcomed her into their lives. One friend, Mary Button, lived with her family on their traditional coastal lands. They welcomed Marie to their country, and taught her about it. *I used to go pippying with them, and picking oysters straight off the rocks and eating them off the rocks and doing all these wonderful things that they were so good at—they were teaching me how to survive almost in the wild, in a way, which I loved.*

The Kempsey community was very politically engaged, too, and when Marie accompanied Mary Button and some other friends to Sydney, to petition the Premier, Neville Wran, for an education facility at the old mission, she got an insight into the discrimination her friends faced.

We pulled up there, close to Neville Wran's office, and we had about four cars and they were all full of Aboriginal people, and me. So, after a little while, all these police motorcyclists turned up, and I said to Mary, 'What are they here for, do you think? Are they expecting somebody really important to turn up here to see Neville Wran?' She said, 'Yes Marie. That's us.' I said, 'No, I don't believe it.' She said, 'Marie, they are here because we blacks are here.' The police in those large numbers came thinking a riot was about to happen. If I hadn't seen it for myself, I wouldn't have believed it. I just was so struck by that.

Marie's friendships with Mary and others from Kempsey helped her understand what Aboriginal people faced every day. *Their pain, their suffering was so tied up with us—with our identity that we forged at their cost—and when you begin to realise that, you think, 'My God, I'm partly responsible for what the Aboriginal people are suffering.'* These friendships became central to Marie's political awakening, in which she understood her growing commitment to both racial justice and environmental justice as part of her spiritual vocation.

I used to go on marches with the Aboriginal people and we all chanted, 'Land rights now! Land rights now!' And one day I thought, 'My God, I know what they're saying. They're saying the land has rights. How come I've missed that?' The land has rights. I don't know what woke me up. Everything changed once I realised that the land has rights. I didn't think the land had rights—the land's there for us. And you know, even though I'm coming from a sacramental background—and you'd think I would have picked up that the Eucharist, bread and wine, comes from the land, and that the land has rights—I'd missed it. But on the march this particular day, it was loud and clear, and I have never forgotten it to this day: the land has rights. I've been saying that ever since.

She and her students put together a book of photographs and words that expressed something of what life was like in Kempsey for a strong and resilient community, still living on their traditional lands, but facing persistent racism. *They were the most wonderful photographers. Their originality—they saw things we never saw.*

Marie was beginning to understand that her move to Sydney was not only about taking her vow of poverty at its word. As well as supporting and giving comfort to those around her who needed it, she was being called to address the cause of that suffering and to do something about it. Ted's message on this subject was very clear. He had told a conference of religious sisters some years earlier that a Catholic vocation wasn't just a question of comforting or serving the poor in their poverty. 'Justice always involves breaking the fetters that hold people down. It does not involve helping people to live with the fetters. It does not involve sending Christmas toys to the poor, so that they can forget their poverty for the day.'[12] Her close friendships with Aboriginal people were teaching Marie how she could be part of a larger movement for radical social change.

+++

Meanwhile, down in Melbourne, things carried on very much as usual. Marian had taken her final vows as Servant of the Blessed Sacrament, and Maureen asked her to take on a new form of leadership for the Armadale Community, since Maureen, still the Superior, was up in Sydney. Marian was to share the role with Charito, the Filipina nun who had now come to live permanently in the Australian community; but very quickly the noses of some more senior sisters were put out of joint, and the dual leadership role did not work particularly well. The division within the community and the resentments it generated had not been resolved. Carol was very busy with her new chaplaincy work at the university, and Marian felt that she wanted to be where Marie and Maureen were, the sisters with whom she had the most in common. She was enjoying the prayer life at Armadale, and the liturgical work, but *I was thinking that I was getting pretty stuffy, and we weren't really moving or doing much there.* When Marian finished her theology degree, *I just plucked up the courage to say, 'Do you think I could possibly come up there?'* So, about halfway through 1981, Marian left Armadale for Newtown.

Well, Sydney was a terrible shock because it was a very old place, like a hundred years old or something—I think there was a stove that went through the floor and there were cockroaches in the seam of the fridge and this sort of thing, so that took a bit of getting used to. While the nuns had managed to buy a washing machine, there were very few other modern conveniences in the house. There was also very little money, which often had to stretch to feed a great many visitors. *A lot of Aboriginal people needed food, and Marie was fantastic at just whipping up food.* There was a choko vine on the back fence that helped furnish many a meal. *We had chokos till we looked like them.*

Marian felt very unprepared for this situation, and she relied on Marie for guidance and support, because almost as soon as Marian had arrived in Newtown, Maureen left. Having travelled to Rome for the latest General Chapter, Maureen had unexpectedly been elected to the General Council of the Congregation of the Servants of the Blessed Sacrament, meaning she would remain in Rome for the next six years.

+++

Vianney was still in the United States, where she was dealing with challenges of her own. The community at Pueblo was stuck in an awkward place between the old ways and the new. The convent had three parlours, and each still had the old grille, while the dining room had undergone some changes—a new television set and a record player had been installed. Vianney was appalled to find that the TV was always on during communal meals. *Oh, it was awful.* Like many convents, the one at Pueblo had suffered an exodus of members and a complete absence of new vocations over the last decade or so, and the remaining sisters were in need of support. As soon as she arrived, they asked Vianney to be treasurer. *I had never done anything of that nature, and I was in a new culture with a new currency. I said, 'Right, I'll be the treasurer.' And in those days, the treasurer also was the person who did all the maintenance work in the place, and I was about as competent as a mouse to do all that kind of thing. But anyhow, the first thing I did as treasurer was to knock down those grilles.*

She turned one parlour into a TV room, so that dinner time became more convivial, and she rejigged the chapel as well. It was immediately apparent that the American Servants of the Blessed Sacrament were more conservative than the Australian ones—they were less involved with the lives of the laypeople who came to their chapel, and they were not doing the kind of creative liturgical work that was being done at Armadale. The sisters had, though, been through enough change that the rigid discipline that dictated convent life up until the early 1970s had given way to greater communication and familiarity between the women. As they became free of some of the old rules governing convent life and interpersonal relations, tensions had arisen, just as they had at Armadale. Those tensions were palpably clear to Vianney, and she found herself once again in the midst of a group of people, living together, but, to her mind, not functioning particularly well as a spiritual community.

One very welcome feature of the convent's life in Pueblo, though, was that its members had a great deal of contact with other local nuns, and Vianney soon made friends with some Franciscan sisters who worked at the local St Francis Xavier Parish. It was quite a lively parish, with a well-attended church, and Vianney soon got to know the priest there, as well as the local bishop. When one of the Franciscan sisters left Pueblo to join her mother house, Vianney was offered her former position as coordinator of a group of catechists, teaching religious education to the parish children.

Pueblo had a very large population of Mexican Americans and migrants, many of whom were undocumented. Most couldn't afford to pay the fees at Pueblo's Catholic schools, so the bishop closed the schools down and focused instead on the parish Sunday school, and this is where most of Vianney's work took place. *Our sisters were a bit shocked with all of this: not only had I turned their own convent upside down but now I was off getting a job in the parish.* Despite never having done catechetical work before, Vianney realised that her liturgical training more than prepared her. So she spent her days riding her new bike between the convent and the parish house until, eventually, someone suggested she move into lodgings at the parish, which she duly did. The atmosphere at her own convent was sufficiently tense that Vianney was rather pleased to leave it.

For the first time in many years, Vianney was earning a wage, and she was doing what she felt sure was good, valuable work: guiding the children through the various sacraments of Reconciliation, First Holy Communion and Confirmation; preparing the liturgical ceremonies; and involving the children's families, as well. Vianney was enjoying life. She liked Pueblo. She was making new friends and had joined the local symphonic choir. Vianney also travelled from time to time, attending religious conferences and special events like the 'Modern Liturgy Festival of the Lively Arts' in the state capital, Denver, and heading to California for a workshop in clown, mime, puppet and dance ministry. She even took a course on Jungian typology. Vianney was really thriving, when, after two years or so in Pueblo, she received a letter from Rome telling her to go back to Australia. The Superior General must have discussed this with the Superior in Pueblo, but nobody had spoken with Vianney. In fact, Vianney had only just heard from Maureen, whose letter encouraged her to stay on in Pueblo if she wished.

Vianney wrote to the Superior General in Rome in July 1981. She kept a copy of her thoughtful, impassioned letter—an important record of her thoughts and feelings at the time. She wrote it after taking a few days of spiritual retreat in the Sangre de Cristo mountains, and making a short holiday trip to Omaha, Nebraska, to visit a friend.

Vianney's letter begins by expressing surprise that her situation was the subject of consideration at the General Council in Rome: *I had no idea that I would warrant attention at such a high level—indeed, it puzzles me, somewhat, that it should need to be so.* While thanking the Reverend Mother General for such attention, Vianney firmly but graciously, *at the risk that it could seem defiance and lacking in a spirit of obedience,* determines to *open her heart* to the Mother General, and, in so doing, offer a fairly unflinching assessment of the health of the community at Pueblo and the future of the congregation as a whole.

Vianney's letter makes plain that applying *abstract principles and norms* to the life of a shrinking group of ageing sisters (the US-based congregation had not received a new postulant for fifteen years) was preventing the leadership from attending to *the life and happiness of the women who presently compose the membership of our Congregation.*

Vianney reminds her correspondent that at Armadale and Newtown, *the sisters have seriously confronted the question of the death of the Congregation in Australia* and notes that of the 320 or so Blessed Sacrament sisters in all of the convents across the world, some 220 were now aged over sixty. She writes that while it might seem that the sisters in Pueblo ought to be living together in a single convent house, *alas, it is not possible, precisely because of those hurts from the past and the clashes of personalities that would and do give rise to frustration and misunderstanding.*

My own part in the life of the community in Pueblo, coming, as I did, tired and somewhat disenchanted from my services as Regional Superior, was to invest myself, as I could, in the life and ways of these sisters. I am a questioner and a challenger; beauty and fun appeal to me; prayer—private, communal and liturgical—is my chosen milieu; Eucharist is my life's passion. Questions of reality and justice, of care for people and quality of life, impinge readily on my consciousness and these I shared with the women with whom I lived. It became clear to me that who I am and the questions I raised were disturbing, in a negative way, to some, most perhaps; and that in my own person, I was a threat to those amongst whom I was living.

Vianney's letter sought to explain and justify her decision to live and work in the parish and argued for its relevance to her vocation. *What I am doing in the parish seems, to me, to be easily recognised as 'Eucharistic' apostolate … With regard to community living, there is probably more real community commitment in the group of four with whom I now live than I have experienced in the last several years as an SSS.*

Vianney proposed that, since the American Vice Province didn't seem interested in what she was doing, nor inclined to approve of her choice to live with the Franciscans and work in the parish, that she be placed once more under the supervision of the Australian community, so that she would answer to the Regional Superior back home. She addressed the question of the congregation's death again—*death does not frighten me and if we must choose death, then I pray that we may follow the example of Jesus with dignity and courage*—as well as the question of transferring to another religious congregation, one perhaps more in line with the work Vianney wanted to do. But *the question of transfer … is a really hard and scary one for me, and one I do not have the strength to face just yet … I have NO wish to leave the SSS family.*

In closing, she reaffirmed her decision to remain: *If we are called as Christian men and women to be mature, self-determining and adult people, I must present my reflections to you. Thank you for your patience in receiving all my heart thoughts, I am somewhat in awe of how vulnerable I have made myself before you. Still, I offer myself to you, as gift, believing you will receive my SELF with reverence and love.*

So, Vianney stayed another year in Pueblo.[13]

The situation Vianney found herself in, both with the nuns in Pueblo and with her Superior General, give a sense of how the Australian community was changing in ways and at a pace that weren't in step with other communities of the order, or with the leadership in Rome. This was something Carol Hogan explored, writing that the Australian community's post-Vatican II lifestyle and theological approach differed greatly from the rest of the global congregation of Servants of the Blessed Sacrament.

'A former congregational Superior General, Sister Mary Catherine Perko, who had always appreciated and supported the Australian sisters, offers a number of reasons for this difference: "The Australian sisters were educated and talented younger women, who could think laterally and were able to read "the signs of the times" more rapidly than the rest of the congregation. Australia's distance from the rest of the congregation gave them more freedom from conventional and revered traditions than other foundations of the congregation."'[14]

In correspondence with Carol, Sister Mary Catherine put it down to 'Australian attitudes to hierarchical structures and authorities … one that doesn't bother too much with rules, especially those coming from outside the country'. It was certainly true that from the time Betty took over, leadership of the community 'continued to liberate rather than repress sisters'.[15]

+++

Meanwhile, back home, Marian continued to find life in Newtown challenging. *My feeling about it all was that it was pretty hard.* The community was fairly poor, the house was very basic and the demands on the sisters' time and attention were ceaseless.

Marian had just finished a long course of study and wasn't sure how to apply it in these circumstances. Also, the lack of any sort of routine, and the difficulty of setting aside time for prayer and solitude, was hard for her to get used to. *People would come and they'd want to sort of stay for hours, and I have to say I wasn't really flexible enough to enjoy that style of living.* Even Marie found it difficult at times to be answering the door at any hour of the day or night. She once swore, in frustrated jest, *'We're going to close the front door. I'm going to go up on the balcony upstairs. I'm going to pour boiling pitch over it, on anybody who comes.'* Of course, the knock at the door came, and was warmly answered.

Marian understood her purpose, even if she sometimes struggled. *I was very conscious that we were saying clearly, 'We're not here for the Aboriginal people. We're here to be with the Aboriginal people.' And that was a very clear statement, and I agreed with that statement. And yet, it was very hard to just do that. And I used to feel Ted got fed up with us whitefellas … He expected others to do exactly what he had done.*

Marian found it particularly difficult to cultivate the sort of community life she needed amid all the very deep and complex needs of many of the people who visited the house at Forbes Street. *Marie adapted to it much better. She was one of thirteen, and she knew what it was like to be in a big group and having to make do and cook. And she was a great cook and she liked cooking and all of that sort of stuff. Plus, she seemed to really make bonds with the Aboriginal people in a way that just couldn't happen for me. I just couldn't. I just couldn't.* Marian was at a loss among people who so often struggled with addiction. *I tried to be as good as I could, but it was just … It wasn't a natural sort of possibility, and I couldn't genuinely say that I was really friendly.*

But Marian's ill ease had little effect on the urgent demands of the people around her, or on her Aboriginal visitors' own capacity for friendliness and connection. *Well, I was in the chapel one morning. It was about six o'clock in the morning and I was there. And 'bang' on the door, and it's Patty. I think I was able to grab my shoes, and she had a taxi waiting outside. 'Sister Marian!' 'Oh yes, Patty, what is it?' 'Come with me into the taxi!' … And she says, 'I've gotta have a drink.'*

Patty directed the taxi to the early opener in Newtown. *So she got a double vodka and something, and she bought me lemonade. And she said to these other people there, 'This is Sister Marian, and if any of youse tries to do anything to her youse got me to answer for,' and I said, 'Oh Patty, that's a bit rough. I'll be alright.'*

Well, I think I had to walk back in the end. And then one of my other great memories, really towards the end, she'd wanted me there at the birth of the last of her children, so I was, which was an extraordinary thing to happen.

Patty herself had been taken from her mother as a child, and she in turn lost all her children to state care. A very vibrant person, she was a frequent visitor to the house on Forbes Street, and on occasion she really knew how to stir things up. Marie recalls one particularly close shave. *She was really, really drunk and she came to stay the night I think, because she said that none of the refuges would take her in. So I made up a bed on a lounge chair downstairs, which she quite liked. There were no other spare beds and I wasn't getting out of my bed—so it wasn't very Christian, you could say.*

Marie laughs as she tells this story. *Patty was sitting in the kitchen with a woman who'd come for a retreat, a quiet retreat, at our house. How bizarre! And this young retreatant said something that Patty took offence to, probably something quite racist, thinking she was speaking to ordinary white people, but she said it to Patty. Well, Patty! 'What?!' She picks up this carving knife from the bench. The retreatant took off, ran up the stairs and tried to lock herself in her room and just … It was very serious, and I thought 'Oh my God, what are we going to do now?'*

And at that moment, as would often happen, Harold arrived at the door. I said, 'Oh, thank God you're here Harold.' I said, 'Patty's got a retreatant upstairs in her room, and she's got a knife!' So Harold goes to the stairwell. He calls out 'Patricia! Come down!' And lo and behold, she did. She was almost crying. She just had this softness and she said, 'You're the only person who calls me by my real name. You call me Patricia.' And Harold took the knife off her.

The retreatant might have still been hiding under the bed upstairs. But Harold then positions all these chairs in front of the stairwell one after the other, stacked them there. And he sat on the one at the front. There's no way Patty was going to get past Harold to go back up there and terrify the retreatant. But he just did it in such a lovely way. Who would think to disarm her like that? By calling her Patricia. I mean, there's this beautiful way. How do you explain that? I can never explain those things, but I could see the dynamic of what happened.

While the sisters in Newtown were connecting with Aboriginal people on their visitors' own terms, Vianney was given a new mission, and one that she was quite reluctant to fulfil.

By September 1982, Vianney had finished her work in Pueblo and was ready to make her way home to Australia. She travelled for a while, visiting friends in the United States, before meeting Maureen in Rome. There, the Mother General asked Vianney to visit India and Sri Lanka before returning to Australia, to see if there were any opportunities to expand the congregation into those countries. *I bet you anything Maureen suggested it, because she'd be there, saying, 'This is silly. It's not what we should be doing. Why don't we send Vianney?' (and she'll come back and say this is not what we should be doing!).*

In India, *it was fairly clear straight away that the bishops were not very keen about having other European-derived cultures in their cities. They wanted Indian sisters to have their own Indian way of life and their own orders and that sort of thing.* Vianney reported her impressions to Rome, and was preparing to travel to Sri Lanka when she received news that her father had died. Vianney headed home for the funeral, and to spend time with her mother.

Despite Vianney's best hopes and wisest instincts, the plan to get a new foundation going in South Asia continued to develop. The

Superior General, a Canadian nun, had paid a visit to Colombo and given her enthusiastic seal of approval to a group of aspiring novices and to the priest and nun who were overseeing their progress. Now Vianney was obliged to go over and help with their formation. *So by the time I got to Sri Lanka, they thought I was coming to make a foundation and they already had half a dozen girls in a house. And when I got off the plane, they welcomed me like I'm, you know, sort of Grace Kelly or something or other. It was just dreadful. I cannot tell you. It was the worst six months of my religious life, almost.*

Vianney was extremely uncomfortable. *I was absolutely sure that it wasn't right for us as whitefellas to come into their life and, as it were, to impose our way of life. It just wasn't right at all. And I kept writing letters back to Maureen, who was my contact back in Rome. I kept writing, saying, 'This is not the right way to do it.' It was all wrong.*

Vianney struggled on there for several months, sending regular reports to Maureen. Maureen was in the difficult position of passing on Vianney's discouraging messages to the Superior General, who remained very much in favour of an expansion into Sri Lanka.

Once again, Vianney found herself in the role of fish out of water, at best, and stirrer, at worst. She was sending unwelcome news back to Rome while struggling in an unfamiliar culture. Trapped in a situation where she was trying to do good while knowing that she was possibly doing harm was really excruciating for Vianney. Eventually, she received a letter from Rome releasing her from her torment, and she went home, somewhat battered and bruised, to join the community at Newtown. (The Superior General kept at it, dispatching sisters from the United States and Canada to pick up where Vianney left off, but it never really worked out and the community in Colombo eventually became part of Mother Teresa's order, the Missionaries of Charity.)

Back among her sisters, and in her home city, Vianney discovered a whole new set of challenges and an unaccustomed level of discomfort. Her sleeping quarters were so tiny she was *scraping my elbows on the windowsills and all the rest of it.*

Vianney immediately took a practical approach. *Well, the first thing was, there was no money.* Marie, Marian and Betty were doing bits of work, guiding retreats, giving occasional lectures on spirituality, and even cleaning houses, *but there was no regular money coming in. At first, they were supported by Armadale but there came a time when Armadale said, 'Well, you've got to support yourselves,' which they were trying to do.* Now Vianney was an extra mouth to feed, and the hospitality side of the convent's activities required a steadier stream of money. *Even cups of tea and bread and butter require some money, so the first thing I did was to try to get a job.*

Vianney had arrived in Newtown in late June of 1983, and by August she had found paid work. *I had said to anybody that I could think of, 'If you've got any kind of job, will you let me know?' I did go over to Sydney University, thinking I could be a tea lady. The guy looked at me and said, 'I think you're overqualified,' so I wasn't getting very far there.* In the end, her cousin Joe, a Patrician Brother and principal of a primary school in western Sydney, offered her a part-time job teaching catechism to the little boys, and Vianney gave an hour's lesson to each year group, two days per week. *I'd go out there on a Monday and Tuesday and do my six classes and come home half dead.* It was a long train ride home after back-to-back classes, but Vianney was able to use her knowledge and her creativity in the job, and the convent now had a regular wage to rely upon.

It wasn't only Vianney, Betty, Marie and Marian in the house, now. From time to time, different people came and stayed for weeks or months, to experience what the sisters were doing. At around this time a young woman was living at the house on Forbes Street, with the intention of becoming a Blessed Sacrament nun and a permanent member of the community. She was the same age as Marian, and the two of them were sharing a room. The house had, in fact, become quite crowded, with occasional retreatants finding it difficult to squeeze in. When a house down the street became available the sisters took it for forty dollars a week, and Marian and Vianney moved in.

In December of 1983, Marian took a study trip overseas. The unexpected duty of training the new postulant would fall to her, and Vianney thought she ought to do some training. Although they sometimes struggled to earn the money that would keep them going week to week, the community had funds set aside for study and travel, and now it was Marian's turn to take advantage of this opportunity.

Marian's ten-month trip took her first to San Francisco, where she spent time with some of Vianney's friends and audited some courses at the Jesuit School of Theology. Then she spent Christmas with the sisters in Pueblo. *The idea was I would visit the different houses of our congregation and see what they were doing with formation.* This wasn't easy, since there were very few novices about—they didn't have any at Pueblo. The Pueblo nuns were still living in that peculiar zone between enclosure and openness that Vianney had experienced. They told Marian about the fun they'd recently had at a Torvill and Dean figure-skating show, and *I thought, 'There's a bit of a contradiction going on here.'* Marian visited the Blessed Sacrament Fathers in Cleveland and stopped at several other places on her tour through the United States, understanding how formation was being done, then called in to the Quebec convent to spend a few days visiting Sister Berthe.

After that, she headed to London where she took a short course in psychology before travelling through Scotland, which delighted her—she connected with it very powerfully as the land of her forebears. Marian also paid a visit to the radical women at the legendary Greenham Common, who had set up a permanent camp to protest the ongoing development of nuclear weapons. *I just was in awe and admiration of them.* Marian and Marie had become involved in the Sydney peace movement, and Marian occasionally made a little

Left: Vianney and her brother Mick, 1940s.
Middle: The Flood family the day they arrived in Ireland after the war, back right is Maureen's uncle, 1940s.
Bottom: Barbara and her sisters at the Moree Show, 1940s.

Left: Jill as a debutante, early 1950s.
Right: A publicity shot of Melissa as a young actress, 1960s.

Left: Marian dressed as a 'Bride of Christ' on the day she entered the novitiate of the Faithful Companions of Jesus, 1967.
Right: Vianney after graduating from university, 1957.

Left: Mother Berthe on the boat from Canada to Australia, 1950.
Right: Vianney as a young nun, New Year's Day, 1960.

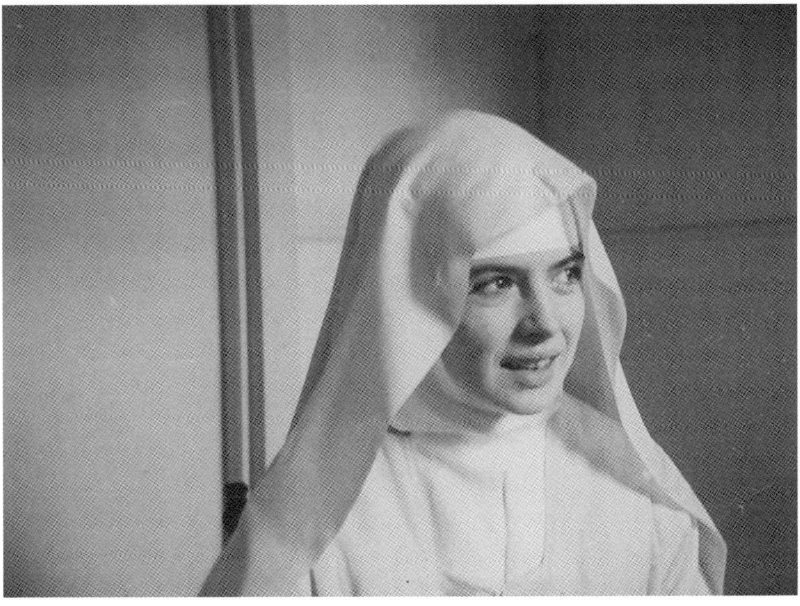

Sister Mary Agnes, formerly Jill Thomas, as a young nun in the 1950s or 1960s.

A group of the Blessed Sacrament sisters —Monica, Barbara, Betty, Vianney, Joan, Maureen, Berthe, Marie, Carol, Elizabeth and Denise, 1975.

Left: Marian, Carol and Marie in the 1970s.
Right: Vianney with a group of young Massgoers, 1972.

Barbara, Elizabeth, Vianney, Marian, Betty and Carol singing in the convent's new chapel, 1978.

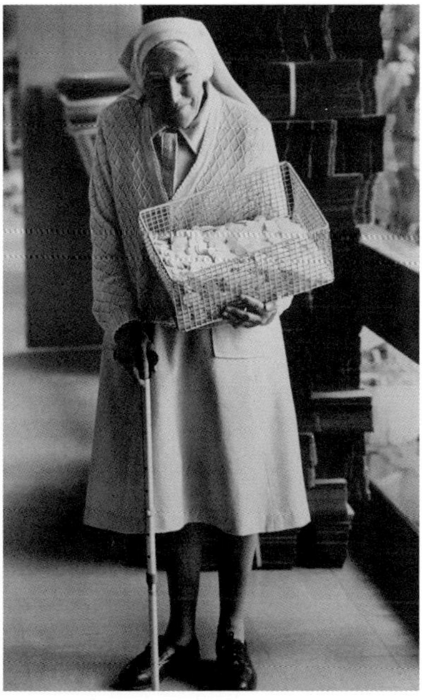

Left: Marian and Maureen at Marian's final profession, 1980.
Right: Sister Pete with a basket full of altar breads.

Maureen meeting Pope John Paul II, 1980s.

Left: Maureen, happy to be back in Newtown, 1980s.
Right: Marian at one of her workshops, 1980s.

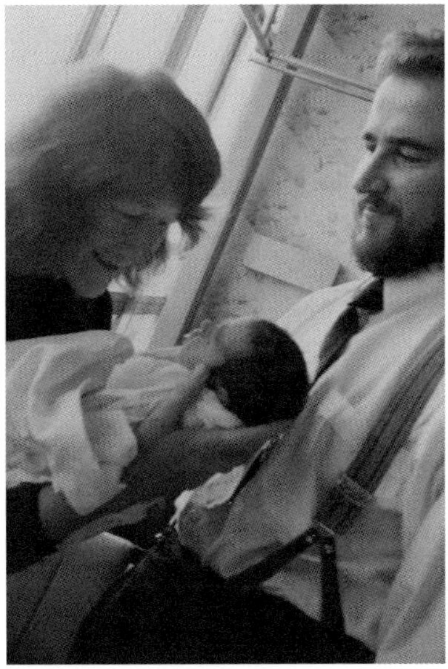

Left: Vianney as a physiotherapist, 1984.
Right: Marie with her son Michael and her newborn granddaughter, Gamel, March 1983.

Left: Vianney took several overseas trips with friends and family—here she is in Turkey, on a trip she made with her sister-in-law, Beryl, 2005.
Right: Marie at work in the Oamaru book bindary, early 2000s.

Left: Kevin and Jill Maher.
Right: Barbara at Rushcutters Bay Park, Sydney, at the time of her interview, 2019.

Left: Marie in her cottage at the time of her interview, 2019.
Right: Marian walking along the Yarra River near her home in Melbourne at the time of her interview, 2019.

money from giving talks about peace, nuclear disarmament and Christianity at schools and communities in Sydney.

Next, Marian visited the Blessed Sacrament sisters in France—*staying with our nuns in Paris was just ghastly. They were so behind in everything*—and spent some time with Maureen in Rome, where she took some courses, before going on a pilgrimage to the Holy Land. As a final stop, she went to India. *I ended up in Puna, at the National Vocation Service Centre, which had short courses in formation and psychology and such-like stuff. And between times I was able to visit our priests in Bombay and to spend time at a Christian ashram.*

Marian was especially struck by what she saw and learned in India. *The experience of being in India was overwhelming. Just the people and the heat and how different it was.* Marian's love of ritual was enriched by the celebrations she enjoyed at the ashram, where the use of fire and singing inspired her creativity. *I learned how to do the Aarti, the waving of the flame in front of the statue of Christ ... that was a beautiful thing. Ah-sa-toma ... Om. Shanti. Shanti. Shanti. I still remember it, see? It's beautiful. And then you would take the flame around and people would take the flame onto themselves. It was just these beautiful ceremonies that they did, they'd taken from the Hindu tradition and they Christianised them, if you like. They did a lot of chanting which I really enjoyed, and they would put Indian elements into the Mass, have all the various little lamps, and would sit on the floor. It was great.*

Though Marian wasn't especially enthused about becoming a Novice Mistress, she had learned a great deal. After twenty years as a nun, living a communal life, she relished the independence and the freedom her trip gave her, and her mind was greatly expanded by experiencing places and cultures that were new to her. *All I would say was, it just opened me out to the world and what a big place it was.*

When Marian returned, she threw herself with renewed vigour into the peace movement. Her postulant wasn't quite as interested in political action and found it difficult to participate with any real enthusiasm. Marian began to wonder whether her friend was really meant to join them. *And I said to her at one point, 'You know, how would it be if I said you don't have to be a nun?' She said, 'Really? Could you really say that?' I said, 'Yes.' 'Oh good.' So that was that—the beginning and the end of my being Novice Mistress.*

While a handful of women approached the sisters over the course of the next decade, it never felt quite right. Marie recalls suggesting to one that she try celibacy for a while. *We talked about it some months later and she said, 'No, I haven't managed it.' So I said, 'Well, you know, that's probably a good sign.'* The sisters realised they needed to think about the future of their community. *As a group we came together to discuss it. Will we continue to take postulants? And after a period of discussion, over a period of time, we decided: no. We're not going to take any more new recruits. If they really love what we're doing, we can find a way where they can be a part of our lives. But they don't have to become a Blessed Sacrament Sister.*

+++

The peace movement had become more mainstream by the mid-1980s. Since the election of Ronald Reagan to the US presidency in 1980, tensions between the USSR and the West were rising—an uneasy détente was replaced by Reagan's goal of freeing Europe's Soviet bloc countries from Moscow's influence. The threat of nuclear war felt real. The proxy war between the United States and the Soviet Union in Afghanistan featured in the nightly news, while films and television programs like *The Day After* and *Edge of Darkness* depicted the dangers of nuclear weapons for both humanity and the environment. Marie recalls it as *a terrifying time, really.* Many Australians were angered by French nuclear tests in the Pacific and the frequent appearance of US warships in Australian ports—tens of thousands of protesters would attend the Palm Sunday peace rallies in Sydney and Melbourne each year. In 1985, Marie and Marian joined a group planning a protest action at Watsonia, in Melbourne, where a satellite dish was part of Australia's intelligence-sharing arrangements with the United States military—arrangements that peace and anti-nuclear activists vocally opposed. Marian was mildly apprehensive, *and I had to go to my mother and father and say, 'Look, I might get arrested but I probably won't. But it could happen.' That was quite an occasion.*

It was Easter Sunday. Marie, who was a little bolder than Marian when it came to breaking the law, had decided to go all the way inside the base, while Marian would stay at the periphery, praying for peace. *So some of us were there, praying these psalms and reading these readings and some had gone right in and Marie was one of the ones who'd gone right in. I wasn't up for that; I just didn't think it was part of my thing.*

Marie remembers that this kind of activity was absolutely part of how she and Marian, with the support of the others, saw their role as Blessed Sacrament sisters and contemplative nuns. *We were very much into what the Church said about war. And the early Church didn't believe in war. They were against war, and the desert hermits wouldn't even go to war. War didn't fit with Christianity.* At this stage, Marie was leader of the Australian community (the women had by now done away with the title of 'Superior') and though some members of the Armadale community would have opposed her taking part, her second in command was entirely supportive. And so, of course, were Vianney and Betty. *I remember thinking, 'Now, I've got to have a good look at my motives: why am I doing this? I can't do this because I think I'm better than anybody else. I've got to realise that I too would not have done this once …' I felt peaceful enough when I finally worked out what my motive was. I can just remember getting through the fence with the others and waiting. Once you start an action like that, what's quite lovely is that the hardest part is making up your mind if you're going to do it.*

Several of the protesters were arrested, but Marie and Marian escaped the hands of the law. In Marie's case, this was the first of many protests. She and her fellow protestors once boarded a US warship amid a tour for members of the public. Marie's large handbag held a rolled-up banner decrying the number of children who *died of starvation while so many billions of dollars are spent on the war machine.* One of Marie's cohort had his camera ready to capture the moment when two others in the group *took out a phial of blood that they had concealed and splashed it on the launch pad for the Trident missile, as I unzipped the bottom of my bag and unfolded this big banner.* The group went uncomplainingly when the police inevitably escorted them off the ship. Some years later, Marie and her friends went on late-night missions into the city to protest the Persian Gulf War. *We prepared stencils and we took some spray paint and we had somebody with the stencils, somebody with the spray paint. We had to keep them separate so that if you were caught they couldn't prove anything … We were so opposed to that war. We could see that that war, if it started, may continue as it still is, more or less—warring against the people and not thinking about the millions that would be made homeless.*

While Marie was protesting, Marian's focus shifted. She had become very interested in new-age spirituality and its connection to contemporary psychology—things like the then-popular rebirthing movement, which sought to relieve trauma through breathing exercises that were supposed to bring back memories of one's birth. Marian spent some very interesting weekends at a rebirthing retreat in the Blue Mountains. *It was pretty confronting stuff. For one thing, you practically had nothing on under a blanket, and you did this very strong breathing. And it brought on sort of altered states, I suppose you'd say. And yes, I remember coming up with a few things, and you could shout and scream and cry. You could let everything out … What it was doing for me was trying to make me a more whole person. That's what I was thinking it would do. It would make … I suppose there was sort of a challenge about, gosh, what would come up? How would this work? It was a time of experimentation in all kinds of ways.*

By 1986, Marian became interested in a writer from the United States named Jean Houston whose spiritual self-help books were based on a process she had developed after working on a government-sanctioned research project on the effects of LSD during the 1960s. Houston was convinced that humans were using only a fraction of their potential—mental, spiritual and physical—and was interested in provoking states of altered consciousness without the use of drugs (which were now banned)—states that might help people reach that potential they held within. Houston's cultural influence has waned, but she once had some very notable fans. John Lennon named his 1973 song 'Mind Games' after Houston's 1972 eponymous book, which, along with her several other titles, sold well amongst the New Age crowd throughout the 1970s and 80s. Marian soon got hold of what was then Houston's latest book, 1987's *The Search for the Beloved: Journeys in Mythology and Sacred Psychology*. She said, *It was quite expensive, but I had saved up and I bought it.*

Soon, Marian was elected to travel to Rome to the General Chapter, the world congregation's meeting, and this time she was asked to stop off in India on her way to see if a group of women who were interested in becoming Servants of the Blessed Sacrament might be part of a new foundation in India. Marian reported back, in much the same fashion as Vianney had years earlier, that the nuns in India were quite different and should be left alone to do their own thing. *Don't import our way of doing things to them. They were doing a great job.* She took the opportunity to pay a second visit to the ashram in Puna and travelled to Gandhi's former ashram at Ahmedabad. All the while, she was reading Houston's book. *It was making a deep impact on me, and I was loving it ... She allows you to go through what she called 'process'. I know I learn by doing. And her way was, you put your whole self in, and you learned about yourself and others and relationships and so on.* Houston's process relied on using movement and imagination to take people into situations from history, myth and fairytale in order to explore their true identity and their full potential. For Marian, who had long felt her life story somewhat burdened by a sense of division, or splitting, this seemed a way of achieving wholeness.

Marian wasn't the only woman at Newtown making new discoveries. Ever since she had appointed herself the breadwinner of the community, Vianney had been looking for opportunities to engage her skills as fully as possible, both to support her fellow sisters and further her own development. While teaching at the primary school in Fairfield in Sydney's west, she made regular enquiries to find out whether she could return to her original profession—physiotherapy. *It did seem to me to be terribly outlandish to think that I could come back to it after all those years, but one person would lead me to another person who would lead me to another person.* A woman who had been a nursing nun and a physiotherapist was head of a local community health organisation, and she arranged for Vianney to do some retraining at a rehabilitation hospital in Dundas, also in Sydney's west. *So I was teaching for two days and then I'd go for three days to do this kind of retraining, and then I had to go before the registration board again.* Vianney was accepted right away, *which was a miracle, a great miracle.* Very soon after, she connected with a friend in Sutherland, in Sydney's south, who needed physios for the local community health team, and Vianney joined them three days a week. Before long, it grew to four days, and she gave up her work as a catechist at the school.

The community at Newtown now had a very good earner in its ranks, and Vianney, who was both treasurer and breadwinner, was satisfied to be doing useful work in service of her sisters and her patients. She knew that her father, had he been alive, would have approved. *He would have been very happy, very happy. He wouldn't have said I told you so, or anything like that, but he just would have been so pleased I had that skill and that profession and that I'd come back to use it.* She also saw the work as eminently Eucharistic. *The Eucharist is the sacrament of healing and the sacrament of nurturing and feeding. And so I think that all comes together very strongly in the work as a physio.*

Though busy in her work, Vianney remained very much part of the Blessed Sacrament community. She had always loved shared communal prayer, and though it didn't happen in the same way as it had back in the enclosed years at Armadale, it still knitted a thread that connected the sisters to one another, to their shared and individual spiritualities, and to different projects in their lives—all dedicated to the search for a deeper truth through contemplation. The women from both houses on Forbes Street met in the chapel early each morning for prayer together, and each did her best to dedicate time to private prayer every day.

Although she did not work as closely with the local community as Marie and Marian did, Vianney, too, was touched by the unexpected interventions of the Aboriginal people in her life and her understanding. *It must have been Christmas eve, and we were cleaning the house and getting it all spick and span. And Harold was there, walking up and down and up and down, and we said, 'Now, Harold, there's nobody going to be here after tonight. Vianney will be here to sleep, but she's going to midnight Mass at Redfern and the rest of us are going to be away, and so we will take you down to town and we've got some money for you to have a bed for tonight.'*

They took Harold into the city where he was to find a bed at a refuge, and the sisters went about their business for the rest of the afternoon, most of them heading to see friends or family for Christmas, while Vianney returned to Forbes Street. *We said goodbye, and off we went. I came home at about half past eight. And I was just sitting quietly in the chapel and then, at about ten the doorbell goes and I come out and it's Harold. I said, 'Harold what are you doing here? Couldn't you get in?' 'No, no, no—I could get in.' So then, I said to him, 'Well Harold, what were you thinking of doing?' He said 'Well, Sister,*

I thought, you've got to walk all that way down Wilson Street for Mass—I thought I'd come back and go with you.' Isn't it gorgeous? He came back to go with me to Mass because I couldn't walk down Wilson Street, which was true. It was pretty noisy and the hotel on the corner was pretty wild on Christmas night.

+++

In 1986, Maureen returned from her time in Rome, with her own spiritual foundations badly shaken. Her unexpected appointment to the General Council should have seen her remain in Rome as second-in-command for six years:

> I survived five. In my fifth year I thought, 'I am going to die if I stay here until the end.' I didn't get along with the Superior General of that time and I didn't like the direction we were going. All the other friends that I had in Rome had gone back home. One saving factor was the people I was working with in the English language department of Vatican Radio. As for Rome, I was beginning to lose faith in the Catholic Church. It was all so male. I had begun to become a real feminist. I thought, if I stay here, I am going to lose my faith.[16]

It was a turning point for Maureen. She sought the counsel of a friend, Tim Quinlan, an Australian priest who was also in Rome,

> and cried it all out while shredding a rather frail handkerchief. Tim just listened until I came to the end. Then he said, 'Maureen, did it ever occur to you that you don't have to stay here?'
>
> And it was like the heavens opened. It hadn't occurred to me that I could just leave. I'd been too brainwashed. I went out of there walking on air. I felt like shouting, 'I don't have to stay.'

> And I didn't. I walked away. It was the best single thing I ever did for myself in my whole life.[17]

Maureen was not alone in her disillusionment with the Vatican. Many Catholics were becoming fed up with their Church. The era of reform that Vatican II had heralded seemed stalled—some felt that it was going backwards. Pope John Paul II, who became head of the Church in 1978, was extremely popular, and he did extend the Council's promise in some areas—he asked forgiveness of the Jewish people for centuries of the Church's antisemitism and worked to deepen ecumenical and interreligious understanding. But in other ways, he was a stickler for the old rules and the old way of thinking. He believed that the edicts of Vatican II had been misinterpreted by over-enthusiastic progressives in the Church, who had convinced themselves that it would soon lead to married priests and women's ordination. But while the ordination of women was happening without any especially calamitous results in other churches, in the Catholic Church it was completely off the table.

The Church stuck firmly to other positions that were falling out of favour in secular society and in other Christian churches. By the 1980s, the Vatican's intractable opposition to contraception was blithely ignored by most Catholic couples in Australia, and in the face of the emerging AIDS crisis, many felt the strict ban on condoms lacked compassion. As more and more people accepted homosexuality as part of human nature, and as more gay and lesbian people were open about their sexuality, the Church's rhetoric on the subject became increasingly hard-line, opposing civil unions and even anti-discrimination legislation. The Vatican's insistence upon heterosexual marriage as the only proper context for sexual life was deeply questioned, if not entirely dismissed, by many Australian Catholics. At Redfern, Ted Kennedy made his position clear both at the pulpit and in his published writings:

> There seems to be a number of contributing reasons for the 'going quiet on sex' phase that our Catholic faithful has now entered. One is natural attrition, a natural pulling away from extremes—away from flogging dead horses. It has allowed for more important responsibilities, like justice, to gain a foothold in our consciousness; like responsibility for the degraded state of our planet; for our having allowed male force and dominating power to develop a one-sided shape of human society, including the Church; for our having allowed racism and sexism to pervade core institutions in our society.[18]

For Maureen, being back at Redfern meant being among like-minded people, and among her Aboriginal friends, who helped her experience her faith anew, sweeping away the emptiness she had felt in Rome.

> One night I was sitting alone in our chapel. The other sisters were out. The doorbell rang and I thought, 'I don't think I'll answer that.' Then I said to myself, 'Maureen, if you don't answer that, you have no right to be here.' So I went and it was Harold and he said, 'What are you doing, Sis?' And I said, 'Just sitting in the chapel, Harold.' And he said, 'Oh I'll come with you.' So we sat there quietly. I was reading a breviary and Harold seemed peaceful. Then he said, 'Is there a prayer for me in that book, Sis?' And I was just overwhelmed. It was like something shifted. I said, 'Oh yes, Harold, there's a prayer in here for you.'
>
> I found the Psalms and read a blessing for him. We sat in silence for four or five minutes and then he said, 'Don't you want me to read one for you?' I was taken aback. I never even considered that he could read or that I should ask him for a blessing. Unconsciously I was putting myself above Harold.

> His words showed me what I was doing, and what I was doing was not right. I passed the breviary to him still open at the Psalms. He read one aloud, perfectly. That moment of being blessed by Harold was one of the best teachings of my life. I learned not to assume anything about a person. Harold was like a prophet in our midst.
>
> And then there was an experience with one of the women. She arrived looking ill, very weak and hungry and said, 'Sis, do you reckon I could have a bath?' We took her into the convent and upstairs to the bathroom, which had a really large tub. We ran a lot of hot water, carefully undressed her and lowered her thin, black body into the bath. She was smiling as if all her dreams had come true. While we sponged her she kept reaching her arms out of the water as if to embrace it. All the time she was repeating a kind of chant, 'beautiful water, lovely water, lovely warm water.' I was overwhelmed by a sense that this was indeed the body of Christ in our hands. That image stays with me always, always. I don't think that I have found the presence of Jesus anywhere more vividly than in the body of that woman and in people like Harold.[19]

At around this time, Maureen, Marie and Marnie Kennedy, Ted's sister, began working together on a new initiative based on the concept of street retreats. The idea was to bring principles of contemplation, of spiritual and psychological openness, to situations where middle-class white people, like the sisters themselves, as well as any laypeople who wanted to, could enter into connection with marginalised people in the community, without imposing themselves. As Marie describes it, *the notion was that you would go vulnerably into their space, somewhere where they could contact you if they wanted to. You didn't make yourself obvious. You might sit on a park bench down the road somewhere and just sit there in prayer and wait and see what God was going to reveal to me today about the people he cares about most—the poor. Ted always said the poor are the beloved of God. And it was another way for people who'd never met Aborigines, that they would meet them and interact and find a way to do that.*

The sisters knew that Aboriginal people were engaged in a life-or-death struggle—against incarceration, deaths in custody, poverty, illness and heartbreak. They wanted white people to be able look that struggle in the face, and understand that pain, and work alongside black Australia for change. The street retreats were a practical way to make those encounters happen, and, the sisters hoped, to help move Australia beyond its racist, colonial mindset.

+++

Back in Melbourne, Barbara was considering taking her turn at overseas study. She hadn't really intended to take a trip at all, *because I felt as though what I had experienced was enough for me to explore in myself for the rest of my life.* But after hearing a lecture by Bede Griffiths, a British Benedictine monk who was part of the Christian ashram movement, *I got the feeling that the Eastern spirituality was very connected, in a way. There was something about it that I could relate to with my experience.* So Barbara asked Vianney, who was in charge at the time, whether she could make a trip to India. *It sounded as if everyone in India was a guru, you know. And even the poorest people who could be sitting in the gutter are gurus because they know the truth. And it sort of ignited a desire to go, and to go on an ashram tour.* Barbara recalls that Vianney wasn't quite sure that this fitted in with the purpose of offering the sisters a period of overseas study. Overseas study was something the community valued and prioritised (above, say, making much-needed repairs to the house on Forbes Street), but the idea was really for a woman to undertake formal study, gaining useful education and training for their work, rather than, in Barbara's words, *to go ashram-hopping, you might say, around India.* Barbara was a little daunted by Vianney's suggestion that she present her scheme to the community at the next meeting, *but I said from the heart why I was making this request to go,* and the community agreed. *It confirmed to me my feeling that God was wanting me to go.*

Barbara spent six months in India. She remembers sitting by the banks of the Brahmaputra River, just watching. *I saw the people take the oxen down and bathe them and look after them. And women were washing their clothes with laughter and joy. And I could see the river giving so much to the people—so much joy. And I could see in the distance a bit of smoke going up. Yes, someone was being cremated, and the smoke was going up. And I thought, 'Yes, great thanks …' And then, the river, I could see, was a manifestation of God. God was the river, giving all this joy and fertility and receiving all back to God with the smoke. So I was sitting there and I think it got me to the idea, 'I can see God everywhere. Everything can speak in the present moment—just stay in the present moment and see God everywhere.' That's what India probably taught me most. You've got to be in the now. India really showed me that the world is a good place. It's all a manifestation of God.*

With Maureen now back home in Sydney, the sisters needed more space. The old convent at Armadale was too large for the remaining Blessed Sacrament sisters still living in Victoria, so the block was subdivided, and the old house was sold. The Melbourne nuns all moved into the newer building that had been the novitiate. The sale meant the Sydney women could buy a new house. They found one in Marrickville, and Marian and Betty moved in, with Charito soon moving up from Melbourne to join them. Maureen moved in with Vianney at the house across the road from the original one in Newtown, while Marie remained at the original house with whichever fellow travellers happened to be staying there.

+++

Marie was planning to take her own study trip when her life took a sudden and dramatic turn. In early 1987, she was on a bus, heading into town, when she noticed a magazine left on the seat beside her. *I picked it up and it had an article about the adoption law in New Zealand changing, where mothers could find their children. And I thought 'What? This is extraordinary!' I got such a shock.*

By the late 1980s, the thinking around adoption had changed. Widespread social change meant the stigma attached to single motherhood had begun to lose some of its power. Forced and coerced adoption had largely ended by the mid-1970s. Many adoptees from that era were now adults, and many of them wanted to find their birth mothers. People were beginning to understand that the complete and irrevocable break between the birth mother and the child that had been understood as fundamental to the practice of adoption was damaging and unjust, and official adoption policies began to respond to this shift.

Marie had never imagined—never allowed herself to imagine—that she would ever see her child again. *A feeling of exhilaration and a shock came up at the same time—exactly the same time. The exhilaration was, 'Oh, I didn't ever think I'd be able to find my son. This can't be happening.' Then the shock was, 'Ooh, but what if he's dead, and what if he doesn't want to see me?' And there was a sort of fear of what could happen. But the strongest one was just this exhilaration. I was so unable to repress that.*

Marie's grief had never gone away. She marked her son's birthday every year in prayer, and the world around her presented her with many occasions to remember him. *There would be triggers—you might see a young mother breastfeeding her baby in town or on the bus or in church. And you just know that that will never happen for you, now, because you've lost a child.*

She had always tried to understand what had happened to her as an inevitability, the mysterious expression of God's will. *I used to often say to myself, 'Well, my son was taken from me and I have handed over all of that part of my life to God. You wanted my son. So I have to believe that you decided you could take better care of my son than I can.' ... And all I could do was to say, 'He's in your hands, dear God. You have to honour what I asked of you: "Make sure he's only ever loved".' That was my prayer.*

As soon as Marie got home after reading that article on the bus, she went to the little Forbes Street chapel to pray. She picked up the Gospel and read the reading for that day. *Much to my amazement it's the story of the dead son being returned to the mother.*[20] *And I couldn't believe it. And I said, 'Oh! That means you are faithful, God. You are faithful.' I kept saying that. 'I'm going to find my son.'*

Marie had never told her fellow nuns, nor anyone in her family, about what had happened. Her friend Rusty knew, *and I used to go to confession and talk to a priest about it every now and then, just when I needed to take the lid off it all.* Now, she knew she needed support. *I just felt an emotional mess, and I said to myself, 'I need to prepare. I need to find him and I need to prepare myself so that if he takes one look at me, he doesn't think, 'She's completely mad!' and walks away.' And I felt completely mad, almost, because the grief hadn't been dealt with.*

Marie made an appointment with a counsellor she knew and trusted, and he helped her prepare to take the next step. The real possibility of finding her son became ever-present in Marie's mind. The convent on Forbes Street welcomed lots of young people from the University of Sydney, just down the road, who came to join prayer vigils for peace, and that sort of thing. Marie would find herself staring furtively into the faces of those young men around her son's age, twenty-one. *I would think, 'Oh, it just could be my son. How would I know?' And I'd been scrutinising, having a good look. Does he look anything like me or Max? That was really, really painful, because you never ever knew. I'd be looking at young people as I walked around Sydney thinking, 'He could easily be here.' A lot of New Zealanders come to Australia, so he could be in Australia looking for me. I realised that.*

After two whole years of waiting and praying, Marie was ready to write to New Zealand and register her interest in reuniting with her lost child. She gave the adoption reunions office her counsellor's address for correspondence, and soon enough, he rang to say a letter had arrived, and that she ought to come by train and read it herself. *I just said, 'Look, I can't wait. Could you just tell me what's in the letter?'* The letter said her son was alive and wanted to find her. *Oh, I could still just weep now. 'He's looking for you!' He said our letters had arrived within days of each other.* Marie went to the nearest bedroom and howled tears of relief into a pillow so that the others wouldn't hear her.

The next step was for Marie to write to her son. She confided in a friend, who ushered Marie into an upstairs room at her house, gave her some of her best stationery, and Marie sat down and wrote. *I needed to make it very clear to him that under no circumstances did I want to lose him. But we were not given a choice ... 'But the greatest sorrow was losing you. And I've never stopped loving you.'*

Not long after, a package arrived. It was full of letters and photographs from her son—his name was Michael. *And one of the things he said was that it was strange getting a letter from somebody he didn't know who had such an intense feeling of love for him. He said it was an extraordinary experience ... But for me, I knew him and I carried him and I always had him clear in my imagination—exactly what he looked like.* Marie wept as she looked at photos of Michael as a baby, as a toddler, as a little boy. His letter was very kind. *He was just so, so concerned that I was coping—did I have enough help? It's very beautiful.* She learned that she and Michael had much in common and shared an artistic bent. He was a bookbinder.

Both Marie and Michael wanted to meet in person as soon as possible. The time had come to tell the others. Marie was making a visit to Marrickville, to see Marian and Charito and Betty, and she sat them down at the kitchen table. *'I've got something really important to say,' and of course then I broke down and cried because I could hardly hold it in. And I just said, 'The son I lost to adoption—I've just found him. We've had our first contact.' In the best possible way, Marian jumped up and said, 'That's fantastic news. We've got to open a bottle of champagne.' You couldn't get a better response than that—she's just amazing.*

Delivering the news to Vianney and Maureen was a different experience. *It was easier to tell Marian and the little community there than it was to tell Maureen and Vianney. But I'm not sure why that was so—I'll probably never know what that was. I think later on when we talked about it, Maureen said to me that she was sad that I hadn't risked confiding in her, because she would have been very good, but I just couldn't. I wasn't sure. I don't know why I wasn't sure, but I wasn't. They both went quiet. The opposite to Marian. 'Marie, you've carried all that burden on your own.' That was another beautiful response—different to the first one. But it came in the right order, so I was very grateful for that.*

Vianney, reflecting on Marie's announcement, recognised the wisdom of Marian's response. *That was a wonderful reaction, and I wished my reaction had been like that. But it wasn't—it was more like the reaction of a woman who'd been a nun for thirty years or more … When I thought about it afterwards, I remembered saying I had two reactions. One was what a lot of sorrow she's had to carry, for over twenty-five years, and nobody knew that—not even Maureen who was her Novice Mistress. And my second one was I was totally envious of her!*

Marie says that some time later, Maureen's keen sense of humour allowed her to share more of her feelings. *Maureen said to me, 'You lucky bastard!' You know, she loved to shock people, in a way, because it was so unusual coming out of her mouth—Maureen was so proper. 'You lucky bastard!' And we both roared laughing. She was such a dear friend.*

Soon after sharing her news with her fellow sisters, Marie told Ted, to whom she had become close. *And he gave me a hug and said that 'it's wonderful news'. All the best things you could ever want, and you just knew that Ted would get it.*

DIFFERENT DIRECTIONS

IN JANUARY 1989, Marie finally boarded the plane to Auckland to meet her son, Michael. With her was her friend, the one who had given her the fancy writing paper and the quiet privacy to write that first letter. They checked into a hotel room and Marie spent a fairly restless night awaiting her appointment to meet Michael in the lobby the next morning. When she woke, she had to take a beta blocker to calm her nerves. *I think it helped me—just so that I wasn't ragingly crazy, with tears all over poor Michael.* He arrived, with his partner Kahren, and the period of reunion commenced. *I was noticing the things that we had in common from the first moment, really, as you can't help it. And every now and then we'd catch each other just looking at each other, taking each other in, because, imagine! After all these years he's in front of me! He's in the room with me—it's just, it's unbelievable. There's no words can say what that was like, really.*

Slowly, each of them, mother and son, unfolded their story, and had their long-held questions answered. *Within days I said, 'How were you treated? How was it?' He said, 'I was only ever loved.' I couldn't believe he used the very same words that I'd used.*

Marie's short visit brought her intense feelings of joy, and marked the beginning of a long process of healing old wounds. Places and moments of past suffering could be transfigured, now, by new experiences and memories. On one occasion Marie returned, with Michael, to the single mothers' home where Michael's adoption took place. *And I said to Michael, 'I'd like to go into the chapel, now that I am back with you again.' I can't put into words how moving that was, having Michael beside me. So, of course, I just had to thank the good God. I said, 'You truly are faithful. I didn't expect this. That it could be completed. And it is. Thank you.'*

Marie returned to Newtown with her heart full, knowing that soon she would have to go back to New Zealand to spend more time with her son. *We couldn't bear being separated now, because we'd just discovered each other.*

Within a few weeks she was back on the plane and spent much of 1989 travelling between Sydney and Auckland. During her trips to New Zealand, Marie continued the delicate work of establishing a relationship with her son, and the difficult process of revisiting the trauma of having lost him. She heard that groups of mothers who had, like her, lost their babies to adoption, were meeting to support one another.

I can remember going to my first meeting with the birth mother support group headquarters at its little place on top of a shop in an arcade in Auckland. And I remember walking to the arcade and thinking, 'I hope nobody sees me going through this door because then they'll guess.' And I thought, 'What? Do I really believe that? They'll guess that I might have had a child out of wedlock?' That's how deep it was in me. Even after I found Michael, I was still nervous that I would be spotted with birth mothers. There was still a sense of shame that I hadn't worked through.

Marie decided she would visit the priest who had supported her and put her in touch with the sisters who ran the home, *because he didn't offer me any alternative other than adoption and I wanted to talk to him about that. I wanted him to know what it was like to have lived all those years without my son. And why couldn't it have been different?*

He still was of the attitude that it was the right thing to do … He said, 'What a great blessing—you've found each other. How faithful and wonderful God is.' 'Yes, oh yes, I agree with you, Father. But it was an absolutely terrible thing to have lost my child. And for all the mothers who have lost our children.' So I was able to tell him that—that was all I needed to do—and let him sit with it ... But the other person I went to see was the nun who was handling the adoption, who took Michael in her arms and took him ... I needed to go and see her because I thought, 'These people have to know what we've been through. I've had twenty-five years of all this grief. I have to tell them.' She was so defensive I couldn't believe it. I thought she'd at least be open to listen to me and she says, 'Oh well. It's been wonderful how God's brought you together.' I sort of thought I was over hearing that. So I challenged her on that. I said, 'But it was terrible for us women. So I just want you to hear what it was like for me.' But she didn't want to hear.

While Marie was away, Barbara moved to Sydney to join the others at the original house on Forbes Street, Newtown. Having lived so long among the Melbourne traditionalists, Barbara soon realised how differently things operated in Sydney. *I am amazed now just how much freedom I had at Newtown. I wasn't told what to do or what I shouldn't do. I did what I was drawn to do.* In many ways, Barbara's ability to be in the moment and to simply sit and listen, or chat for as long as her interlocutor wished, made her particularly suited to the nature of hospitality offered at the house. She found an immediate affinity with the Aboriginal people of Redfern. *I saw them as friends, as beautiful people, you know? I had the experience that the true self was in everyone, so that gave me reverence for everyone, really. They just accepted you as you are, I think. They welcomed me into the group, and I valued them.*

The fact that many were struggling with mental health issues, with drug and alcohol addictions, was no barrier for Barbara. *I always thought if I hadn't received that experience when I was so young, I could very well be like them now. But their true self is in them just as much as in me. And one day they'll wake up to it.*

Barbara quickly befriended an Aboriginal man named Leo. He introduced her to many others around Sydney and she soon felt at home, and grateful to discover that what she had thought were the two choices she faced when joining a convent—to either work with the poor or become a contemplative—were both available to her here in Sydney. One evening, Leo took Barbara to a meeting at a hospitality house on Bourke Street, in Surry Hills, and afterwards, as they walked towards the bus stop to travel home, *we stopped at the lights to cross Oxford Street. I became aware that I was standing beside a tall person dressed as an angel. I felt like laughing. I thought, how amazing is God? I entered an enclosed order, to be there for life. Now, I'm still a Servant of the Blessed Sacrament, in Oxford Street, at Mardi Gras!*

Marie returned to Sydney from New Zealand in time for what would be a significant event for the Australian Blessed Sacrament sisters. The Melbourne and Sydney communities came together only rarely. They would meet in Armadale every three years for a Regional Chapter, or for anniversary celebrations to mark the decades since the foundation of the Cenacle at Armadale, or, Marian says, *whenever the need arose to settle questions that had arisen between the two communities.*

The old divisions had never fully gone away, and these meetings were often tense. But in the winter of 1989 a week-long meeting was held for all the sisters at Stanwell Park, in the bush just south of Sydney. *It was a very good meeting,* recalls Marian. *We had an outside facilitator there who helped us come to some very good financial decisions. They turned out to be good decisions.* The community's money, which had been hard-earned by the sisters who worked in altar breads for all those years, increased after the sale of the old building at Armadale. The presence of the financial advisor helped keep a lid on the old tensions, and reaching those important decisions helped, too. *It settled us with regard to how the money was going to be administered between the two communities,* says Marian. Henceforth, the sisters could apply to the Regional Council (made up of the leader and two other

Australian sisters) if they wanted funds for study or travel. *It was a good experience. We knew where we stood, and we could go from there with more confidence about the just distribution of things.* In the evenings, the women would relax and enjoy one another's company—at least, those who actually enjoyed the company of their sisters would stay up for a drink and a talk. Others took themselves promptly off to bed. In one of her several reports as Regional Superior, Carol acknowledged the meeting's success and remarked that *the evening rages and brandy Alexanders really helped. Thanks to Vianney for this.*[1]

The following January, in 1990, Marie finally took the study trip she had been planning to take before she found Michael. It began with a three-month course in cultural analysis at the Mexican-American Cultural Center in San Antonio, Texas. Marie had hoped it would give her an extra analytical and practical framework for understanding and working with the Aboriginal people in Redfern. Now, she also believed the course could help her better understand what had happened to her and the many mothers who shared her experience with forced adoption. Marie began to understand that as an unmarried, pregnant young woman, she became part of a marginalised, misunderstood and misjudged group in society. It was not so much God's will that had caused her to lose Michael, but society's prejudices. *What would the Gospel say about women who were in my situation? The Gospel would be very compassionate. Take them in and care for them because they're the most vulnerable.*

After her time in San Antonio, Marie travelled to Europe for a holiday, staying with her fellow Blessed Sacrament sisters in France—*they were still almost strictly enclosed, but they were very open to me*—and spent time enjoying herself at the Louvre and wandering the streets of Paris. Soon after, she visited the mother house in Rome, where a fellow sister showed her around, and she went to Mass at St Peter's. When Pope John Paul II appeared, Marie was embarrassed to see a number of nuns hopping up and down with excitement. *I was in my early throes of feminism, and he was not saying helpful things about women at the time. I was feeling quite annoyed with him, really ... And I thought, these silly little things—this is no way to behave! He's only a person, after all.*

In Assisi, much more than in Rome, Marie felt a real sense of holiness. *I always loved Saint Francis, of course, and was struck by the tiny cell in which he spent great lengths of time in solitary contemplation. It was like a little box ... the extraordinary things that people in the medieval times did in the name of God and religion.* Finally, she visited her ancestral home in Germany, and made her way to what is now Marszewo in Poland, but had been the German town of Marsdorf. Marie carried with her a postcard her father had received decades ago, showing the town's church and two young oak trees planted in front of it. She was moved to see that the oak trees were now enormous, their canopies shading the entire forecourt.

Refreshed, Marie headed back to the United States for more study. She spent some time at the Maryknoll convent outside Ossining, New York, and immersed herself in the teachings of Thomas Berry, an American Catholic priest and theologian who was grappling with the emerging climate crisis. It was there she met Sister Miriam McGillis, a Dominican nun who was experimenting with sustainable agriculture and drawing on Berry's teachings. Marie took a course on theology and the natural environment which drew heavily on these ideas. Berry's writings, which were heavily influenced by Teilhard de Chardin, would come to have a profound impact on her thinking. *I came back with five tapes that absolutely spelled out the whole thing, with the story of the unfolding of the human community within the Earth community, and the mismatch of those two, and where we've started to go wrong. And he actually says Christianity has to wear a huge responsibility for it, because of our understanding of God as being distinct from the Earth and not being part of the Earth.*

Marie thought of her own relationship with the Earth, and of her family farm in Queensland, and she made herself a promise: *I said, 'I've got to be on some land somewhere within five years.' That was a commitment.*

All throughout her travels, Marie had been missing Michael. *We wrote lots of letters to each other. I've got a whole lot of letters that I've kept from my time overseas. Letters are an amazing way of communicating and expressing your deepest feelings. And with Michael, it was so easy to communicate deeply. It wasn't superficial stuff.*

At the end of her seven-month trip, Marie returned home to Newtown knowing that she needed to be near Michael. In late 1990, she moved to Auckland with the blessing of her fellow Blessed Sacrament sisters. It was a big change for the community and unknown territory. What would Marie's role as a Blessed Sacrament sister be, so far from her fellow nuns? Nobody had the answers, but they were prepared to go along with Marie and find a way. The community promised to support her until she settled down and found a way to earn a living in New Zealand.

By the end of that same year, Vianney had left Newtown, too. Vianney had always valued the communal life of the Servants of the Blessed Sacrament, and she valued having a peaceful home. But things at the house could be unpredictable, with the street retreats being hosted there. *We had people living there and staying there and I got to a stage where I thought, 'Is this really my home?'* It wasn't just her own household—the communal prayer life of the general Sydney community had died. *I'd come down to prayer in the morning and nobody would be there. They were all off doing other jobs and I said, 'Well this is not working—nobody is here!'*

Vianney spoke to Carol, who was leader at the time, and said she needed to live closer to her work (the commute to and from Sutherland, where she was practising physiotherapy each day, was tiring) and asked whether she might be able to rent a flat on her own. In the end, the decision was made to buy a property, and Vianney moved into her own little place, just as she'd done at Berkeley. *I was the first one to go out on my own.* Vianney saw much less of the others, now, though they stayed in touch on the phone. Vianney still came to Sunday Mass at Redfern occasionally, but she soon became active in her new parish of St Patrick's in Sutherland, where she was able to contribute her skills and knowledge to the liturgy—something that St Vincent's, with Ted's distinctively shambolic approach to the ceremony of Mass, hadn't offered.

That year, 1990, was also very significant for Marian. The house at Marrickville was host to a very interesting array of people and pursuits. Betty had become interested in Jungian psychology and Marian was still studying the ideas of Jean Houston. They each attracted people who shared those interests and there were study groups and social gatherings that drew a great many people to the house. The place had a large front room—big enough to hold meetings and movement workshops; anything the sisters were experimenting with. Marian hosted a weekly gathering where people would use Houston's book and go through some of her imaginative exercises. *I met a lot of interesting and strange people.* One couple she met was keen to bring Houston out to Australia, and when the woman herself arrived in 1990, Marian was engaged to help promote the tour and arrange some of the logistics.

Marian had already written to Jean Houston asking whether she could undertake a kind of scholarship with her to learn more. With her career as a Novice Mistress over before it began, Marian was searching for meaningful work that tied in with her vocation. Just as Vianney had found that healing people's aches and pains as a physio, and helping them live fuller and freer lives, fitted with being a Blessed Sacrament Sister, Marian wanted work that was Eucharistic in spirit. *We were saying that the Eucharist was pretty broad, at that stage. So I thought I could be a proponent of this kind of work, which was all about life, and God was in all of life.* Marian had no wish to evangelise, but she saw this as a way she could help people grow in spirit.

When Jean arrived that May, she was just what Marian had hoped and imagined she would be. *Powerful. Oh yeah. She came into the room, six foot something and you just stopped because she had such a presence. And she'd be going around almost sniffing the air to see what was in the room, you know, and using all her senses all the time.*

Houston was receptive to Marian's idea of a scholarship, or apprenticeship, and they discussed it further, agreeing that Marian might be able to join Houston in the United States for a few weeks, to study how she did her work. Down in Melbourne, Carol, who was still the leader, had to be convinced of Marian's scheme. *But I said, 'Well look, there's a scholarship. All we have to pay for is the trip over and back, more or less.' And I could make a career out of it, because we were so amorphous as to what we were doing. I mean, it was alright for Carol. She was still doing the chaplaincy stuff.* But the others were supportive. *The community was wonderful in this sense: they always said, 'Go ahead', and there was none of them that really was as interested as I was. And, of course, my mother said, 'This is psychology. Aren't you supposed to be doing religion?' So I didn't have much to say to that. I'm saying, 'Well, it's the whole person,' you know?*

By October, Marian was off on her four-month-long tour with Jean Houston. Houston was enjoying a successful career as an author, public speaker and workshop facilitator. Her method involved the use of myth, religious texts and fairytales to explore questions of untapped human potential and spiritual fulfilment. Houston believed that all humanity shared a collective unconscious whose wisdom could be unlocked by meditating on foundational stories and key figures from the past. She reached the height of her fame in the early 1990s, thanks to news that she had run workshops for the then-First Lady Hillary Clinton at the White House—the press called her 'Hillary's guru'. *She had a house outside of New York. It was like a little castle—it was an amazing place—and I had my spot in the little house at the back, which was lovely. And Jean had dogs and cats and I was in my element—I love animals. So we travelled. We travelled around the country, we travelled down to South America, doing all these different courses and we finished up in India and we met up with Bede Griffiths, a Benedictine who was also in an Indian ashram. They were marvellous, marvellous, marvellous times; I met wonderful people. And Jean gave me a letter saying I was authorised to teach her stuff, so when I came back at the beginning of '91, that's what I wanted to do.*

Marian threw herself into the work of running Jean Houston's workshops out of the house in Marrickville and at retreat centres in Sydney and beyond. Often Marian would draw on stories of some of the leading figures of the Catholic tradition—Hildegarde of Bingen, Francis of Assisi, and Pierre Teilhard de Chardin. *These people were like models, in a way, and the sorts of things they'd had to face … It would help you I suppose if you went through that a bit, with them. You would feel more able to face life and the sorts of things that happened. I did take this stuff to most states. I got invited to go to Tasmania and South Australia and Queensland. Obviously Sydney, Melbourne, country areas. So 'have Jean, will travel' took me quite a way. I was loving it! It was feeding me.*

Marian held a Jean Houston retreat down at Stanwell Park. Several people were there, including Maureen and Vianney. Marian could tell that the exercises had been *freeing and life-giving and sort of saying, 'Well if I've come to have life, have it to the full.' It was like that. And you could see people brightening up and livening up, and seeing new possibilities in themselves.* In the heady atmosphere of the retreat, Maureen and Marian even found themselves running into the sea, fully clothed, for a bracing dip, *which was something I wouldn't have thought about doing—we kind of egged each other on.* The retreat's success gave Marian confidence that she could do this sort of work—it had real value, and it could be Eucharistic, generating a connectedness within and between people.

For Maureen and Vianney, the 1990s were an equally productive period, creatively and intellectually. Vianney enrolled in a master of science degree at Wollongong University, not far from where she was now living, and wrote a thesis on innovative approaches to ageing. She had realised that many of her physiotherapy patients needed help in understanding what to expect from old age—its impact on body and mind, and its demands on a person's inner and outer strength. She wanted to help her patients find a positive, growth-focused approach to this phase of life. When she graduated, she applied for and won a prestigious Churchill Fellowship to travel overseas and study the way ageing was approached in other countries. While she was very busy with work, study and her role as treasurer for the Blessed Sacrament community, Vianney always had plenty of energy left over for new friendships and new forms of pleasure and enjoyment. She had always loved live performance, and now Vianney was a regular at the opera and the symphony. It wasn't just pleasure—like all forms of beauty, Vianney saw music as another manifestation of the divine. *I've been heard to say I'd rather go to a concert than go to a lecture on spirituality—much, much, much more.*

Carol Hogan was fulfilling her intellectual dreams, too. She travelled to Boston to study with leading feminist theologians Elizabeth Johnson and Sandra Schneiders. Back home, she left her job as Melbourne University chaplain and undertook her doctoral studies. Her thesis on Eucharistic women told the story of her community's transformation and examined their spirituality in the light of the latest feminist theology.

Maureen was also very busy. She had done quite a lot of radio work over the years, and in 1996 she wrote and narrated an eight-part program on human sexuality for Vatican Radio. Maureen's rich, mildly patrician voice speaks from decades of accumulated wisdom and experience—experience that was still teaching her, and which she was still incorporating into her whole self as a Blessed Sacrament Sister. Having begun her religious life in a convent that saw the body as an impediment to spiritual achievement and required its nuns to wear a chemise while bathing, she had learned how to celebrate her body as herself. *Joy in our sexuality goes with having a body and it runs through the whole course of our lives ... It is enmeshed with our total being and we can't allocate it just to bits of ourselves. ... It's about a whole set of ways of relating to God, to self, to others and to the rest of creation too. ... Building loving and respectful relationships may be the deepest meaning of our sexuality. And it seems clear that doing the hard work of building loving and respectful relationships is the clearest manifestation of what it means to say that we are body, soul and spirit made like God.*[2]

Some of Maureen's insights on this topic may have come from a close relationship she had formed with an Australian priest while in Rome, where both of them had found the atmosphere extremely stifling. Like Maureen, her friend was a free, life-loving spirit. Maureen always stayed true to her vows, and he to his, but they formed a very warm friendship that became an important part of Maureen's life.

Maureen was enrolled in a Master's degree of her own around this time, studying English Literature at Sydney University. She had discovered that where her religion could not give her the answers she needed, poetry might. She became particularly interested in the work of the Australian poet and activist Judith Wright, who had grown up in the New England country of Maureen's childhood—a landscape to which Maureen was very attached. Wright's poetry became the subject of Maureen's thesis. Maureen wrote about it in a personal reflection:

> The language of poetry may speak where 'religious' language fails. It may speak without saying too much, and without filling all the silences. In the course of this study of spirituality in the poetry of Judith Wright, spaces and absences have taken on a different quality for me. Absence becomes presence, with difference but no opposition between the two.[3]

The spiritual crisis Maureen had begun to experience in Rome hadn't ended. She had once been sure that the spiritual and intellectual journey she'd been on since the early 1970s—the renewed liturgical practice, the intellectual rigours of interpreting the Gospels anew, and reading literature, philosophy, poetry—would only enrich and enlarge her faith. But her intellectual growth was accompanied by profound spiritual bereavement. Maureen eventually lost her faith in a personal God. 'I didn't realise that following paths that led to life and gave so much energy, hope and understanding, required a death, such a death ... When the time came, it was long drawn-out agony.'[4]

> The death of God came as a great shock to me. It was a shock whose waves rolled through the entire structure of my life and my world. The realisation of such loss came not as the result of reading about it in philosophy or 'radical' theology or through any process of rational thought but in dark personal experience. In a part of myself I thought the loss to be temporary and that it was a matter of just getting through this difficult time. But somewhere within myself I knew this was not to be. The loss was not only necessary, it was irrevocable. The transcendent God vanished and was not going to return. A huge void opened and there was nothing ...
>
> It is hard to understand, let alone describe, how it is possible to be in nothing but that is where I was and it became the only place I knew for a long time. There was no light, only darkness and it was in no way consoling. Any 'dark night' I'd lived through before was nothing like this. Everything I'd been able to call upon before was gone, with a sense of utter finality.
>
> Yet in an obscure, never able to be spoken way, dark-nothing seemed the right place to be. This 'seeming' was not conscious thought, it was more blind, dumb instinct. Slowly some vague sense stirred with the faintest suggestion that what I regarded as terrible loss was, perhaps, the lifting of a series of thick veils through which I had seen the world and everything in it.[5]

In the midst of her crisis, Maureen remained closely connected to her sisters. She seemed to understand this moment as an essential part of her life as a nun, rather than a reason to abandon that life.

+++

Now that Betty was getting older, the leadership of the community was shared between Carol in Melbourne and Maureen in Sydney—the two other women who had the time, energy and inclination for the leadership role. The two communities supported one another and respected their differences, but they only rarely came together.

Every so often Marie would receive a visit in New Zealand from the community's leader, whether it was Maureen or Carol, and Vianney visited, too. *You know, you've got to check how your nuns are getting on in remote parts of the world! I felt very supported by them all the time.* Nonetheless, Marie was very much making her own way. She had at first set up house in a tiny attic flat above the bindery where Michael had his workshop. She reconnected with the support groups she'd encountered on earlier trips to Auckland and attended regular meetings with women who had shared her experience of forced and coerced adoption. *The thing was just to sit around in a circle in a hopefully non-judgemental way and listen to the women's stories, or the stories of the adopted person. And often they were in enormous grief. You'd have to listen through untold grief. It was just because it was so raw and so new. And they've just found the child, or the child didn't particularly want to have anything to do with them and then they had to deal with that.*

The workshops were very emotional. *Lots of tears. Honestly. There was no moment when there wasn't lots of tears … I cannot describe the waves of grief that would come up in you and you didn't understand why. 'Are they still there? Am I still crying? I can't believe this,' I'd say to myself.*

Marie was financially supported by a stipend from the community in Australia, and she made extra money helping Michael in his work.

Because I had the graphic art background, he said, 'Well, it's not that different because it's working with your hands and making sure everything is straight.' … So it was that sort of attention to detail you had to have, and I had that, and I quite liked the fact that you could hold this book—I probably preferred it to graphics because you had a concrete thing in front of you and I liked that feeling of a real thing. While Michael did the complex restoration work, Marie made new cloth covers for worn out second-hand books. *I couldn't believe it. I sort of still can't believe it. I would look at him and think, 'My God, who would have thought this was going to happen?' Every now and then out of the corner of my eye, I'd notice him again because I was still getting used to the fact that this is the son I'd lost for twenty-five years, and now I've found him.*

When an opportunity came along to work for the New Zealand government as a social worker serving adoptive mothers and children, Marie applied, and she got the job. Soon she was running her own workshops, drawing on what she had learned during her study trip, but also on her experiences with Aboriginal people in Newtown: *If you're in pain, don't try to help us, but come with your own pain and let's work together. We'll all be healed then.* Marie was still coming to terms with all she'd lost by missing out on Michael's childhood, while managing the very complex sensitivities that their reunion had created among the other members of his family. *I'm still being healed. And the mothers would pick that up. They'd know if I thought I was more healed than they were.*

Marie was happy in Auckland, and her reunion with Michael was going very well. In 1993, he and his wife, Kahren, had a daughter, Gamel—Marie got a call in the dead of night and was among the first to see the baby in hospital. Living in inner-city Auckland was not unlike living in Newtown, and Marie had made many new friends, but she hadn't forgotten her promise to herself, made while she was studying with Sister Miriam McGillis in the United States. When an opportunity arose to leave the city and form part of a spiritual community tied to the land, Marie took it with both hands.

Marie, along with Michael, Kahren and Gamel, as well as Kahren's mother and stepfather and Michael's adoptive mother, all packed up and moved to the South Island. Marie, along with a handful of Dominican nuns and laypeople, moved in to Teschemakers, an old country estate that had once served as a Catholic boarding school, some 100 kilometres north of Dunedin and just back from the moody north Otago coastline. Its new residents planned to establish a retreat and reflection centre to host people looking for a new way of living that respected and cared for the natural environment. Marie ran courses and retreats, sometimes hosting up to fifty people on a weekend, giving talks and running discussions while also helping to prepare the food and make everyone comfortable.

It was hard work—not just preparing and running the conferences but also caring for the century-old stately home and its small farm, which Marie and her companions were hoping would furnish most of their earthly needs. One of the Dominican sisters was a skilled gardener, *the food just absolutely sprung out of the earth*, and Marie's job was to take care of the orchard. People from neighbouring farms would lend their sheep to graze among the trees, trimming the grass and getting rid of the weeds, and Marie carefully harvested and preserved the fruit. *It was a gorgeous orchard. I loved it.*

Whenever she had any spare time, Marie would do some book binding for Michael, who had set up a new workshop and store in one of the old limestone buildings in the still-decrepit Victorian precinct of Oamaru, a harbour town on the nearby coast.

I used to ride my bike in once a week on my day off from Teschemakers back into Oamaru. It was wonderful. It would take me about an hour, but I used to love being out in the quiet of the countryside. It's a lovely feeling—everything is so immediate, and you can hear the birds fluttering around and even the wings of the birds flying past. Every now and then I'd just get off the bike and listen to it all. So that was like a meditation, cycling in the morning. And I'd stay with Michael's mum for a night, not always with her, but she was very welcoming for me to stay a night, and then I'd go back the next day.

It was here at Teschemakers that Marie recalls receiving one of Maureen's visits. Maureen took her role as leader of her little community seriously, yet she had by now developed a deep scepticism about the institutional church. *I saw her pacing up and down in the garden from my upstairs window. 'I wonder what's going on? Maureen's having a bit of a pace.' So I grabbed her later and I said, 'Are you okay?' She said, 'I don't know how you can stand living with all these nuns!'*

+++

With the others busy with work and study, and Marie overseas, Barbara was the only Blessed Sacrament Sister left at 40 Forbes Street, though there were other fellow travellers living there and helping the household along. Barbara had renamed the house 'Dadirri', an Australian Aboriginal word meaning something akin to 'contemplation'—Barbara learned the word while listening to a cassette tape recording of Miriam-Rose Ungunmerr-Baumann, the Aboriginal activist, artist and teacher.[6] The deep listening the word evokes was by now a central part of Barbara's life and spiritual practice. She listened to her inner voice, her truth, as well as to the many people who came and went at the house. In 1990, Barbara wrote a reflection about her time there so far:

> It seems obvious to me that Dadirri has been called to be a place of love and simplicity where particularly the little ones in the eyes of the world come to experience their own preciousness in the heart of God's family … A distinct Aboriginal spirit pervades the house. It holds within its walls the joy of meetings and

reconciliation between Aboriginal and non-Aboriginal brothers and sisters, who hold each other in mutual love and respect.[7]

Barbara's old friend Leo was still a regular presence, visiting most afternoons, and Harold remained an ever-faithful visitor, calling in each day, sometimes several times a day. 'He brings a blessing even though we sometimes feel reluctant to answer yet another doorbell,' Barbara wrote.

The place had fallen into even worse disrepair over the years, but those sharing the house, as well as some young people who used to visit, helped patch things up so that plaster wasn't falling from the walls and glass panes weren't being blown out of the old wooden window frames. Barbara enjoyed frequent visits from her sister, Mercia.

As well as hosting Eucharistic celebrations in the very warm, spontaneous style that suited the house, Barbara was finding new ways to explore and express her own spirituality. Sometime during the 1990s, she began hosting weekly meetings at the house, based on a book she'd read called *A Course in Miracles*, a 1974 book by American psychologist Helen Schucman that gained enormous following in the early 1990s after Oprah Winfrey promoted it on her high-rating show. Schucman always claimed the book was dictated to her by an inner voice she identified as Jesus, but it drew on a range of New Age ideas and many people began to form groups based on the spiritual practices it described. Barbara soon gathered a crowd to do the same at Newtown.

People from across the road came over, the lesbians who lived next door, whoever it was. They all knew they were welcomed, and respected. So that's how it all grew, somehow. The main idea is knowing your true self, and to change from illusions to the truth—that was the big miracle. And to change from fear to love was a miracle. It was actually changing from who you thought you were to who you really are, which was what my experience taught me. So, really, the Course in Miracles gave me a language to share.

As well as running her meetings, Barbara was managing the house at Newtown, providing hospitality and welcome, and producing the endless cups of tea and sandwiches, as well as laying out mattresses on the floor whenever emergency accommodation was required—a still far from seldom occurrence. There was still Mass every Tuesday night, and a meal afterwards, to which all were welcome. When a suggestion was made that she, too, ought to be doing some paid work, *I think I did say, 'Look, if I'm going to earn my own money, then give me a unit and I'll work from there. I really can't earn money and run this place at the same time.' I thought, 'How can I do that? How can I go out doing work and have an open house? How could they expect me to go out working when I could hardly keep the place I'm in clean?'* Barbara felt she didn't have the skills or training to do the kind of engaging, enriching work the others were doing. She would only be able to clean houses. *And I thought: it's time to leave. It's time to leave, because all this is making me feel the last and the least. And it doesn't feel right. I put this on myself, wanting to be the last and least, and I think I've had enough of it, and I'll go.* Barbara moved out of Newtown in early 1997, and formally left the Blessed Sacrament sisters later that year.

In 1998 Sister Pete died. Her funeral was one of those rare occasions on which the two communities from Sydney and Melbourne came together. Barbara had just had an operation, but she was well enough to make it to Melbourne and stayed at the convent at Armadale, along with all the Sydney sisters who had travelled down for the funeral. Sister Pete had worn her cream-coloured nun's outfit and her veil to the very last. She had always remained a true original, and a much-loved member of the community. As Barbara recalls, *she would sit you down with a cuppa and a piece of cake—probably one she had just baked—and we all loved her, somehow. Just being herself, she was very lovely … She was very free. She could easily break rules if she thought it was better to do it. I think she was just true to herself. She was free enough to be herself.*

+++

The late 1990s saw Marian reach a difficult turning point. Her spiritual work using Jean Houston's methods was not the success she'd hoped it would be. *I just could not get enough people to come. It was too exhausting. And by about 1999 it was really starting to die and that triggered the greatest spiritual crisis of my life, I think, because I could not understand what I'd done wrong ... And so I was just left and, somehow—this is what happens in people's lives, in my life: everybody disappears, there just wasn't anybody—and I spent several months, really, without work, wondering, thinking, 'What have I done wrong?' And praying, and thinking, and going into a deeper spiritual place, and staying there for some months.*

The house at Marrickville was lonely. Charito was away, and by this time Betty, after suffering a stroke, had gone into an aged care home. Vianney was living down in Kirrawee in her flat, and Maureen had moved into a small flat by herself in Dulwich Hill. *Everybody seemed to be away. I was on my own quite a lot and had to come to terms with what was happening, and what would I do. And somehow, I was in touch with Melissa, because I remembered that Melissa was an extraordinarily spiritual woman.*

Melissa Jaffer, who had left the Blessed Sacrament sisters long before Marian joined them, had always stayed in touch, and paid occasional visits to the house at Newtown, as, in fact, had Jill. Marian telephoned Melissa, who was living in Picton, a small rural village just west of Sydney. *And I said, 'I'm going to come and see you.' Strangely, I didn't feel I wanted to talk about it with any of our current sisters, just Melissa. And I said, 'I just want to come and see you and talk to you and see what's going on here.'* Marian spent a night or two with Melissa, who helped her through the crisis, *and somehow through her I learned that there was a liturgical job in a parish going, and I thought, 'Well, I can do that. I've got training in liturgy, and I've done it in my theology degree.'*

So Marian found herself working in the somewhat genteel inner-city suburb of Forest Lodge, near Glebe, at St James' Church. *I had to prepare the Eucharist and sometimes to run a communion service. Some of the kids from the school would come over occasionally and I'd try to get them to prepare a special Mass. It was involving the laity and getting to know the parishioners a bit. And I introduced the idea of a cup of tea after the Eucharist, after Mass, and that sort of thing, and running the liturgy group. That kind of stuff. Look, there wasn't that much to do, frankly.*

But she got on well with the priest, and the work was Eucharistic, and Marian was able to recover from her disappointment.

A couple of years later, in 2002, Marian celebrated her silver jubilee—twenty-five years as a Servant of the Blessed Sacrament. She celebrated with a trip. The overseas trip to mark the important anniversary had been introduced some years back. *You had three months of refreshment. If you wanted to study—like Carol, of course, would always want to study. Vianney, I don't know what she did. I think she went to Greece.* Most of the sisters used it as an opportunity to relax and enjoy themselves. *I desperately wanted to just go and see Scotland because that was my forebears' place. And Maureen wanted to go back to Ireland. And I thought, 'Well she's coming with me. We'll go back to Ireland.' I said, 'I don't want to go by myself. I've done everything by myself. I want to have someone come with me, and Maureen, would you come?' And she, being herself, said, 'Of course I'll come.'*

Two of them going away meant the trip would be more costly, and so it was curtailed to just five weeks, taking in Ireland, Scotland and France. *I knew about the labyrinth on the floor at Chartres Cathedral, and I really wanted to walk on that labyrinth. So they were the three places.*

Marian and Maureen stayed at bed and breakfasts, or with other nuns who offered them hospitality (many of them from Marian's former community, the Faithful Companions of Jesus—she had called ahead to let them know they were coming). By this time, communal prayer was no longer part of their practice, but Maureen and Marian went to Mass together each week. Otherwise, they left religious obligations to one side and just enjoyed themselves, driving around Scotland and Ireland, with Marian behind the wheel, visiting historical sights. In Scotland, the women had an experience—more spooky than spiritual. *Well, we'd heard about these spirits of the woods and spirits of the rivers and we met this lady who had photos of all these things. It was very interesting, and I thought 'What does it matter? We're here. We'll just see. We'll go along with it.' I never saw these spirits, but Maureen did.* In Ireland, they spent time with Maureen's relatives—*Maureen of course was totally at home with all the Irish*—and sought out the kinds of sights and experiences any other tourist would look for. *We went to a few Irish pubs. We actually saw a bit of Irish dancing. There wasn't a lot, and in Scotland it was very hard to find bagpipes, too, which I kept looking for.*

In France, they were astonished to see that their sisters in Paris were still pretty much cloistered. *It was a terrible shock. Maureen couldn't get out fast enough, and I was pretty much with her. We went back to about the 1940s the minute we walked through the door.* All the nuns were still in formal habits and would sit around stiffly at recreation, just as they had at Armadale more than two decades earlier. *So Maureen said to me, 'God, we've got to get out of this.'* They left the convent straight after morning prayer and headed to the Louvre, and sat around in elegant cafés on Paris' boulevards, avoiding recreation hour at all costs. *Then we got the train down to Chartres, and it was lovely. We went to the cathedral, we got there as Mass was on, so we went to Mass. And then the big moment: I walked on the floor.* The medieval labyrinth at Chartres Cathedral maps a symbolic pilgrimage, *and in the centre there's a flower shape and you spend some time in the centre. And then, interestingly, the way out is exactly the same as the way in, but you are supposed to be sort of somewhat different, because you've made the journey. It's a journey, and you don't have a goal in mind. I thought, thousands of people have walked this, there must be a lot of energy in all of this. And I walked it and prayed the whole way.*

Maureen and Marian experienced all the usual pleasures, disappointments and pitfalls of travel. *Well, Maureen lost her luggage on the way. And this was another thing: I was starting to think something wasn't right.* Maureen—now aged sixty-seven, and twelve years Marian's senior—seemed unusually forgetful.

It did worry Marian, but once they were back in Sydney, her attention was soon taken up with more immediately pressing concerns. Marian had not been comfortable at the house in Marrickville for a while. Charito's health wasn't good, and the two of them were not getting along very well. Marian had confided in Maureen during the trip, and Maureen supported her decision. *I'd said to her on the way, 'I can't stay in this place much longer.' So really very soon after I got home I was able to say to Charito, 'I think I have to be on my own.'* The sisters soon bought an apartment in the same building as Vianney's, and Charito moved to Kirrawee. The house at Marrickville was sold and Marian moved into a rented townhouse nearby, not far from Maureen's place. It was Marian's first experience of living alone. *I'd been there for less than a year when I got a cat. My first cat—Mr Morse. He was a beautiful cat and I loved him. So I had a companion. I had a feline companion.* Marian was glad to be close enough to keep an eye on Maureen. *She was getting discernibly more forgetful and we were all getting more worried. She was going to see various doctors all the time. We weren't sure what would transpire.*

Things for the Sydney sisters were beginning to fragment. Vianney, who had retired from her work in physiotherapy, was very involved with her local parish at Kirrawee, though she still came to Redfern occasionally. There, the St Vincent's parish was running itself, more or less—Ted had suffered two strokes, and had retired to the Southern Highlands. In 2004, Marian changed jobs after the priest at Forest Lodge died. She returned to her original setting, a Catholic girls' school, taking a part-time role at Kincoppal-Rose Bay, where she provided some pastoral care for the boarders and ran liturgical gatherings for each class. *There would be big feast days where you'd have to do liturgical things, special Masses and so on. It really wasn't enough to keep me occupied, frankly. I think they wanted to tick a box that said 'nun doing liturgical coordinating'.* She still met regularly with a small group of Jean Houston enthusiasts at her flat, and she did her best to support Maureen.

In May 2005, Ted Kennedy died. An enormous funeral was held in Redfern, where Ted had wanted it, starting with a smoking ceremony at St Vincent's church and making a procession down Redfern Street towards the Block, where a giant marquee—the biggest his friends could find—held more than a thousand mourners. All the Sydney sisters were there, of course, along with many Aboriginal people from the local community and beyond, as well as two former high court judges, several current and former politicians, and at least seventy priests, three bishops and a cardinal. A didgeridoo accompanied the coffin's journey to the altar; Aboriginal children brought the bread and wine for the Eucharist; and the congregation shared the warm, authentic and joyful kiss of peace that was always shared in Ted's church. The prayers, songs and eulogies—some planned, many spontaneous—lasted three hours. Ted's friend, the former priest and judge Chris Geraghty, described the deceased as 'upright, uncompromising, a living treasure, hard, earthy, compassionate, welcoming sinners, a pebble in the comfortable boot of establishment, a man who spilt his guts for others'. He prayed:

> Our Father Ted comes before you, Lord, with a life poured out for all, with empty pockets and dirty hands … Raise up an army of Kennedys in our midst to bandage the wounded, to

> bury the dead, to share the fruits of your earth, to protect the weak and welcome the stranger.[8]

+++

By the middle of 2005, Maureen's health had deteriorated, and her memory was becoming worse. She had long understood what was happening to her. That year, she wrote:

> My life is coming to an end. The path ahead is not so long. I walk in darkness, yet the darkness is luminous. My memory is becoming very bad … That's a bit scary. And I'm losing eyesight. Not reading, not being able to see what others see, is a huge loss. At first I was very, very depressed and angry. Now I look on myself as having all the time in the world to do what I want. I don't have to do anything and I've got so many loving people around me. I don't have to rush off. I think that this is what contemplative life is meant to be like.[9]

Marian was the leader, now, and she could see that a decision had to be made about Maureen's care. *She was getting quite a lot of help, but somehow, between us we realised that she couldn't really stay in the place by herself. We kept her there as long as we possibly could.* There was a place run by the RSCJ sisters in Kensington, where a number of elderly nuns were living. The Sacred Heart sisters offered to keep Maureen with them for as long as she needed. Marian and Vianney sat Maureen down, at a meeting at her brother Sean's place. The idea of being permanently reinstitutionalised, and surrounded by nuns, cannot have been easy for Maureen to accept. It was Marian who broke the news. *And the darling woman … Really, she had enough nous to know, and she said, 'What's this meeting all about? You know, I suspect something.' And I had to tell her, being the leader. And she sort of went,*

'Agh!' And then she said, 'Yes of course I have to do this.' It was like the old obedience coming through, and saying yes, she would do it. And so anyway, that's what happened. She went into care.

Vianney, who was still treasurer, thought it would be best for Marian to join her and Charito in Kirrawee, and when a nearby unit came up for sale, they bought it. It was a garden apartment, and Marian could bring her cat. In the midst of Marian's move, in late 2005, Maureen took a turn for the worse. *I knew that once she went to hospital, that was going to be it, really.* She went into hospital with heart problems, but the staff didn't know how to manage her dementia. *They'd bring her food on a tray covered with plastic stuff. She didn't know how to get to the food. She was practically starving. And they'd taken her glasses away, so she couldn't see. It was really terrible when I think about it.*

Marian and Vianney spent many hours at Maureen's bedside. *There was one beautiful moment where she was a bit clearer, and Vianney and I were both there, and she said, 'You know, I just want to thank you two for all you've done.' Oh, I was nearly in tears. I'm in tears now. She said, 'You know, you've kept me in my place as long as you could. And you've been wonderful. You've looked after me.' It was probably the most lucid thing she said for a long time.* Maureen had always been a very important spiritual leader for their little community, and Marian found it extremely hard to watch her decline. *Oh, she was a leading light. It was kind of incomprehensible in a way.* When Maureen's physical health improved, the hospital said she had to go. Marian and Vianney scrambled to find somewhere to take Maureen, who needed extra care now. In the end, they found her a place at a fairly grim aged care facility in Surry Hills, where Maureen had to share a room. Marian had already cleaned out the Dulwich Hill flat, and now she cleaned out Maureen's belongings from the place at Kensington and moved Maureen to Surry Hills.

It was the most awful moment leaving her there. It was the beginning of December, about December the 5th, 2005. The place was kind of all being decorated for Christmas, and I remember just being there, with her in that bed, and she was asleep, I think. And I'm saying … I was really saying, 'God, take her.' I was just so upset. And I came away from there, I remember stopping the car and bursting into tears. 'I just can't do it.'

A little while later, Maureen's sister, Margaret, announced that she was going to throw a seventieth birthday party for Maureen. *And she organised that we'd have it at the RACV Club in the city. Poor Maureen! We sort of got her dressed. It was on the 22nd of December, her actual birthday. And Carol came up, and she had friends there. She had some lucidity on that day, and she sang 'Paddy McGinty's Goat'. It was just extraordinary. The whole song! We were all laughing and clapping and all that. And she thanked everybody for being there. And I had this feeling I was at her funeral, but she was there. It was a very wonderful occasion.*

On Christmas morning, Marian and Maureen had Mass together at the chapel, and Maureen sat down to Christmas lunch with all the other aged residents being cared for there. *The thing that broke my heart—she couldn't find her mouth. They had to feed her the ice cream.* Marian said goodbye to Maureen, and left to share Christmas dinner with Vianney and her family. *And I never saw her alive again. She died the next day—I'm grateful she did. Thank God she did.*

ENDINGS, 2019

MAUREEN

Maureen died on Boxing Day, 2005, and was buried in January 2006. Marie flew over from New Zealand, and all the sisters from Melbourne came up to Sydney for her funeral. Even Betty, who had been in aged care for years, was able to join that sad, joyful reunion. A huge funeral was held at Redfern, and Maureen was buried at Rookwood.

Maureen had arrived at the end of her life without earthly possessions, and without the same faith that had motivated her to become a nun almost half a century earlier. She remained, nonetheless, a deeply faithful, spiritual woman. In her final essay, she wrote:

> I live alone in this little unit. This is my convent. I try not to be too concerned about what might happen to me. My spiritual practice is mainly sitting still. Focusing on the breath, but gently, not worrying about it. Sitting still and letting myself become perfectly quiet, no thoughts. The distractions come, but I let them go. There is the sense of knowing something, but not knowing what it is. Sometimes I simply gaze at the beautiful green leaves of the pot-plant in the corner of my room. Gazing at the plant, my mind slows down and I go very still. There is something divine in the plant, as there was in the monstrance

> so many years ago. Yes, it is the same thing. A sense of presence; of God, Jesus, angels, saints, even my brother Peter who died a few years go. I know for sure they are all around me these days.[1]

Her many grieving friends reflected upon one of Maureen's most well-worn quips, that she had been *the best possible nun of the worst possible kind.* Her vocation had led her to unforeseen challenges, joys and losses, and she had stayed constant to it. At Maureen's funeral, Vianney claimed a place for that incisive, critical, rebellious, but ultimately loyal woman in her Church. *She was never other than a daughter of the Church, but she came to eschew mediocrity and the institutional structures that bound rather than freed people. She was equally intolerant of hypocrisy and patriarchal oppression.*

The assembled Blessed Sacrament sisters shared a night of storytelling the evening after the funeral, together with Maureen's family and friends. Maureen's obituary, published in the *Sydney Morning Herald*, reported one of her confidences, shared from the pulpit that day: 'If I believed in reincarnation, I'd like to come back and have lots of sex.'

VIANNEY

Living alone suited Vianney. She was not lonely—by early 2006 she had Marian as well as Charito as close neighbours. Betty was also nearby, at a nursing home in Cronulla. Vianney's flat was not far from where her brother, Mick, and his wife, Beryl, lived, and she enjoyed their regular company, along with a generous number of close friendships. Vianney had always stayed in touch with dozens of people—from her university days, from her time in California, her years in Pueblo, and from her professional life as a physio. She was an honorary aunt to the children of her closest friends, always taking a keen interest in their activities and great joy and pride in their accomplishments. Her friend Wendy, whom she met working as a physio in southeast Sydney, shared Vianney's passion for live performance and the two of them went to the symphony together, and later cultivated an interest in opera, too. Her friend Mary, whom she'd met just before entering the convent, remained among her closest friends until Mary's death, and Vianney made regular trips to visit Jenny, an artist who lived on the central coast. *I'm really blessed because I have these three wonderful women friends.*

She stayed in touch with Ray, too, but never regretted choosing to remain a Blessed Sacrament sister, forsaking the attractions of coupledom. *I'd like to say that I was being faithful to my own calling, which I hope I was … But I've fallen in love with a few people. I suppose it happens, doesn't it?*

Vianney visited Ray in Winnipeg at the end of his life, when he was unwell and suffering from early dementia. *I think it was probably a mistake, because I got there and after we talked for a while, it was as if there was nothing more to talk about … I thought 'What can I do? He can't talk. He's getting tired; I'm getting tired.'* Vianney kept herself busy by helping with the housework. *There was a whole lot of ironing there, and I just went to this little alcove and ironed all his shirts. What could I do?*

Memories of her time in California, and with Ray, were precious to Vianney. *I'm glad I had that experience, even though it was painful. I was able to say that I truly and really felt I was loved. And we can go through life not being sure of that, you know? And so, I've been able to hold on to that as a reality and as something that's really important for me—that I really felt from him that I was loved. And that's a great learning.*

In 2003, Vianney wrote a short essay, which she named 'Unfinished thoughts'.

The essay asks what Adoration means for Vianney at this time in her life, and attempts to describe where she has arrived in her spirituality. She begins her answer with a quotation from Drusilla Modjeska's *Stravinsky's Lunch*, which describes a painting by Grace Cossington Smith:

'A cup and saucer, two vases and three jugs are arranged on a table beneath a window in the studio, drawing our attention inwards, although above the table we are shown a narrow band of window, a last glimpse out into the garden. The weight bears down on the table. The one in the middle has a fancy handle, but the others are modest, everyday kitchen jugs, the sort that might be used for vases. The cup and saucer are very white, a translucent white, waiting to be filled.'[2]

When I come to describe my spirituality now, it is imaged in this painting. It is not my favourite painting by this Australian woman artist but it captures a number of elements that are important to me in my life now. I like its ordinariness, the daily-ness of it. Each morning I have my coffee from a large blue cup. It has a wide-open circular rim and it signals the start of my day … waiting to be filled. I like the jugs … they are a feminine symbol … round, chunky, able to be filled and able to pour out what they contain.

My spirituality is pretty ordinary. Life is embraced anew each day. I find myself tired at the end of a day but refreshed by sleep and able to begin again to be filled and poured out. The jug is a pleasing symbol.

The image of a jug, filling and emptying, might also represent the contrast between what was long understood as the two kinds of sisterly vocation: the active and the contemplative. Yet Vianney had long since come to reject the distinction between so-called active and contemplative nuns, and especially any suggestion that the contemplative life was the higher spiritual road. *You can't pluck one value and put it at the top of the list of who we are and what we do and how our spirituality is lived.* Vianney was both the filled jug and the self-emptying jug, drawing sustenance from prayer and a curious, questioning approach to the scriptures, but also from her action in the world. Filling herself with prayer, with walks in the bush and nights at the symphony that brought her closer to God; pouring herself out and sharing herself with her family, her friends, her sisters and her church community.

This sense of balance, perhaps, along with her practicality and her wisdom, helped Vianney to remain open and adaptable in the face of constant change. *Even though we changed so much, it never bothered me that the so-called contemplative life was changed, because my vocation was Eucharistic. And once my understanding of Eucharist changed, then, yes—the whole possibility of what can happen changes.*

Throughout most of her retirement, Vianney remained quite energetic and industrious. As she wrote in 'Unfinished Thoughts'

> In practice, then, my spirituality … my adoration is my daily life. Un-spectacular, unnoticed, unsung, unremembered. The day to day involved times of silence and reflection, work for the administration and financial management of our Community, care of our Sisters in Aged Care or in our community. Time on the telephone, the computer, at the stove, in the laundry, at the supermarket, in the theatre, on paths near the beach …

She fulfilled her duties as treasurer of the Australian community and managed its funds very well. She made a trip to Vietnam with Marian to welcome a new and growing province of Blessed Sacrament sisters into the congregation. Vianney also served her local parish community, conducting regular communion services at St Patrick's in Sutherland, and delivering homilies at weekday Mass. If there was one thing that Vianney always missed from her years as a cloistered nun, it was the beautiful singing. She sang in the St Patrick's church choir for many years.

In 2011 Vianney undertook only her second term as community leader. It was around this time that she began to feel some stiffness in her legs. Assuming it was muscle fatigue, Vianney treated herself as any physio would, but the pain didn't go away. When she eventually saw a doctor, she was diagnosed with bone cancer, and began a difficult course of chemo and radiotherapy. In 2016, Vianney moved into residential aged care in Sutherland, close to where she had been living for more than twenty-five years. Marian had moved to Melbourne the year before, but made regular trips to Sydney to visit, and Vianney was never short of company, with her many friends, as well as Mick and Beryl, calling in on her very often.

Vianney had given her youth, from the day she entered in 1957, aged twenty-one, until a decade and a half later, to a contemplative way of life to which she hadn't been especially attracted, and whose spiritual value and common sense she always questioned. She is not prone to regrets, but near the end of her life, she could reflect upon the ways in which being a nun had set her apart from others. *I don't play cards. I'm not even interested in playing cards, but I look at some people playing cards and I think, 'I really wish I knew how to do that.' Or I go to the singing on a Tuesday night and there's all these different songs and I don't know the songs. And I think, 'Oh, dear me, I wish I knew some of those songs,' but I learn them. There's a whole lot that you do miss out on, so you have to recognise that.*

Yet those difficult years of enclosure and silence gave Vianney inner resources that have nourished her during these final years of her life. *I learned a lot in those first fourteen years, I think. Learning to find ways that I could grow within myself. You had to learn to be happy in yourself, and part of that probably goes back even to my years in boarding school. You had to learn to be independent, and to look after yourself … And I think that maybe some of those skills are not so well learned in society today … People are lonely, people are sad, because nobody has helped them to recognise their own gifts and to recognise the strength that they've got, that they can draw on when they're alone. Many old people haven't learned how to be alone, and for it to be a nurturing and a fruitful way of life. If you don't grasp that when you come into an aged care facility then you can be very lonely. And I see it in people around here.*

The process of remembering and speaking about her early life as a Blessed Sacrament sister wasn't always easy for Vianney. She was quite sick during the time the interviews for this book were conducted. Often, she felt tired and sometimes frustrated by the difficulty of recalling a particular detail or of bringing to mind the word she was looking for. Her cancer treatment made her immune system very vulnerable, and she was easily hospitalised by the mildest and most common of infections. After one afternoon of interviewing, Vianney said she'd suffered an upset stomach. *And I'm wondering to myself is it because I'm thinking of these things that I'm a bit emotional …*

I was surprised after the first time we spoke that I was stirred up. Talking about some of those early days, you touched on some ways of looking at those early days that I hadn't thought of. And I thought that I'd thought of every kind of possibility. But a number of the questions you asked me were new. So that took a certain amount of re-thinking about things. So I was stirred up and I wasn't well the next day.

And then I began to see that as you asked me different sorts of questions, it meant that I opened up to a whole new way of looking at things that was different and that expanded my understanding of what those early days had been. So that was interesting.

And also, somehow or other, talking about those early years made me realise they were tough and it made me realise how we really had to be strong. We had to be strong, but we had to also be sure about what we wanted to be and to do and to become as sisters … I think it made me think of the people who stayed and the people who left … and the fact that we had only sixteen who actually stayed and made final vows, so it's not many. I was thinking that a number of people who left included people who shouldn't have been there in the first place, and that's not a fault against them. But it's a fact that it takes a certain amount of … I don't know what it takes … a certain kind of character to be able to sustain this kind of life. I agree with that, and I agree that the life itself is very good, if it's lived well.

Vianney's reflections on those early years have led her to form two great certainties: that people need friends, and that they need intellectual and creative nourishment. *Of all things that I'm absolutely sure about, I'm sure that every person needs friends, and needs the possibility of communication with those friends.* The privation that came from not being able to communicate with Maureen and her fellow sisters, and from what she called the rather 'flimsy' nature of the spiritual formation offered to them as novices, left their mark. But Vianney has never wished to leave the sisterhood she chose as a very young woman. She wrote a reflective essay in 2003, describing how she had come to live and understand her faith.

> I have not outgrown my interest in things of the spirit and my quest for the holy and the sacred. I read, I listen to music, I look at beautiful art works, I walk in the bush in the early morning and God's presence is often a conscious reality at these times. I value my family and friends and my associations with older women from many different walks of life. I especially value my companions who help me in the search to live a holy life.
>
> My images of God are changing. I am still able to relate to the God who is the Father and who has been the object of my love and commitment for so long, but I am disillusioned by the constant images of a male God, a Lord, a monarch, a king, authoritarian and unchanging. My most helpful image of God is as my Friend. I need to feel connected and somehow recognised as equal and of value to this God.

At the same time, Vianney never ceased being a questioner and a keen, analytical critic of the institutions to which she belonged.

> I try to be loyal to a church, (none so ugly, none so beautiful—JH Newman) of which I do not always feel proud, and to

intentionally belong to a Religious Congregation whose articulated vision often seems narrow and uninspiring.[3]

Compared with the 1950s, very few Australian Catholics these days attend Benediction, or pray before the Eucharist with any particular fervour. Jesus's presence has expanded. Yet Catholic dogma maintains that something mystical happens when a priest, granted the power to do so by ordination, consecrates the bread and wine at the Mass.

Yeah well, I have to tell you that I don't believe in that magic trick as such. From my time at Berkeley and our liturgy studies there, it's not those words but the whole prayer that is what you call consecratory. Now, I won't go further than that. I don't think there's a magic trick. We haven't thought that for a long time, have we?

If you ask the question about the magic moment, you're asking a question about transubstantiation: how does it happen? And I'm saying we don't have to believe the 'how' of it. We don't know: it's a mystery. But that it happens—that, we have to believe, if we choose to believe.

When we come to Mass on Sunday what it should be is an occasion when the people of God gather together to celebrate who they are as the people of God, chosen and called. And they do that by listening to the Word of God and by sharing bread and wine. We believe that in doing so, Jesus is present with us—because we came together, and because we shared bread and wine. Now, I might be a heretic, but that's my believing, now.

Vianney no longer prays before the Blessed Sacrament. She became too unwell to attend St Patrick's for the monthly exposition. *But we've got a little quiet room downstairs with a tabernacle and if I was Vianney of 1952 I'd be down there in front of that tabernacle.* Instead, Vianney prays in her room. *I believe that Jesus is everywhere.* She sits in a comfortable chair, alongside the glass door that gives onto her balcony, overlooking the nursing home's courtyard. *There's a lovely tree over here that I'm a bit attached to. It's lovely against the sky.* The gum reaches its graceful branches upwards, its loose crown waving grey-green leaves among the blue.

Vianney has never stopped questioning, never stopped learning and thinking. *I read a lot, and so I'm grateful that I'm still able to both see and concentrate.* Marie and Marian stay in touch with her by phone, and Marian visits several times a year. The three of them share what they've been reading and thinking. They continue to form a community and to support one another—emotionally, intellectually and spiritually. They respect and value their individual gifts and differences.

Vianney compares the spirituality that compelled her to the convent with her experience of God now. *I thought that I had beauty and that that's what I could give. Now, having sat at the feet of some great theologians, I know we can give nothing to God—nothing at all ... We can give nothing because all is given—it's all given by God.*

As she wrote in 2003, the spirituality she has come to know and practise at the end of her life 'is un-spectacular ... yoked to Eucharist, and worthy, because all life is gift and worthy of the Giver'.

JILL

Newly married Jill and Kevin Maher embarked upon their life together with humble resources and high hopes, settling down in Melbourne's northern suburban fringe. *When we bought the house at Greensborough, which was within six months or nine months, I walked in—there was the main bedroom, the second bedroom—'Oh I can fit three beds in here, and I can fit two beds in that little one. Oh, five children. Oh, this will be great!'*

But Jill didn't fall pregnant, and after they'd been married for nearly a year, Jill and Kevin decided to try adoption. About six months later, they brought home an eight-week-old blue-eyed baby boy. *Michael was a beautiful baby!* Not long after, they adopted a daughter, Michelle.

Jill loved motherhood, and though she was mostly focused on caring for the family and the home, she also did some paid work, selling encyclopaedias door to door, pushing Michael in the pram. The extra money came in handy. *We bought a caravan, a second-hand caravan, with my earnings.*

When Michelle was ten and Michael had just started high school, Kevin lost his job. He had worked for decades at a Melbourne yarn factory. *He wasn't in the union. And he'd had TB and they wouldn't put him on super. They put him on a life insurance that would have only paid out if he died, something like that. And in the end, he was made redundant after thirty years with no thanks from anybody. It destroyed him.* Kevin was only fifty-two—not ready to retire, with a young family to support, but old enough that he struggled to find a new job. He couldn't bring himself to apply for the dole, and though he did find some work, he never found a secure, full-time job.

Jill and Kevin joined forces as salespeople in the garment business, but they struggled to make a comfortable living. Jill applied furiously for any permanent full-time job she might be qualified for, but she had limited experience. *No qualification—I couldn't even type … and I was one of five hundred with every application I put in.* After six months she got a call from the Victorian Department of Education to come in for an interview. Jill accepted, but she was terrified. *I was so acutely stressed I was physically sick. Anyway, I got the job.* The stress didn't end there, as Jill was now working full-time while doing most of the domestic work. *Did the shopping, cleaned the house on the Saturday, did the washing, prepared meals for the week … And after nine months I got angina, and I had a coronary bypass. And I was so frightened of losing the job that I was back at work in six weeks. Yeah, it was tough.*

After her health scare, Kevin began to help Jill more around the house. *Kevin learned how to use the washing machine and the vacuum cleaner while I was sick in hospital … He'd actually do the whole washing—hang it out, bring it in, sort it out, put it on your bed. He was good. If I was pruning, he'd pick everything up and put it in the bin.*

When the children were in their late teens, Jill and Kevin thought about moving. They had been to the north coast of New South Wales a couple of times, caravanning with the kids, *and we were very happy up here. I loved it.* They saved their money—Kevin was now on a disability pension, due to his partial deafness—and moved up to Coffs Harbour when Michelle was finishing high school. It was a fresh start. *We used to picnic during the week, Kevin and I. We'd go out for lunch on a different headland. You know, it was all so new and beautiful. And then we got into the retirement way—Probus on this day and the pool on a Friday, and travel club on Saturday, and out every other Sunday.*

Jill and Kevin made lots of new friends in Coffs Harbour. *Kevin did, and he took me along with him, thank God, because otherwise I would have stayed home gardening and not bothered. I'm very shy.* They had a happy marriage. *We were good friends. We were understanding.* There was very little conflict between them—not just because they got along well, but also because Jill found it difficult to disagree with her husband. *It took me seventeen years to answer him back. I just went into my shell. And he'd know, and he'd be so upset.*

Jill thinks her fearfulness and meekness were a legacy of her time in the convent. *Oh yes. Oh yes … I'll put up with anything rather than upset anybody.*

The last five years of her marriage with Kevin were particularly enjoyable, *mainly because Kevin got the travel bug. Going away, it was good for us, and the cruises were good except you get the flu quite badly.* They travelled to many places in Australia, and to New Zealand as well.

Kevin died in late 2018, and eighteen months after his loss, Jill was still very much grieving for him. *It's just so different. You don't have anyone to share. And even if Kevin was difficult, he was besotted with me, and he did care for me. And you've got no one to share it with. No one really cares. You've just got to cope with yourself.* Michael lives with his mother, and like Jill, he is shy. Michelle and her husband and daughter, Grace, live in Queensland. They visit every Christmas and Easter and Jill tries to go up and visit once or twice a year.

Jill still finds it hard to communicate—another legacy of the convent. It's more noticeable now that Kevin isn't by her side when she is at a social event. *I mean, I went to New Zealand with the travel club in May, for seventeen days. I didn't communicate because of my lack of skills.* She talks on the phone with Michelle, *and she talks! She's very loving.* But even answering the phone can be a challenge for Jill. *You didn't use the phone in the convent. I might have spoken once to my parents on the phone, but not otherwise. So I find it hard to pick up the phone, now.*

Looking back on her life as a nun, Jill has very mixed feelings and impressions. When she considers the rules—about how often you could wash your hair, for example—she says *it was ridiculous really, when you think about it ... I think you accept sacrifice, but you don't make it deliberately, right?*

Yet Jill couldn't see much sense in all the changes the sisters who chose to remain went through, either. She would visit them quite often while she lived in Melbourne, taking the kids to Armadale during the 1970s. *I just thought they were crazy. And I thought, 'There's no way I would ever have joined them if they were that sort of people.' My perception of the order was complete devotion to the Blessed Sacrament. It was more the meditative side of it. I know there are a lot of bad things in not being allowed to talk and all of that, but it was the spiritual side of it, and I couldn't see how spiritual they were when they were rushing round doing things.*

Jill was surprised to receive a card from Vianney a couple of years ago, with a generous cheque enclosed, acknowledging and honouring the contribution Jill and her years of work in altar breads had made to the welfare and financial position of the Servants of the Blessed Sacrament in Australia. *I was delighted! Absolutely delighted! ... And I did appreciate it—the fact that they still considered me part of the family.*

Because, you know, you feel you've dishonoured your vocation in a way by leaving, and you don't really deserve anything. But no, it was nice.

Jill feels grateful that her life took the direction it did, and that she and Kevin were able to give Michael and Michelle a home. *Kevin and I have lived for the kids. We haven't spent anything on ourselves. Always, the kids have come first.* And she is still thankful for her time in the convent, too. *I think it's been very enriching, and I think that I would have found it hard to get through life without a deep love and faith in God because there's an awful lot of stress in life. It's really hard.*

The best thing about her life in the convent, Jill says, was *a closeness to God. That was definitely there.* She has always retained her faith. *Oh yes. That won't change. That's immutable. Everything else can go, but not that. So I don't look at the bad things in the Church. I look at what's beyond.*

The changes in the Church, changes that were part of the Vatican II reforms, have been good for Catholics like Jill. *Like when we go to Mass, these days we're not so all wound up in the silence and what have you. You go up to Holy Communion, then you go out and have a cup of tea with everybody. And I feel, at this stage of my life, certainly I need company, but every person that I meet in my age group is very lonely and I listen to them and I empathise with them. And it does everybody good. And I think that's what God wants.*

BARBARA

Barbara's spiritual life didn't fundamentally change after she left the Servants of the Blessed Sacrament in 1997. *It's taken me on turns just as it began … It was in tune with my experience.* Just as she accepted the strictures of the Rule of Life when she first entered the convent at Armadale, she accepted each and every change, every challenge, that life presented to her. *Because the essence of it was stable. The essence of who I was could never be changed, and it could never be destroyed. It was how I felt all along, because that was my truth.*

When Barbara decided to leave the Servants of the Blessed Sacrament, her sister Mercia, who had also left her order of nuns, invited Barbara to retire and join her in Redcliffe, on the edge of Moreton Bay, just north of central Brisbane. There, the two of them continued to hold their Course in Miracles meetings out of a spare room in their house. Barbara was very happy living with Mercia, who was really a fellow mystic—like Barbara, she had experienced a revelatory moment in her childhood where *she felt a ray of golden light go into her. And she said that pierced her with an incredible joy.*

Living with Mercia was *very easy, because we both had the same spirituality. We are very different personalities, in the sense that she was very outgoing. Her experience was joy, so whenever we were going to visit someone, she would send her light and her joy ahead of her. Because joy was her thing. And somehow she always spoke something that she knew would give somebody joy.*

Barbara still goes to Mass most Sundays, at a parish where the priest is very open-minded. In any case, differences between herself and her Church have never bothered Barbara. *No, I didn't care what the Pope said. If he said something contrary, I wouldn't challenge it—I didn't take any notice of it … And even the local priests, if they preached something, saying we were all sinners, I would think to myself, 'Oh, God only sees our innocence.' I can't say it, because the Bible says those who say they're without sin are doubly sinful, so there's no challenging this, but I just … in my own self I kept to my truth.*

Mercia died in 2009, and Barbara has lived alone in Redcliffe ever since. Before moving to Queensland, she received a proper send-off from her sisters in Sydney. *Before leaving Newtown we did have a Eucharistic Meal of thanksgiving together. Since then whenever I meet up with the sisters we meet as very good friends. Thanks be to God there is no 'least or last mentality' to get in the way.* Barbara has no regrets about leaving, any more than she has for the years she dedicated to the life of enclosure at Armadale, or to the house of hospitality at Newtown. *I give thanks for it all.*

Barbara still holds fast to her experience—that moment of revelation she had as a little girl on the farm at Moree. *I didn't know it was to lead to the greatest blessing. The True Self was there always. There when I didn't know. The profoundest gratitude that I woke up to the wellspring of all thanksgiving. The True Self is complete—nothing can be added to it or taken away. I am grateful I was saved from misery so early. Each brand new day has its own thanksgivings where nothing is impossible. The love story continues and I am still surrendering separation to oneness.*

MELISSA

Melissa remembers her final months in the convent, from Marius Garail's visit to her return to her family and to the stage, as an intensely exciting time of new possibilities. *It was like a huge surge of the Holy Spirit. It's like the Holy Spirit went, 'Wham! Out you go! That's where I want you.' And of course, it's followed on. It's wonderful.*

And when she decided to leave for good, she had no regrets and no recriminations. *I'd had the most wonderful experience that I could ever have hoped for, because it was an internal spiritual experience. Look, the trappings of it weren't important to me. They didn't worry me at all. I was hell-bent on this spiritual journey—this level of consciousness that I was seeking. I was hell-bent on that. So the peripherals didn't matter a damn. I wouldn't have cared where I was.*

Nor did she experience any breach between her past in the convent and her future as a performer. She felt it was all an act of grace. *I was buoyed up. It was as though I was being carried along. And that's what I mean by grace.*

Her return to life as a performer presented her with challenges, but even those only served to illuminate the ways in which the Holy Spirit was at work. *What I knew I had to do was to learn to act properly.*

I mean, I had to because I'd had four years not doing anything. So I thought, 'I have to smarten myself up, you know. I have to get back into the routine of this, back into the aura of this. It's a new world to me now, because I've been away for a long time.'

And I began to understand that principle that it wasn't me doing the work; that I was there doing my bit but it was the creative spirit within me doing the work. I began to understand the Spirit of Creativity, which I think that any actor or any musician—anybody in the arts—knows they have, but doesn't quite understand it. You know, when you're working on a script or something, you get an idea, and you think, 'Where did that come from?' There is an inspirational flow, I think, to all creativity. And that's buoyed me along. That took me along. And, of course, I had to work hard. I had to work very hard.

Never interested in motherhood—*I think it's a gift, and I don't have that gift*—Melissa dedicated herself wholeheartedly to acting, and has never stopped working. In 1974 she gained her first film role as Beth in Peter Weir's debut feature, a horror comedy called *The Cars That Ate Paris.* Two years later, she shared an AACTA award for Best Actress in a Supporting Role opposite Jacki Weaver in the historical drama *Caddie.* During the 1980s she became a very familiar face on Australian television, with many roles, including in the long-running series *Mother and Son* and *A Country Practice,* as well as the mini-series *Land of Hope.* In a particularly apt bit of casting, Melissa played Sister Attracta in the immensely popular ABC miniseries, *Brides of Christ,* which told the story of a convent school in the 1960s, its nuns struggling to come to grips with the changing times that the schoolgirls embodied. Later, Melissa was a member of the *Police Rescue* and *All Saints* casts, and in 2015 she appeared in *Mad Max: Fury Road.*

Melissa always remained passionate about the stage, and her face is as familiar to Australian theatregoers as it is to TV audiences.

When she was interviewed for this book, she was preparing to travel to the UK for performances of *The Secret River* at the Edinburgh Festival and London's National Theatre.

After a brief and ill-fated marriage, Melissa found lifelong love—she and her partner spent the next forty years together. *If you're lucky enough to catch that, you can sail through the difficulties of life much easier. Sandy was a musician. She wrote music for theatre, and her creative spirit was very much alive, and she was open to all possibilities of life. We met, and it was as though we were meant to be together—talk about soulmates.*

Love became part of Melissa's experience of God's revelation. *It's such an important development in the contemplative journey, to realise and accept the love, which is a gift in itself, from a human being who doesn't fit the stereotype that I had in my mind as a Catholic girl growing up. It never occurred to me that the love that God would give me would come from another woman. I was perfectly straight, and quite actively so, before I entered the convent. But then I met this person.*

When Sandy died, Melissa moved back to Melbourne, to be close to her sister and the rest of her family. Now in her eighties, she is grateful that she can still find plenty of meaningful, fulfilling work. *Scripts are awful sometimes for elderly people.* On the other hand, her age can be an asset, and directors are keen to cast her. *If you are old and you can still walk and talk and not fall over the furniture, you can stagger around.* Melissa and her friend Peter Carroll seem to almost monopolise roles for older actors in Australia. *They're either dead or they can't do it anymore—it's by the grace of God that I can do it.* And she still enjoys it. *I love the company of actors. I love the company of actors! I always have. There's nothing as much fun as sitting in a caravan full of actors on a film set when they're waiting, you know, the day's dragging on … Honestly, it's so funny sometimes. It's just wonderful.*

Throughout her busy career, Melissa maintained her connection with her former sisters, and remained particularly close to Maureen, who had been her Novice Mistress. *Maureen was wonderful. I lived in Chippendale and she lived in Newtown, and so we saw a lot of each other. I stayed in touch with her until she died.* Through Maureen, Melissa met Marian, who entered the convent at Armadale after Melissa had left it, and she saw the other sisters from time to time, both at the house on Forbes Street and at Mass in Redfern, which Melissa attended occasionally. *Oh, I loved that church! I loved that church. Now, that was an exception. All through the changes, that was a wonderful church.*

Melissa has always felt a powerful sense of having been led along her life's path. *I feel that very, very strongly—that the initiative was never mine.* Whether it was entering the convent, or deciding to leave, she says *it was a shock to me, and I was drawn … A lot of people wouldn't agree with me and say, 'That's nonsense, of course. It's your own willpower.' But it's not just that. It's the awareness of that presence that is drawing you.*

The awareness of the presence of God, which first compelled her to the convent, remains at the heart of her life. *My spiritual practice is being, and there is an alertness to being, and there's an awareness of presence. It's about presence, really. It's about presence.* For Melissa, this practice is essentially the same one she devoted herself to as a young nun, subject to the rules of the convent and the requirements of the Divine Office and perpetual Adoration. *We were witnessing to a presence. I mean, all right, we did it in white clothes, we knelt down. For twenty-four hours, there was somebody there in front of the Blessed Sacrament exposed. That was what our forms were doing, but what our consciousness was doing was being aware. Our consciousness was aware of that reality.*

She lives alone, with her little dog, and her spiritual practice is very simple. *I have a cup of tea every morning with the dog on my lap and that's it. God is in the water. You can't see anything apart from God. I look out the window and see these lovely flowers, I have this lovely dog, and I nurse her on my knee and feel the life in her. I just know—there is only God.*

That contemplative practice sets her up for the day. *At my age, I have to be aware of that presence all the time, and when my mind starts thinking about things I think, 'Uh oh, just be in the space between the thoughts.'*

Melissa eschews labels like 'Catholic' or 'ex-nun'. *When I came out, that was one of the first things that occurred to me—that I didn't want to be labelled anything.* And although she no longer needs its rituals or dogmas, she is disappointed in the Church. *The institution itself has suffered greatly because it hasn't moved with the Holy Spirit. It's stayed there, and the Spirit's been pushing. So it's happening in other ways, now. They've had opportunities but …* She recognises that what she experiences as continuity in her spiritual life, others would see as something quite different. *Most practising Catholics would say, 'That woman is seriously deluded, and don't listen to her.' That doesn't worry me in the slightest.*

Melissa no longer goes to Mass—*anything that takes me away from that awareness of the presence of being is a distraction*—but she rejects the idea that she has left the Church. *I am the Church, you know—we are the Church. The people are the Church. And when the people are moved in various directions, the Church has to move with them, or the Church remains this establishment. I mean, that was one of the first things they said at the Council: 'The Church is the people of God.' And that means all people. It's not an institution, it's not a building, it's not an establishment, not a boys' club.*

Melissa remains a believer. *I can't explain how this has happened to me, but I have never been more aware of the presence. I've never been more alert to the love. And I've never wanted less to go through the rituals of religion.*

MARIE

About two years into the experiment at Teschemakers, Marie was becoming disillusioned. She felt the group had lost its original focus. *Something in me said whatever it was that attracted me originally to the nuns, I'm over it. I felt that we were spending so much time on sort of superficial interaction. In the meantime, the Earth is possibly burning and we need to concentrate on these really big issues, and we were pettily fighting about who's in charge of what. I just didn't like it.* There were other problems, too. *Well, we had no money; we weren't making anything from workshops.* The Dominican nuns in New Zealand who supported the project from the beginning now expected the community to be financially self-sufficient *and we couldn't possibly do that—an old place with buildings over one hundred years old, needing repair.* The unravelling of Teschemakers was a blessing for Marie, in a sense. *I think the good thing was it helped me overcome my belief that I could go back into a community like a religious order.*

Marie had to decide what to do next. *So am I going to go back to Australia? Or am I going to stay here? And I felt I had work to complete here. I wasn't ready to go back yet. So the next thing was to rent a house. I got a nice little house almost at the heart of Oamaru. A hundred dollars a week.* The Servants of the Blessed Sacrament in Australia supported Marie with a stipend, and she earned her own money working at Michael's book bindery, for which she now had much more time. *We were really getting big orders for books, and I was the main book maker at that stage.*

Oamaru suited Marie. *It was different—small town living, which I'd never done before ... I loved it. And the family was there, so I was close by.* Marie felt a strong need to remain close to Michael and Gamel, her granddaughter. *And I had the privilege of Gamel staying with me sometimes for a night. I loved how Kahren and Michael would just trust that I would know how to look after her ... even though I had no experience of raising my own child. And Gamel loved staying.*

As Marie settled into life in Oamaru, she began thinking about finding a more permanent home. Before long, Michael spotted an old place, just across Oamaru Creek and the town's public gardens, atop the opposite hill from where he and his family lived. *Michael said to me, 'I've been looking at this little cottage. It's derelict; I can see it from my verandah.' And I went and had a look at it.* The house, first built in 1860, was in a fairly bad state, but it was on a quarter-acre block and was selling for just five thousand dollars. *There was grass almost up to my shoulders, and I'm sort of pushing the grass aside to make my way up to what is the front door with no door—no windows and no door!—and I'm thinking, 'I think he's gone mad! But remember that Michael's got a very good imagination.'*

Marie's mother had died in 1994, leaving Marie ten thousand dollars. Marie thought, *'Well, that's half of it. Maybe I can use the other half on boarding it up to make it weatherproof.'* She spent the next weeks and months looking on with joy and excitement, lending a hand where she could, as two local artisan builders, friends of Michael's, restored the place. They replaced the broken windowpanes, laid a new floor, and added shelves and a kitchen sink, along with a wood-fired stove and a working bathroom. It was still very basic. *To get connected to the grid was, I think, about thirty thousand dollars or something—just to put the electricity on. So I thought, 'No, no, no. I've always thought I'd like to try this romantic way of living again, how I grew up.'*

Marie moved into her candlelit, wood-warmed cottage in 1996. She was fifty-eight years old.

I wanted to live simply: poverty, celibacy, obedience. Poverty is just about living simply. That's how we interpreted it. For some people that would be living very poorly. But our charism never ever said that we had to live really, really poorly—just simply, and they emphasised that. So this was clearly a much simpler life.

The cottage became Marie's convent for one, and she got straight to work on its garden. Reaching above the head-high weeds were the beginnings of an orchard—an apple and three pear trees. *So I put in hazelnut trees. I think I have got about three up there—heaps of hazelnuts, now. And I put in a few more apple trees. I put in a feijoa tree and unfortunately the frost finally killed that one off. Two or three apple trees, a peach tree. And I've put in wattle trees because that creates such hot wood and it's very good for my stove.* She also planted a herb garden.

Marie began to make lots of friends in town (she is known around Oamaru as 'the nun with the son'), and threw herself into all manner of local activities. She helped arrange a New Zealand speaking tour for Sister Miriam McGillis, the nun she'd met on her study trip to the United States who focused on sustainable agriculture. She joined with neighbouring farmers and environmentalists to set up an organic food co-op, and she banded together with local activists against unwanted development. On one occasion Marie was with a large group protesting the construction of a public swimming pool in the town's main park. *That was the central green space and it was also an important place for the Māori people. And we were saying, there are other places in Oamaru where the swimming pool can go.* Police ordered the crowd to move on, but Marie dug in along with most of the others. *So I got escorted off towards the paddy wagon. And lo and behold, I couldn't believe it, there was Michael in the paddy wagon! I had never been in a police cell before. A once and only time … it was a bit of an adventure.*

One of the things Marie got involved with in Oamaru was the community garden. When she and her fellow community gardeners learned that the monarch butterfly had become a threatened species, they researched the creature's life cycle and Marie was amazed—*I had come very late in life to finding out how butterflies evolve.* She wanted to help, so she bought some milkweed plants, which came complete with the butterfly's tiny larvae on their leaves, and placed them inside her kitchen window, looking out onto her orchard.

I could see those little caterpillars getting fatter and fatter and fatter. Probably as fat as my little finger. And one day, one amazingly curled up—its tail came up towards its head as I was looking. It was like it devoured itself, turned inside out. It looked like a beautiful jewel, green with gold dots on it, and so the caterpillar that I'd seen crawling around is now inside that very small shell. And stays there I think nearly a week. He's made his cocoon. And he's waiting there. And I'd be watching it—such a wonderful thing to be part of seeing this unfolding. So later, as I was watching, I saw it was starting to shake a bit. It's alive and it's moving and I think it's trying to get out. And so the little cocoon breaks. And the butterfly with its big blackish wings flops out, still holding on with its legs and it stays like that for quite a while. And then after a bit longer it begins to want to move its wings, and dry the wings. And eventually it can actually take off and fly. And I watched them fly off. Extraordinary!

The whole process held great meaning for Marie. *Like with the enclosure: you know who you are, but then you go into this hidden state and you don't know who you are. And I'd lost my identity, I felt, when I joined the nuns, and I really went into … It was like a cocoon experience. The enclosure was really enclosing me, it was almost like a physical thing. Yes, that's quite like what it was like for me, to go inside this cocoon and then eventually, when the time is right, and you know when the time is right, you start moving enough to break the shell—to emerge. And emerging—well, for me, from our community, it took quite a while to really emerge and then eventually find my feet. But I could see the cycle of the butterfly fitted so beautifully with what happened to me. And I am sure others had romantic images like that as well. It's just nature teaching us what happens.*

For Marie, life at the cottage feels like a return to her roots—living the simple life she'd grown up with, and the contemplative life she'd sought as a young nun. *It's not unlike how it was when I joined the nuns, when we were making altar breads and we just had our prayer life and it was all very simple. I keep saying I feel I've done a full circle. It's very like my early years of living in enclosure, except I can go out and do my shopping and even, if I want to, go to the theatre occasionally. I can do all that.*

Marie's spirituality remains fundamentally contemplative. *Normally I get up, depending on the weather and the time of the year, probably six-thirty, sevenish, and I have about an hour where I have a long slow process of drinking a herbal tea.* Marie sips mate, a stimulating infusion especially favoured by the gauchos and rural people of Argentina, Uruguay and southern Brazil. She has an Argentine friend, Guillermo, with whom she engages in long phone conversations about matters spiritual, and he supplies her with it.

And it's in a one-litre flask—a nice lot of fluid to start the day with. I always think that's a good thing for my body and it feels good. So I sit in my comfortable chair there and I just quietly sip tea … My sacramental tea-drinking first thing in the morning … It's about just being in the present moment, of being awake in the here and now. I think that is what prayer is. Prayer is not thinking about God. The minute you start thinking you're not fully present—you're in your head again. So it's just being really awake and present … I used to be drawn to those books written by the mystics—they would talk about the grace of the present moment. Well, it's as simple as that. It's living with the grace of the present moment.

Marie contemplates, as she sips, all the properties of the tea—its warmth and smell and flavour, as well as the earth that it grew in, the human hands that harvested it. It's a Eucharistic contemplation. *So you're in your senses, which … I think we've made a big mistake over many years of moving away from our senses because we thought it was sensual—that the senses would tempt us to do things that the mind tells us we shouldn't do. But I've realised that befriending your senses is the most grounding and healthy and wholesome thing you could ever do. And I think that probably is the essence of prayer.*

The need to attend daily Mass has long since passed for Marie. *I think because I found a way to live Eucharist, being in the sacramental moment, I didn't feel the need then to go to all the individual Masses once a day like we grew up with.* Marie has suffered chronic vertigo since 2008, and can't make it down the hill to Mass on her own. *Nathalie, my neighbour two doors down, she often picks me up on a Saturday night and we go to the five o'clock Mass. And I love going down there with her.*

Still, it's not like the Masses Marie and her fellow sisters used to hold at Armadale in the 1970s, or the Tuesday night Eucharist at the chapel on Forbes Street. *I mean, if we nuns were running the Eucharist, we would probably do it quite differently. But you know, we've got clericalism in the Catholic Church and so the clerics are still doing it. And I don't think they even think twice about what would happen if they stepped back and let the women come forward … Even mentioning it is a bit of a joke. And I don't think this present Pope is ever going to allow women to be ordained priests … I think if the Mass was a bit more like we would do on street retreats, when we were running such retreats in Sydney, then that would be a different story. But they're not. They're still very much like the very early renewal times in the sixties. They're sort of stuck in that era. They can't get out of that.*

The typical Mass for Marie still carries that sense of separateness that she believes is antithetical to Eucharist. She has arrived at this understanding via more than one path—her reading of thinkers like Pierre Teilhard de Chardin on the one hand, and on the other, the key moments in her life when the truth of God's real presence revealed itself to her: in the gently waving mallow grass at the farm in Queensland; the moment at Benediction in Auckland's Cathedral; the state of prayer she entered into with her sisters at the convent in Armadale; what she saw and felt among the Aboriginal people of Redfern and Kempsey; the experience of Michael being restored to her. All these experiences point, for Marie, to a profound truth about God, and about the Eucharist.

They're threads, aren't they? Little epiphanies. They're like watering holes for the faith tradition. Yeah. It's sacramental. You see? It's the sacred in the midst of the ordinary and just to be able to … I suppose that's why I felt I had a vocation to be a Blessed Sacrament sister, because it's a sacrament in the midst of what could be just considered ordinary. And this is extraordinary when you see it for what it really is. I think that's what sacrament is. These moments are life-giving. It's transformative. It's just like the Eucharist—a transformation happens when you can see beneath the surface of the thing. Yeah, I think that's the gift I was given—to be able to see that.

Marie is still reading, still discovering new connections between her experiences and our collective understanding—through science, philosophy and psychology—of ourselves as humans, and of the universe around us. She reads and she talks about the latest idea that has caught her attention with Marian and Vianney and her many other friends. She watches Eckhart Tolle's YouTube videos on the computer (she uses one down at the bindery) and she relishes the work of thinkers like Thích Nhat Hahn, a Vietnamese Buddhist monk, and Masanobu Fukuoka, a Japanese scientist, ecologist and philosopher. She still feels bonded to her Blessed Sacrament sisters back in Australia. She knows that her decision to go to New Zealand and remain there affected them. *I think a lot of them missed me a lot.*

Growing old and maintaining her independence in the cottage has not always been easy. Marie's garden sits above a steep slope, *and I fell down that embankment one night because there'd been a lot of rain and there were no steps … I had a severe break.* Marie had handrails put in after that, and more recently she has had raised garden beds put in so that she doesn't have to climb for her herbs. *This one was just put in last year and I've got my summer greens in it.* As well as her weak ankle, Marie's vertigo, which comes and goes in its intensity, adds an extra challenge to living independently in her cottage.

Marie has no fear of death, and spends no time dreaming of the afterlife. *I don't want to go anywhere. Dying and going to God in Heaven? Well, if Heaven is not to do with the earth, then I actually don't want to go to Heaven. I just want to be part of this amazing universe. I've fallen so in love with it—I can't imagine being anywhere but here.*

As she contemplates the Eucharistic mystery that first drew her to the convent at Armadale—*real presence and my real presence mirroring each other*—the presence of God continues to reveal itself afresh to Marie.

I often sit outside on a nice day under the pear trees and drink my herbal tea out there and just be aware of the sounds around me and the movement of life and the birds and the blossoms breaking out on the tree. I was under the pear tree. And I just remember being so overwhelmed by nature. The beautiful world. We never see it because we're too familiar with it, so we don't really see. I was overwhelmed by this sense of the divine. And I just was looking out saying to myself looking at the landscape around me, saying 'This is the body of Christ. This is the body of Christ!' I repeated that. I was completely overcome by that. I'm living the Eucharist. This is the body of Christ. Take and eat: the elements of the earth; wheat growing beside the pear trees and the fruit and the nuts. It's all of the Earth, and God chose this medium to be present with us until the end of time. And I thought, 'This is amazing.' So, I've had that one many times since.

It was like the experience Marie had in the cathedral in Auckland, only much larger. *Very similar—very similar, but then Jesus was totally located in the wafer, in the monstrance. There was no extension into anything else. Here it was completely the breadth of the universe. The whole universe. And the sound, everything that I was exposed to in the natural world outside my door, was shimmering with the presence of the divine. It's the only way I can say it.*

MARIAN

In 2005, Marian became leader of her little community of Blessed Sacrament sisters. After Maureen's death, the group included just ten women: there were four in Sydney, four in Melbourne, one in Adelaide and one, Marie, in New Zealand. The last house at Armadale had been sold in 2000, and each of the sisters lived either independently or in aged care.

Communities of Blessed Sacrament sisters in America and Europe were shrinking, too. In 2005, the congregation sold the apartments that housed its Generalate in Rome, and moved to Sherbrooke, in Canada, where there was a large house, home to a dwindling group of nuns. Meanwhile, communities of sisters in Asia were growing. In 2007, Marian and Vianney made a trip to Vietnam, where groups of women had been coming together to live their vocations since 1968. They survived through the war by operating in secret, and their work was both contemplative and apostolic—they cared for adults and children with deafness and other disabilities. While the Vietnamese sisters didn't practice perpetual Adoration of the Blessed Sacrament, they had a Eucharistic emphasis, and by the 1990s their wish to join the Servants of the Blessed Sacrament was granted. In 2007, they became a Province of the order, giving them a new measure of self-determination and independence from the Generalate. The Vietnamese sisters now make up about two thirds of all Servants of the Blessed Sacrament the world over—there are around two hundred Vietnamese sisters in a global community of some three hundred women.

Marian and Vianney made a two-week trip to Bien Hoa, just east of Ho Chi Minh City, to celebrate this milestone with their Vietnamese sisters. This time, Marian and Vianney stayed with the nuns. Somewhat isolated by their inability to speak or understand Vietnamese, the Australians communicated as best they could in French and were otherwise left to quietly observe the differences between themselves and their hosts. *We were in a big dining room with a lot of these young women! We hadn't seen young nuns for so long, it was sort of amazing.* The special Mass and the celebration that followed drew a very large crowd. *They were all sort of accommodated on the grounds, on the floor, in the halls, somewhere, overnight. And the sisters fed them all. And, of course, they spilled into the chapel and out of the chapel and all of that. But the sheer numbers were overwhelming for Vianney and me. I mean, we'd never seen anything like that.*

The liturgical renewal that Vianney, Marian and the others at Armadale had helped promote and lead had lost its energy by the early 1980s, when the flush of enthusiasm that followed Vatican II died out in most Australian Catholic churches. But in Vietnam, it was still alive. The festivities on this occasion went on for the whole day and into the night. *There were biblical plays, all in Vietnamese, and all that sort of stuff—outside, with lanterns and things. It was very picturesque. It was very lively.* It couldn't have been more different from the quiet, fairly separate lives lived by the remaining women of the little Blessed Sacrament community in Australia and New Zealand.

In 2008, Betty died. Charito followed in 2010. Carol, who was suffering from pancreatic cancer, moved into palliative care in 2014. In an email to her friends, she wrote, 'I am at peace … and hopefully will live this last stage of my journey with integrity and trust in my loving Sophia God Mother who holds me in her embrace.'[4] Carol died a few months later. In 2015, two other Melbourne sisters, Joan and Elizabeth, died in aged care.

Now it was just Marian and Vianney in Sydney, Marie in New Zealand, and two others—Mary and Monica. Monica, who had entered the convent at Armadale on the same day as Maureen and Vianney, had spent several years working in prisons, and now worked with a Men's Shed in her native Adelaide. Mary remained in Melbourne. She was an organist at a St Kilda parish for many years, and had worked in pastoral care, delivering the Eucharist to sick people.

In 2015, Marian lost her mother, and realised she wanted to be closer to her siblings. She decided to move back down to Melbourne, and, with the permission of the General Council, the community bought a house in Ringwood, with a double garage so that she could both park her car and store the community's archives, inherited from Carol.

So I left Sydney with the cat and came here and the house has been such a gift, such a gift, and it's just been the right thing: it's been in the right place; it's a wonderful parish here that I'm part of. There are sisters around that I've got friendly with, family is close by, and I keep in touch with all the others. I visit Vianney every, say, two or three months and Marie at least once a year. Monica doesn't want me visiting, so that's all right—I talk to her on the phone, and I see Mary.

Living alone suits Marian, and she has long since detached herself from the idea that members of the congregation ought to live together, or even nearby. *It was tremendously important to me through the seventies and the eighties, and probably the nineties. After that, when we were sort of really moving into separate ways of living, it was helpful, really, that we were on our own because when you saw people it was, generally speaking, a really good experience.*

The disagreements and clashes of personality that were let loose in the 1970s are still there, though they've eased. *I can say my own relationship has improved with the ones that I've had trouble with. I think that's the grace of God. And yet, the last time we all came together here, in 2016, the tension was like that, and there were only five of us. So I thought, 'This isn't such a good idea, to get together.' We won't be able to, thank heaven, to do this again. It's the last hurrah.*

Marian's connection to Marie and Vianney has remained strong. *I still would say they were my primary relationships as regards human beings—I suppose God's my primary relationship. It's terribly hard to be together now in the sense that Vianney gets so tired so quickly—we can only spend a couple of hours and then she's exhausted. So we have to kind of have that sense of community in small bits, and they're lovely and they're memorable.*

Marian has made a great many new friends and connections in Melbourne and beyond. She is an active member of her local parish, celebrating Eucharist most mornings with a small group at the parish chapel. She sings with the church choir and practises at the weekly rehearsal. She has remained a faithful Catholic, even if she isn't always satisfied with the Church's direction, or the experience it offers the faithful.

The great passion and energy that she and her fellow Blessed Sacrament sisters brought to the celebrations at Armadale's chapel in the 1970s represent a high point for Marian—a sign of what liturgical celebration could be, and of what a truly open-hearted Church might both embrace and offer. *And it's why I get so annoyed on Sundays when there's none of that. And it's so kind of mechanistic or something. Even though we try and make the music nice and so on, there's nothing to excite the spirit. But those times did. I felt my spirit was absolutely fed. It was just a spirit of almost being united with each other, in a palpable sort of a way.*

Prayer remains central to Marian's life. She spends time each morning in solitary meditation, a 'centring prayer' that she thinks she probably learned about from Vianney. It's inspired by Mechthild of Magdeburg, a thirteenth century German mystic poet who wrote a ground breaking account of her ecstatic mystical experiences (and whose vivid descriptions of hell are thought to have influenced Dante's *Divine Comedy*). *You're trying to get out of the way of your own ego and your own thoughts so that you let God work. Or 'Let God be God in you,' as Mechthild de Magdeburg said. Let God be God in you, and not sort of mingled up with you and your thoughts.*

And through the parish, Marian has met two others—*these two women have prayed all their lives, and they're very spiritual*—who join her regularly for a centring prayer. *So we just sit here for twenty or twenty-five minutes in silence. We normally have a little prayer to lead in. Maybe a very short reflection, and sometimes I read a psalm. I've got a beautiful psalm book … We just sit and hopefully let the thoughts go. I always call it a thickening when there's others. You feel there's more of an atmosphere or something, and it's nice to do it with others. I'd like to do it with more.*

I loved the idea that we would gather together and pray together. Collective prayer is something Marian continues to miss from her first years as a young Blessed Sacrament sister, after she left the Faithful Companions of Jesus for the very vibrant company of Maureen, Marie, Vianney, Carol and the other women at Armadale. *And Vianney will say that. There was an atmosphere and an energy and a feeling of a shared call and shared vocation … I get this warm glow when I think about it. I thought it was like religious experience, shared.*

The power of a collective state of prayer still draws Marian, and she's found new ways to practise it, and to expand her understanding of what prayer can mean. She is undeterred by how esoteric these spiritual and intellectual endeavours might seem to the institutional Church. Since moving to Melbourne, Marian has joined and formed reading groups where she and others study the work of thinkers and writers like Teilhard de Chardin, and contemporary figures like Ilia Delio, a North American Franciscan sister and theologian who researches connections between theology, evolutionary science and neurology. Marian still meets up with others to practise the Dances of Universal Peace that she first learned about when she was into Jean Houston's ideas. She regularly socialises with like-minded nuns from other orders in Melbourne.

One of the most significant new practices Marian has taken up is the process of Continual Blossoming. She learned about it from a friend, a Sister of Mercy. *You have this face-to-face sort of meeting in ten minutes, where you say what's arising, what's happening. And I thought somehow, 'I'd like to do that with Marie, face-to-face.'* Sometime later, when Marie and Marian were on retreat together (it was a silent retreat, but they bent the rules), they decided to try it out. *It was like we just opened out into a completely different sort of realm of existence together. It was so powerful, this thing. I was able to say, 'Marie, I love you.' I'd never said that in my life. And she said, 'And I love you,' and it had never been said. And I don't ever say that easily. It never comes easy to say those words, and I thought, 'My goodness, this is some process! This is really something.' And so we hugged and cried and I said, 'We've got to keep this going.' And she said, 'Yeah, we do.' And so, we have.*

Marian and Marie call each other almost every week and share an intense exchange of thoughts and feelings—a very deep listening and attentiveness to one another. Marian is also part of a larger group whose members—most of them nuns, and nearly all of them women—meet online, from all over the world, to practise Continual Blossoming. *You meet with one person for half an hour or so in which one person only speaks, answering the question, 'What is happening, what are you experiencing, what's occurring?' So we take it in turns to do that and it's amazing how that takes you to a deep place with people you think you've known and with people you've never met—it's probably one of the best things in my life at the moment.*

Marian's love of nature and concern for the planet continue to motivate her, in both prayer and action. She stopped eating meat in 2015. She continues to enjoy the company of animals—of her cat, Cassie, and the magpies who visit her, and whom she feeds each afternoon in her garden. She takes long walks along Mullum Mullum Creek, which runs near her house, and along the Yarra River at Warrandyte. And she drives around town in her hybrid car, meeting with her many friends and fellow spiritual seekers. Amid all her activity, her vocation remains fundamentally contemplative.

Maureen said to me once, 'You can't help yourself. You're a contemplative. It has to be this way.' But I've got a very active side of myself. And again, perhaps my Capricorn nature says, 'Why aren't you out in some particular job doing one thing all the time, helping people?' And the other side of me says, 'Because this is the way I've been called.' And there's this big tension. Year after year, I see it in my retreat notes, the same thing: 'Be content. This is what you're doing. What the world needs is people growing in awareness and consciousness.'

There are parts of Marian's spirituality that she cannot describe. *I'd say I've had some religious experiences that were deeply spiritual, but they were religious experiences on my own. I'm not talking about those. They're too private.*

What Marian is looking for, still, is expansion—a greater deepening of her understanding and awareness. *If you want to keep growing, you do keep growing and it will never end. It will just never end, and I owe that to the openness of my community, which has allowed and encouraged these things here in Australia.*

The inevitable death of the Servants of the Blessed Sacrament in Australia does not perturb her. *I've known this for such a long time, probably twenty years, that we're dying, and according to the law of averages I would be the last one left standing … I don't feel too much about it, one way or the other. Reality is reality. We can't fight it. There's no point. I always think the Holy Spirit is miles ahead of us. We don't know what's coming.*

Despite seeing herself as someone who places great value on stability, Marian appreciates the important role change has played in her life. *This is the thing: things don't last forever. I mean, some people do stay with one thing forever. It's just never been that way with me.* Yet there is a deep sense of constancy, too. *God has been faithful to me all these years. I don't think that's going to change. And I hope I have been faithful, by and large, to the call—with all the human foibles that go with that, and one's own sort of faults and lazinesses and all those kinds of things that are there.*

Nevertheless, it is like a golden thread is there and I'm sort of following it, and sometimes it's through a mist and sometimes it's sort of dangled in front of you … I am exploring, still, and will continue; trying to see everything in the light of the presence of God. It's a life's work and it will only be completed when you breathe your last breath.

EPILOGUE

AT THE MELBOURNE General Cemetery lies a rather curious grave. Its large black granite headstone bears the names of eight women, all of them Servants of the Blessed Sacrament. They are Sister Monica O'Leary, who died in 2020, and Sister Mary Kelly, who followed her in 2021. Sister Pete is there, and Sister Carol Hogan, along with two others who formed part of the Armadale community, and who were laid there in 2015: Sister Elizabeth Mills and Sister Joan Lawler. In anticipation of the inevitable, the tombstone also bears the names of Marian and Marie.

That does sum it up, laughs Marie. *When Marian first suggested it to me, I thought, 'That sounds very strange—I don't know.' But then I thought, she's right.*

Marie and Marian are now all that is left of their little Australian community. Not long before Monica and Mary died, they lost Vianney.

While Vianney was quite sick during most of her interviews for this book, her final interview in May 2019 saw her feeling much stronger. But by the end of that year, she was very ill again. Her cancer specialist told her there was nothing he could do for her. *She was very down*, remembers Marian.

Vianney went to hospital while the terrible bushfires were burning through New South Wales, and a veil of smoke had settled over Sydney.

Marian was in regular contact with Vianney's brother, Mick. *I kept thinking, should I go to Sydney or should I stay? I regret that I didn't go earlier. I was waiting for the hospital to tell me when was the right time to come. I talked to Vianney probably for the last time on 8th December. We didn't say anything of real pith and moment, but she was making sense. The next day I couldn't talk to her.*

A couple of days later, Marian flew to Sydney to sit at Vianney's bedside, and she slept on a cot next to her. *I didn't sleep much … She couldn't talk, she was completely unconscious. I was just hoping that by this time she would let go.*

Mick and his wife, Beryl, came, as did Vianney's dear friend Wendy.

Marian prayed by Vianney's bedside. *I wasn't sitting there saying the rosary—that's not my thing. But I was praying that she could go soon. It was Saint Lucy's Day—Lucy is the patron saint of light. I said to Vianney, 'Go into the light—it's the feast of the light—the light is drawing you.' The nurses had changed her into another night dress and turned her. 'Darling, go, go into the light.' I just watched, and her breath got less and less, and finally petered out. It was a terrific privilege. It was just me, just her. And she had always said, 'Who's going to be there when I die?' Because she had been with others. And I thought, 'I'm lucky I'm here.'*

Marian remembered Vianney washing Charito's body when she died. *So I asked the nurses for a facecloth and I wiped her face and neck and arms. I said, 'I'm trying to wash you, as you washed the others.'*

Vianney's funeral was held at St Patrick's in Sutherland, and she was buried at Rookwood with some of her Sydney sisters: Charito, Betty and Maureen.

Soon after, the fires burned out and within weeks the pandemic made its way to Australia. Marian became sick, though not with

Covid-19. *A very important thing for me was the pleurisy that I had in March 2020. It made me reassess many things in my life. I had had far too much going on and I had to let things go—I had to let certain activities go … I could not keep up that level of intensity. The thing about the pleurisy was that I couldn't breathe. I mean, I could breathe of course—but it was saying to me, there's too much, I can't breathe under all of this.*

Marian couldn't be with Monica when she died in Adelaide, after a series of strokes. The pandemic made interstate travel almost impossible.

Mary Kelly was living in aged care, and when she fell into a coma during the last days of her life, Marian was at her side a great deal. She sat with Mary, and spent time clearing out her things. When Marian went home for a break the phone rang, with the news that Mary had died.

And so now at the time of writing, in 2024, it's just Marian and Marie. *And that's made a big change for me.*

There was one other death—Marian's cat. But Marian has recently acquired a new one, and she still gets about—just not so much as before the pandemic. *I still keep up with certain groups and try not to get too busy, And I am more focused on the subtler level of things, which is influencing the field of consciousness by the way I quietly live my life, on a conscious level.*

So it was like a refocusing on what really mattered, and I think for me it's been part of a movement of trying to lift the consciousness of the planet, really. Why not just go broad and say the planet? But there's a lot of people who are doing that in their lives. We need to up the level of consciousness in our planet or we will not be able to take the steps we need to.

Marian believes the Eucharist is at the heart of that project. *I am very aware that Saint Peter Julian Eymard said, 'Jesus is in the tabernacle, go to him.' And that was the spirituality of the congregation. It was very focused on Jesus in the Blessed Sacrament. Now my understanding is that the Eucharist is everywhere. Because it's the presence of Christ in every person. And I believe there is a presence even in animals and in the rest of creation, if we have eyes to see it.*

And yet the tabernacle remains a part of that. *I want to say that the ritual of the Eucharist has a real place. It celebrates the presence of Christ in a way that gives us a physical, symbolic—that is, real—sense of his presence among us and within us: a moment of almost another dimension of the divine presence of Christ. I think it's a multilayered presence. I see the presence of Christ in you, and I call that Eucharist. But when we gather for the ritual, it's there on another dimension. That's why I think it's important to keep going.*

Across the Tasman, Marie has also experienced great change. In addition to having suffered vertigo for many years, she now has osteoarthritis. *It's very crippling—I've got it in the ankles and the knees. It's making walking very difficult. But because of Covid we're not going anywhere at the moment—it's finally arrived in Oamaru. But I had five years of strict enclosure, so I don't mind being on my own.*

The vertigo meant Marie couldn't fly across to be with Marian at Vianney's funeral. So the two haven't seen one another for several years, now.

Marie can't manage things in her cottage the way she used to. *I've got the power on. I've even got a heat pump now. I was having to light the fire every morning and keep it going all day. But with the osteoarthritis I wouldn't even manage to get the wood inside—I walk with a walker. So my life has changed dramatically in the last few months. I didn't know that the osteoarthritis would move so quickly. I spend a lot of time sitting. I remember Vianney said when she first found out she had cancer she couldn't even pray—she just used to look at the tree out the window. It's a feeling of helplessness. That's starting to lift just in the last few weeks. I'm still cooking, and that's easy to do—I am a good cook and I've always liked cooking. But I can't get out in the garden. So I'm learning how to be helpless and to be grateful for what people do for me. My friends are rallying around, and I'm so fortunate I've got good friends like that who ring me up and can see what I need. It's becoming childlike again, where you have to depend on others.*

But Marie's spiritual understanding continues to unfold for her. *Going from a God of fear to a God of love—that's the main story of my journey.* Years of strict enclosure, perhaps ironically, helped her discover that. *I had to look at everything in my life because I couldn't get away from it anymore—there was nowhere to go. I was faced with who I am.* She had to stand still, and grapple with her fears, and accept herself. *And if you can do that, you're a free woman.*

I came very much from a God of fear. We grew up with the Fatima stories and the three children of Fatima. One of their visions—I've never forgotten this—souls were falling into hell. Think of that! That's some of the stuff we had as kids growing up. I went from that to the understanding that God is pure love. That was a massive shift for me. I have got that on my headstone: 'Love changes everything.' That's the opposite of fear and the God of fear. That's a big philosophical leap that I've made. I've been given so much comfort from discovering the God of love. There were elements of it from the beginning, but losing and finding Michael—if ever I needed proof that God was love, it was all there in that unfolding story. The all-forgiving God, who is there for us. God is love—there is no doubt about that—and God is faithful.

Marie still frets and fears for the world, though. *The IPCC, they've issued the last warning—if we don't do something it will be too late … Their last statement was really scary. But we're still not listening. We don't get it. It's like we are just sleepwalking. We don't even want to know—even those of us who can do something. But we're not doing anything like what's enough. We're frozen into inaction.*

And we're facing a massive war in Europe. I was born during the Second World War and that made a massive impression on me. It only ended when I was at primary school. Here we're facing what could be—and I'm hoping desperately won't be—a possible third world war. I'm focusing on that a lot. It's absorbing a lot of my life at the moment. What I'm doing is when I come back into the present moment, I try to unite my breath in this love of the divine, and breathe with the Ukrainians and anyone suffering anywhere. Somehow or other I'm with them. As long as I'm taking a conscious breath with them, I'm with them. It's just my prayer. It's how I can be close to them. It helps me, and who knows? It could even help them. But it certainly helps me cope with this terrible thing that's unfolding.

Though they lived far apart for many years, Marie feels Vianney's loss a great deal. *Vianney and I talked on the phone regularly and she kept me up to date with what was going on in Australian politics, and I loved that—I was always interested. I only had to ask her a few questions and I got all the information I needed. So I miss that a lot and just her lovely friendship and the warmth of her laugh. That's been hard. It was expected, but nonetheless I still miss her. It leaves a big gap in my life—but that's what death does. I can cope with that.*

So there's just Marian and me—we are down to the last two.

As leader, Marian's attention to all the community's needs—even in death—has occupied her greatly. She has organised and stored the community's archives and will leave everything in good order when their story reaches its end.

Marie can easily accept the fact that the community's story will end with her own death, and Marian's. *We faced the fact that we're dying as an order and we were okay with that when we came to terms with it. And so it's similar to having the headstones done. We're the last ones! This order in Australia dies with us so we might as well put the finishing touch to it.*

Marian is both looking squarely at that end, and living out her days in a strong and peaceful faithfulness to her vocation. *I'm very happy to be a Eucharistic sister until I die.*

ACKNOWLEDGEMENTS

THIS BOOK WAS written on the sovereign Gadigal lands of the Eora nation—land which its people have never ceded. I pay my respects to their elders past and present, and offer my gratitude for their ongoing care of the land on which I live.

I want to thank the Blessed Sacrament sisters—Vianney, Marie and Marian—for entrusting me with their story and for their great patience as I completed the work. Marian in particular worked hard to correct my drafts and offered useful feedback throughout the writing process.

I also want to thank Melissa, Barbara and Jill for sharing their experiences with me for this book.

Thanks also to Sean Flood and Elizabeth Fink, as well as Averil Fink, who helped share Maureen's story and offered feedback on the draft, and thanks to Mick and Beryl Hatton, who helped share Vianney's photographs and her story.

My gratitude and appreciation to Aunty Donna Ingram, who provided very thoughtful cultural advice for this book.

Thank you also to Clare Monagle, whose encouragement was extremely helpful to me.

Thank you very much to my copyeditor, Anna Thwaites, who so carefully corrected my stumbles.

And my very fond thanks to my mother, Kathleen Gilbert, who helped me greatly as a meticulous transcriber, proofreader and editor.

SELECTED BIBLIOGRAPHY

Archives of the Servants of the Blessed Sacrament are held at the Melbourne Archdiocese. The oral history interviews can be accessed there, along with most of the archive documents cited in this book.

Campion, Edmund, *Australian Catholics,* Viking, Melbourne, 1987.

Campion, Edmund, *Ted Kennedy, Priest of Redfern,* David Lovell Publishing, Melbourne, 2009.

Carey, Hilary M, *Believing in Australia: A Cultural History of Religions,* Allen & Unwin, St Leonards, New South Wales, 1996.

Evangelisti, Silvina, *Nuns: A History of Convent Life 1450–1700,* Oxford University Press, Oxford, 2007.

Flood, Maureen, 'About Redfern [Social work among Aborigines in Sydney]', Asian Bureau Australia newsletter, 38: 15–16, 1978. This is held in the AIATSIS archives.

Flood, Maureen, spoken in interview with David Busch for the ABC Radio National program, *The Words to Say It*, 1996. An audio file of this program is held in the convent archive.

Flood, Maureen, 'Bits of Yarn, Calico and Velvet Scraps: A Journey through the Death of the Father', *Women-Church: An Australian Journal of Feminist Studies in Religion*, 20 (March): 30–35, 1997.

Flood, Maureen, 'Presence and Absence in the Poetry of Judith Wright', *Women-Church: An Australian Journal of Feminist Studies in Religion*, 24 (April): 16–20, 1999.

Flood, Maureen, 'Walking in the Dark', in Australian Catholic Women, *And the Dance Goes On: An Anthology of Australian Catholic Women's Stories*, John Garratt Publishing, Mulgrave, Victoria.

Flood, Maureen—an online archive which includes slightly different versions of 'Walking in the Dark' and 'Bits of Yarn, Calico and Velvet Scraps' than those that were published. Appears on Maureen's profile on Dazed.org.

Hogan, Carol, 'Eucharistic Metamorphosis: Changing Symbol, Changing Lives,' in Power, K, & Elvey, AF (eds), *Reinterpreting the Eucharist: Explorations in Feminist Theology and Ethics*, pp. 10–30, Routledge, New York, 2014.

Kennedy, T, *Who is Worthy? The Role of Conscience in Restoring Hope to the Church,* Pluto Press, Sydney, 2000.

McNamara, Jo Ann Kay, *Sisters in Arms: Catholic Nuns through Two Millennia*, Harvard University Press, Cambridge, Massachusetts, 1996.

O'Brien, Anne, *God's Willing Workers: Women and Religion in Australia,* UNSW Press, Sydney, 2005.

Ryllis Clark, Mary, Heather O'Connor, and Valerie Krips (eds), *Perfect Charity: Women Religious Living the Spirit of Vatican II*, Morning Star Publishing, Northcote, Victoria, 2014.

Wilson, Mary, *Servants of the Blessed Sacrament: Eucharistic Communities 1950–1990*, published privately by the Sisters of the Blessed Sacrament, 1991.

NOTES

AUTHOR'S PROLOGUE

1 McNamara, pp. 9–6.
2 Ibid., p. 3.
3 Ibid., p. 2.
4 Makowski, E, 'Cloister Contested: Periculoso as Authority in Late Medieval Consilia', *Jurist*, 71(2), 2011, p. 334.
5 McNamara, p. 5.
6 Evangelisti, p. 8.
7 Goldstein, Darra (ed.), *The Oxford Companion to Sugar and Sweets*, Oxford University Press, Oxford, 2015.
8 Evangelisti, pp. 91–2.
9 McNamara, p. 6.
10 Ibid.
11 Pitt, Helen, 'Sisters of Charity Go from Ladies in Black to Sisters in Street Wear', *Sydney Morning Herald*, 9 June 2019. <https://www.smh.com.au/national/sisters-of-charity-go-from-ladies-in-black-sisters-in-street-wear-20190607-p51vln.html>.
12 O'Brien, pp. 166–7.
13 For an important analysis of the history of Catholic nuns and mission work in Australia, see Hilary M Carey, 'Subordination, Invisibility and Chosen Work: Missionary Nuns and Australian Aborigines', c.1900–49, *Australian Feminist Studies,* 13(28), 1998, pp. 251–67.

14 'MacKillop banished after uncovering sex abuse' at ABC online, posted 25 Sept 2010. <https://www.abc.net.au/news/2010-09-25/mackillop-banished-after-uncovering-sex-abuse/2273940>.
15 See Franklin, James, 'Convent Slave Laundries? Magdalen Asylums in Australia', *Journal of the Australian Catholic Historical Society*, vol. 34, 2013, pp. 70–90. <https://web.maths.unsw.edu.au/~jim/magdalen.pdf>
16 See Choo, Christine, 'Daughters of Our Lady, Queen of the Apostles—the First and Only Order of Aboriginal Sisters in Australia, 1938–1951: History, Context and Outcomes', *Journal of the Australian Catholic Historical Society*, vol. 40, 2019, pp. 103–30.
17 Campion, *Australian Catholics*, p. 230.
18 Reid, Stephen, Robert Dixon and Noel Connelly, *See, I am Doing a New Thing! A Report on the 2009 Survey of Catholic Religious Institutes in Australia,* John Garrett Publishing, Melbourne, 2010. The report (see p. 6) shows that there were increasing numbers of women religious in Australia from 1911 until 1966, when they numbered 14,622. By 1976 their numbers had dropped to 12,619.
19 See Turner, Naomi, *Which Seeds Shall Grow? Men and Women in Religious Life*, Collins Dove, Melbourne, 1988.
20 Thomson, Alistair, *Moving Stories: An Intimate History of Four Women across Two Countries*, University of New South Wales Press, Sydney, 2011.
21 Portelli, Alessandro, 'What Makes Oral History Different' in Perks, R and A Thomson (eds), *The Oral History Reader*, Second Edition, Routledge, Abingdon, United Kingdom, 2006, p. 39.
22 Ibid., p. 36.
23 Ibid., p. 38.
24 Ibid., p. 37.

BEGINNINGS

1 'Blessed Sacrament Cenacle Opened at Armadale', *The Advocate*, 4 October 1951, p. 7. <https://trove.nla.gov.au/newspaper/article/172521009>

2 While the Australian Bureau of Statistics tracks religious affiliation, the National Church Life Survey studies religious life in Australia. <https://www.ncls.org.au/articles/religious-service-attendance/>

3 The Australian Bureau of Statistics' census of population and housing shows that from the end of World War II, Australia's total number of Anglicans—the largest Christian denomination since settlement—fell steadily, while the number of Catholics rose. By 1986 Catholics had taken over as the largest Christian denomination. <https://www.abs.gov.au/ausstats/abs@.nsf/2f762f95845417aeca25706c00834efa/10072ec3ffc4f7b4ca2570ec00787c40!OpenDocument>

4 Carey, *Believing in Australia.*

5 'Blessed Sacrament Cenacle Opened at Armadale'.

VOCATIONS

1 Flood, 'Bits of Yarn, Calico and Velvet Scraps', p. 31.

2 Ibid., p. 32.

3 Ibid., p. 30.

4 Flood, 'Walking in the Dark', pp. 138–9.

5 Flood, 'Bits of Yarn, Calico and Velvet Scraps', p. 31.

6 Ibid.

7 Flood, *The Words to Say It.*

8 Flood, 'Walking in the Dark', p. 139.

9 Ibid.

10 Flood, *The Words to Say It.*

11 Flood, 'Walking in the Dark', p. 139.

12 Flood, *The Words to Say It.*

13 'The Inhuman Comedy', *The Bulletin*, vol. 84, no. 4306, 1962, archived at <https://nla.gov.au/nla.obj-680307065/view?sectionId=nla.obj-696388848&searchTerm=melissa+jaffer&partId=nla.obj-680370158#page/n33/mode/1up>

14 Jones, Jennifer and Josie Castle, 'Women in Australian Universities, 1945–80' in *Vestes,* vol. 26, no. 2, 1983, pp. 16–20, p. 16. <https://files.eric.ed.gov/fulltext/EJ291805.pdf>

THROUGH THE CONVENT DOOR

1 From an oral history given by Carol Hogan and edited in Clarke, Mary Ryllis, Heather O'Connor and Valerie Krips (eds), *Perfect Charity: Women Religious Living the Spirit of Vatican II,* Morning Star Publishing, Melbourne, 2014, p. 206.
2 Hogan, 'Eucharistic Metamorphosis', p. 13.
3 Constitutions, no. 18, quoted in Hogan, 'Eucharistic Metamorphosis', p. 13.
4 Clarke, O'Connor and Krips, p. 203.
5 Flood, *The Words to Say It.*
6 Flood, 'Walking in the Dark', pp. 139–40.
7 Flood, *The Words to Say It.*
8 Flood, 'Walking in the Dark', p. 140.
9 Ibid., p. 139.
10 Flood, *The Words to Say It.*
11 Ibid.
12 Pope Saint John XXIII, 11 October 1962. Translation taken from <https://www.catholicireland.net/the-opening-speech-of-the-second-vatican-council/>
13 Flood, 'Walking in the Dark', p. 140.
14 Flood, *The Words to Say It.*

SMASHING THROUGH THE GRILLE

1 Flood, *The Words to Say It.*
2 Clarke, O'Connor and Krips, p. 208.
3 Arrow, Michelle, *The Seventies: The Personal, the Political and the Making of Modern Australia,* NewSouth Publishing, Sydney, 2019, p. 23.
4 Flood, 'Walking in the Dark', p. 140.
5 Flood, 'Bits of Yarn, Calico and Velvet Scraps', p. 33.
6 The proportion of female university students rose from about a quarter to a third between 1966 and 1972—see Arrow, p. 23.
7 Flood, 'Bits of Yarn, Calico and Velvet Scraps', p. 32.
8 *Unitatis redintegratio*, the Second Vatican Council's decree on ecumenism, promulgated by Pope Paul VI on 21 November 1964.

ANOTHER FACE OF CHRIST: THE MOVE TO NEWTOWN

1 Flood, *The Words to Say It.*

2 This is from Issue 28 of *The Smouldering Wick*, June–July 1981, held in the convent archives. *The Smouldering Wick* was printed and distributed by the Asian Bureau Australia, a centre for research, reflection and action on Asian social justice issues, set up by Father Mark Raper in the 1970s. It was later subsumed into another Jesuit social justice entity. The convent archive holds some examples of the newsletter, but very few.

3 The draft essay is held in the convent archives. The draft essay is entitled 'The Contemplative in an Unjust World'.

4 *Octogesima Adveniens,* Apostolic Letter of Pope Paul VI, 14 May 1971. <http://www.vatican.va/content/paul-vi/en/apost_letters/documents/hf_p-vi_apl_19710514_octogesima-adveniens.html>

5 Flood, 'About Redfern [Social work among Aborigines in Sydney]', p. 15.

6 This document is held in the convent archive.

7 Ibid.

8 Kennedy, *Who is Worthy?*, p. 133.

9 Kennedy, Ted, 'No Need to Leave a Note', published in Nelson, Venetia (ed.), *On Being Human: Meditations on Experience,* David Lovell Publishing, Melbourne, 1990, p. 193.

10 Campion, Edmund, 'A Father to the Poor and Dispossessed', *Sydney Morning Herald,* 19 May 2005. <https://www.smh.com.au/national/a-father-to-the-poor-and-dispossessed-20050519-gdlcmf.html>

11 Flood, 'Walking in the Dark', p. 140.

12 Campion, *Ted Kennedy: Priest of Redfern*, p. 69.

13 The document is held in the convent archives at the Archdiocese of Melbourne.

14 Hogan, 'Eucharistic Metamorphosis', pp. 26–7.

15 Ibid., p. 27.

16 Flood, 'Walking in the Dark', p. 141.

17 Ibid.

18 Kennedy, *Who is Worthy?*, p. 71.

19 Flood, 'Walking in the Dark', pp. 141–2.
20 Luke 7:11-17.

DIFFERENT DIRECTIONS

1 Report from Carol Hogan on her six years as Regional Superior. This document is held in the convent archives.
2 A recording of this interview is held in the convent archive.
3 Maureen Flood's *Born of Fire, Possessed by Darkness* is an essay on spirituality in Judith Wright's poetry, written as her thesis for the Masters in English Literature at Sydney University, completed in 1997. This quote is from the personal reflection at the end of the essay.
4 Flood, 'Bits of Yarn, Calico and Velvet Scraps' (online version).
5 Flood, *Born of Fire, Possessed by Darkness* (thesis reflection).
6 See Ungunmerr, Miriam-Rose, 'Dadirri: Inner Deep Listening and Quiet Still Awareness', *Earthsong*, vol. 3, no. 4, pp. 14–15.
7 This document, 'The Story of Dadirri, 1989–90', is held in the convent archives.
8 Campion, *Ted Kennedy*, p. 196.
9 Flood 'Walking in the Dark' (online version).

ENDINGS, 2019

1 Flood, 'Walking in the Dark', p. 143.
2 Modjeska, Drusilla, *Stravinsky's Lunch*, Picador, Sydney, 1990, p. 328.
3 Vianney quotes John Henry Newman (1801–1890), an English theologian, poet and scholar of significant fame and influence. He was canonised by Pope Francis in 2019.
4 Carol's theology had evolved to imagine a female deity, and her phrase, 'Sophia God Mother', uses the ancient Greek notion of Sophia, which in the Christian tradition refers to the female personification of divine wisdom. This quote appears in the obituary written for her: Clark, Mary Ryllis, 'Theologian Saw Feminism as Social Justice', *Sydney Morning Herald*, 13 July 2014. <https://www.smh.com.au/national/theologian-saw-feminism-as-social-justice-20140713-3buwf.html>

INDEX